Leaves in the Wind

Leaves in the Wind

Thirty Years Spanning the Continents

Elko von Krogh Stillfried

VANTAGE PRESS
New York

FIRST EDITION

Copyright © 2005 by Elko von Krogh Stillfried

Published by Vantage Press, Inc.
419 Park Ave. South, New York, NY 10016

Manufactured in the United States of America
ISBN: 0-533-14956-8

Library of Congress Catalog Card No.: 2004093624

0 9 8 7 6 5 4 3 2 1

To my husband, Dominik, my son, Gebhard, and my daughter, Christiane, and in memory of our oldest son Franz.

Contents

Preface

As I began writing down memories of the past, I found these to be a collection of often unusual events. I experienced a rush of long forgotten incidents crowding in on my memory. There are many old letters, a few skimpy pocket calendars, and many photographs. All of these helped me to recall the first thirty odd years of my life that formed what has become "me." Our "extended" family members will partly corroborate these memories. Perhaps you or they will find contradictions of timing and incidents. To this I can only state that I wrote events down as I saw and understood them at the particular age or period of my life. I cannot claim "political correctness" for any of it.

It is significant for me to realize, how a rather disciplined but protected upbringing, seems to have prepared us to cope with unusual, often difficult events, without losing sight of happiness and the joy which can always be found even in difficult situations.

Early childhood memories of beautiful Colombia where we grew up in the "Shadow of the Andes" were interspersed with steamer trips to Germany. The experience of going to Germany in the middle of World War II placed us squarely in the horrors of steady heavy bombardments, evacuation to the eastern part of the country, and having to flee from the Russians to the West again, at the end of the war. Tremendous difficulties were faced trying to get back to Colombia or the U.S.A., respectively. A high point of my life was the employment as airline stewardess and the first transatlantic flights, from South America to Europe in 1950. Finally—marriage and becoming farmers in Virginia—what a change of pace!

I found great enjoyment in reliving my rich early years. I thank my children, particularly Christiane and nephews like Georg, to whose memory I dedicate these pages. They repeatedly urged me to get busy with this project. I hope it gives you a few hours of entertainment.

Leaves in the Wind

1

Where the Seed Takes Root

The murky waters of the Magdalena River swirled and churned by the tin shacks of Colombia's Girardot waterfront. The over 100 degree temperatures barely cooled down at sunset, to start up with renewed energy early the next day, every day, all year round. Two rainy seasons brought some change, not so much to the temperature as in a heightened humidity. Then the air became so heavy that a piece of paper in the hand felt like a spongy mass. The brown river boiling through Girardot and below our own sheet metal balcony formed the earliest impressions of my childhood.

I was born May 21, 1927 in the beautiful city of San Francisco (California, USA), where my parents, Harald von Krogh and Ada Riess, resided for a few years. They had first met in Brazil where they lived after the effects of World War I spewed out these two young Germans in search of a livelihood that the post World War I conditions in Germany made almost impossible there. Both young people had found companionship in a group of other émigrés and fallen in love with each other. Ada was an intelligent, warm, adventure loving woman. Her motherly nature must have appealed to the two years younger, early orphaned young man. He had hardly known the warmth and protection of a family. Harald had been offered a position with Grace Co. in San Francisco, which he had to take up immediately after acquiring the

1

necessary visa. It required more time for Ada to get her visa and follow Harald to the United States, after saving up enough money for her passage. A very simple ceremony performed by a Justice of the Peace united the young couple soon after Mother arrived from South America to join Harald.

There were no relatives, no friends present, nor was there any money. The meager inheritance my father used to boast about was a teapot, the only remaining possession of a large family fortune that dwindled away during the Depression and inflation. Father's mother, Elizabeth Heintzen, had been born in Manila in the Philippines, of a wealthy sugar-trading dynasty from Bremen. She died young and my father was placed in the cadet academy of Lichterfelde at the age of nine. Training at the academy was strictly military. Even the smaller boys were handled and addressed as adults. His father was then Commander of troops in Cameroon, a pre-World War I German colony in West Africa. It was no place for a motherless boy to be raised. Grandfather died when Father was fourteen years old. His only brother, Eberhard, was more than ten years older and independent in his own way. Friends of the family were supervising orphaned young Harald and he went with them to Chile in South America after finishing with the academy.

This did not take place before he was involved in a battle as a graduate young cadet in command of a tank. It was to be the only action in battle for this descendant of a General, who, on the Danish side had once defeated the Prussians. Now in 1921, Harald's troop was shipped to fight in a brief clash at Annaberg in Silesia. Half of this province had been turned over to Poland in spite of a plebiscite in which the majority of the population had opted to remain a part of Germany. Many such bloody insurrections had to be quelled before a kind of peace was finally observed throughout Germany during the implementation of the harsh conditions of the Treaty of Versailles. The uprising in Silesia was quickly quelled and Harald was free to leave for South America.

My mother's parents were living in a small apartment in Berlin. Grandfather Max Riess had been involved in engineering. Grandmother, Berta Raedisch, came from a rural setting in the Bohemian Sudetenland. The hardships of war and rampant inflation had left them without any means or ability to help their daughter. She was an art student aspiring to become a sculptor. Like a few spirited young women in those days, Ada had joined the "Wandervogel" (German youth movement). They hiked Germany's beautiful countryside singing, declaiming poetry and clamoring for women's rights. But she soon had to give up her art dreams and take a position as companion and nurse with a German family leaving for Brazil. Besides her parents, she left behind a beloved brother, Heini. The family was still reeling from the loss of the younger brother, Walter. He had been a student and was killed during one of the many battles that raged in Berlin between the factions of different political entities during 1919. Her departure for Brazil was a hard separation for Ada. In those days the travel distances were almost insurmountable.

After Ada's arrival in the USA and their wedding, my parents settled in San Francisco. Finding a studio-type apartment, my mother was able to convert it into their first cozy home. They fully expected to stay in California and to become United States citizens some day. However, only the birth of their first daughter Elko, made a legitimate American. Mother's grasp of the English language must have been rather poor. She never developed a good ear for languages even though her vocabulary in German, English, Portuguese and Spanish became quite encyclopedic in time. I am sure the nurse who recorded the statistics at my birth, also lacked imagination. Whatever the reason, I ended up with the unusual name of Elko. Surely my mother meant and said, "Elka," a Scandinavian name. Thanks to the pronunciation in English it came out as Elko on the written document. There is a saying: "What's in a name"—Well, try to live up to the name "Elko" for 70 years!

I was eight months old when Grace Company transferred my father as an apprentice to their coffee export company in Girardot, Colombia. That hellish hot place became home of my first awareness and for eight years. Some of the first things I learned were that in Spanish a name with an ending of "o" is for males. And secondly, according to my nanny's superstitious beliefs, that a child not baptized in the Catholic religion had an evil mark and would end up in limbo or shadow-land where the dogs went. This became one more disadvantage for me to live down although I had no compunction about dogs. The arrangement even seemed cozy to me.

Our life in the tropics was a good one. It was basic and simple. Our house of very plain, one-story construction, had no conventional windows. The tops of the walls were open to whatever air would stir, allowing free access to little critters and huge roaches with great wingspans. Of course, scorpions also inhabited the premises. It was not wise to slip into one's "alpargatas" (straw sandals) without a thorough inspection of their insides. The window openings of the house contained decorative iron grates for safety. Mother soon converted the terrace into a lush garden, in which a hammock offered much enjoyment for swinging and playing. Carpets and elegant furniture were non-existent. My mother was a genius in transforming indigenous mats, pots and carvings into decorations and furnishings. The "estera," colorful straw mat used for sleeping and carried around by the population on their backs, had always been a favorite in our homes. Of course, we only used them as floor mats.

The food prepared by our cook was of the local custom produced with whatever the "mercado" (market) could offer. A great variety of fruits and vegetables of the tropical kind was always available. The meat, covered with flies, hung in the heat or sun for an unknown period of time. It was usually extremely tough and exuded a rather unappetizing odor. Settling for a chicken, one had to carry it home alive and squawking, for the cook to butcher. These birds were free ranging, but really still tasted the way chickens used to taste before mass production and supermarkets. They actually were delicious.

What I remember most about our house high above the Magdalena was the exciting view of the river. There were floats and dugout canoes piled high with "platanos" (plantains). The picturesque mound of lush green bananas made the haphazard shipping contraptions look quite flimsy. With the help of long poles, men navigated them around currents, debris, and paddle-wheel riverboats loaded with sacks of green coffee to be transported to ocean ports for shipment overseas. The muddy banks often were lined with washerwomen. They carried their heavy baskets of laundry to and from the river gracefully balanced on their heads. Using large stones as washboards on which they pounded their laundry, they wore only a "chingue," a sort of shift that could get wet and dry again fast. Naked little children were always part of the scene together with their scrawny dogs. The sound of their happy voices would drift up to our house.

With alarming frequency a woman would lose her life by slipping under the strong brown current or when a huge crocodile crashed out of the muddy water and pulled her under. When it rained in the distant mountains, the waters began to churn and huge clumps of all sorts of refuse floated by. Sometimes we saw entire trees, banana plants, and even huts, or carcasses of animals. It was a regular occurrence along this waterway.

Above all, Girardot prided itself for having one of the few bridges spanning the mighty Magdalena River. On the other side of the bridge was the hamlet of Flandres. The train used the bridge for crossing, on its way south to Neiva. Every place had its own odor. The special smell that emanated from the river and its surroundings, while not necessarily pleasant, has stayed in my memory forever after.

Our daily routine started at five A.M. before the sun came up. Father would go to work in the "trilladora," a huge flat-roofed shed containing the coffee processing plant and offices. The coffee was brought in on mule-back and dumped on the roads and open spaces all around to dry in the sun. Coffee drinkers, enjoy! Mules and other animals, doing what animals do, as well as people with or without shoes, and vehicles of different varieties, traveled over this carpet of coffee. The purpose of this was dual. The coffee would dry in the sun while some of the hulls were crunched off, the work to be completed later in the "trilladora" (mill). There the beans were bagged for shipment on the riverboats. Father would return from the "trilladora" for lunch and the customary long siesta. From eleven A.M. to three P.M. life stood still during the glimmering heat of noon. Even the flies drowsed away while the Magdalena River boiled along on its uninterrupted search for its Caribbean Ocean destination.

In the early morning dusk and before many people were about, my nanny took me for a walk in the park. Our dog, Niko, always accompanied us. He was of undefined breeding and very intelligent. My words "no me toque," (Don't touch me) were enough for him to come to my protection with a menacing growl. My almost white blond hair, an unknown in those parts, stigmatized me. Sadly, many leprous and otherwise very ill and gangrenous people walked about freely and in abject poverty. Bad odors and all the associated unpleasantness of untreated diseases were a part of street life in those days without antibiotics and medical care. And so was superstition. These unfortunate people believed that touching the clean blond hair, maybe obtaining a few strands of it, would cure them. They sometimes would come to our house to beg for hair or urine from "la monita" for a treatment.

I loved my nanny, Isabel, "Tita," as I called her. She was always singing and knew the most exciting games. Frequently our dog, Niko, joined us. I hardly had other children to play with. In the evenings, after the worst of the day's heat, Tita would take me to the "Club de Tennis." The club consisted of an open sided tin shed with a "bar," some rickety chairs and three tables on which leather "cascos" (leather cups) with dice, were rattled and slammed down for a popular game. Sometimes a deck of cards would turn up. There was also a tennis court used regularly by the adults and even a swing for the children. As night descended with tropical speed, fireflies alighted in the old trees and a hand-cranked gramophone produced creaky music, which competed with the increasing chorus of frogs, crickets and myriad other insects attracted to the lights and enjoying the slightly cooler evening breeze.

The members of the club were always the same.

There were a few visiting foreign bachelors but otherwise seldom changing faces. There was Father's new boss. Papi had switched over from Grace Company to the coffee "in and export" firm of "Schaefer-Klaussmann." Erik and his wife, Elsa Klaussmann, had a nice home in Girardot, before they transferred to New York a few years later, after Papi became manager of the Colombian branch of the company. Elsa Klaussmann was an old nag and very proud of her home bakery. My father, in disapproval of her bossy nature, never ate apple pie again, this being her specialty. It was a recipe she never shared with anybody else. Other members were Rudi and Julia Stahlman, a German couple. He was a friendly fellow, she a transparently thin and anemic woman with an eternal smile. Then there was Edgar Schwarz, an American businessman, in Girardot without his family, and the Canadian, Cecil Schuler, married to a tall imposing Italian.

Years later I discovered that she was the sister of the composer, Gian Carlo Menotti. They had a daughter my age. Nini and I were club playmates when the nannies had their evening chat. On one occasion, on our way to the club while the two women were walking behind us deeply engrossed in conversation, we little tykes were skipping around and navigating a multiple line railroad crossing on which freight trains were often switching back and forth. Fortunately, this went on at a very slow pace. Just as the train was backing up, my foot got caught between the rails and I fell. Instantly, my dog, Niko, grabbed me by the arm trying to pull me off the track. As the train crawled closer, the nannies came running, screaming, and picked me up just in time. This event instilled in me very early, the realization that animals must have some intelligence. This was in spite of the native disregard for all living things except humans.

8

I cannot remember a time in all the years of moving around, that we did not have at least one dog, or were trying to get one fitted into our life style. Fortunately, many other animals became part of our family. Our beloved Niko, with his fiercely protective attitude, made enemies around town. So it happened that I witnessed the horror of him being run over by a truck. Niko was furiously barking at something or someone. I saw the truck driver move his vehicle off the curb and right onto my dog. He had a nasty grin on his face when he moved his vehicle back to the curb. Somebody wrapped the dying dog in a blanket to carry him home, followed by a weeping Tita and me. My parents were also devastated; my father had been called from the "trilladora." But we were unable to do more than hold the dying dog. My playmate was gone. No longer could Mami cover Niko's eyes while I would hide somewhere in the house and wait, with tingling excitement, to hear Mami say to him, "Such die Nena" (find the girl). He would storm in and soon discover where I was hiding and we would have the most joyful reunions.

Gerrit and Iris Gothals, a German-English couple, also lived in our vicinity. He was a friendly, burly sort of fellow with a skinny, tall, bucktoothed wife who was extremely mean to her stepson (also named Gerrit), a gangly teenager. The boy Gerrit sometimes came running over to our house when the whipping he got for misbehavior became too much and he needed to confide in someone, even a five-year-old. I learned to hate his stepmother as much as he did. Once he ran into our house so fast that he did not see an open shutter. An ugly gash and blood from a head wound were the results. There was just as much blood as my kneecap produced when, some months later, I was watching a violent thunderstorm from our small balcony. A bolt of lightning struck it or something nearby

9

and threw me down, causing a deep gash in my knee, which I cut on the tin flooring. Even now storms and lightning fascinate me and I cannot resist watching them.

Such early impressions stay. The sadness, the hardships, the emotional pain are stored together with joys and happiness. I believe they are the most valuable treasures in our lives' collections. We obviously cannot be really happy without knowing real pain and also the other way around. A very disturbing experience hounded me all my life. As usual, I had gone to the "mercado," (market) with Tita to buy the daily supply of fruits, vegetables and meat. The approach to the open market hall was through a large lot teeming with vendors displaying all kinds of produce. The trash and garbage, mostly of rotting fruits and vegetables, was repulsive. These were the days before refrigeration and plastic packaging. Almost everything was wrapped in large banana or other leaves. The odors and flies were unbelievable. Dogs, pigs, and naked children prowled around this field of filth. The vendors' loud calls tried to attract buyers and I held on to Tita's apron so as not to get lost while I enjoyed the excitement.

Startled, I froze in front of a pile of refuse in the midst of which stood a small wooden contraption on roller skate wheels. On it hovered a figure, grotesque and shriveled, with arms and legs twisted and entwined in the oddest configuration. The little man was emaciated, had a large, triangular shaped head and a wispy beard. He held his finely shaped, long-fingered hand out to us in the way of a beggar. Was the stab of pain that went through me a premonition of the future? The medical term, "Osteogenesis Imperfecta," which, years later, marked our life at the birth of our oldest son, had not yet been coined. It was unknown then. Why did this experience when I was a four- or five-year-old stay with me so vividly for the rest of my life? Poverty, beggars, disease were all around us, were part of life in the tropics. But also there was no show of great wealth to be seen. The medical profession was still in its humble beginnings. That umbrella of security and protection did not exist.

Girardot is a river town, not only serviced by riverboats but also a railroad and occasional buses. These were actually rather rickety contraptions that served as transportation and connected the town with other villages. The "ferias" (county fairs) that converted Girardot into a steaming cattle pen a few times a year, were well known. Most of the town's streets, generally unpaved, then held multiple herds of cattle, mules, horses and other livestock. The "arrieros" (cowboys) under their large hats and wearing leather "samarros" (chaps), would crack long whips and accompany the din with loud shouts and bravado as they went about the business of buying or selling their animals. For several days traffic could not use the town streets. An attempt to negotiate them and the sidewalks on foot produced very dusty or "green" results. But these events offered entertainment and occasional excitement for us all. The pall of dust eventually settled back on everything in and around the house and for days after the "feria" was over.

We lived a simple life of day to day importance without the hassle of a telephone or radio and, of course, no TV or computers. However, we enjoyed ourselves just as much without all of these entrapments. The Magdalena River, (upriver from town) looked brown and dirty, but was not polluted, and offered wonderful bathing areas and picnic spots. If one had an old or new Model T, the possibilities for bumpy, dusty rides into the countryside were numerous and really adventurous. Sundays often

11

saw us all drive out to a "piquete" (picnic) along some nice river beach. We enjoyed these family outings with our friends and the refreshing dip in the cooling brown waters. There were few children in our group and always the same faces.

At home my mother, with much ingenuity, came up with surprisingly exciting homemade toys. She made me a schoolhouse with authentic-looking miniature books, people and a blackboard. She constructed a village of painted wood blocks. It had a church and a train station in it, too. Above all Mother taught me how to read in German at a very early age. This was the language we always used with our parents, even though we spoke Spanish everywhere else. There was no limit to the imagination awakened when reading those wonderful fairy tales and sagas that had been brought from Germany. Mami had been a budding artist and had hoped to become a sculptor. Alas, the opportunity never again presented itself and she gave up all those ambitions, busying herself with her family instead.

Even Christmas was duly celebrated. A dry scrub tree of the variety that grew in the arid plains around Girardot was decorated for this purpose. A vague memory of one of these events has stayed with me, the time when Erik Klaussmann gave me a live lamb for Christmas. I was standing in awe looking at the candles on the tree, when the sheep moved, or some other incident caused a huge puff of flames and the tree disintegrated in seconds in front of my astonished eyes. Fortunately, no major damage was done to the bare cement and stone construction of our house.

My world began to expand. I finally found a friend in Erika Meyer, barely six months younger than I—but we were well-matched in our little concerns and interests.

Erika's father was a pilot for "Scadta." Don Pablo Meyer and a few other World War I flying aces were trying to establish flight routes through the dangerous Andes Mountain passes to open up Colombia to the modern age. The Scadta was later taken over by Avianca during the early years of World War II. Avianca was a subsidiary of Pan American that benefited greatly from the work done by these courageous young men, many of whom lost their lives flying into some rain shrouded, high peak, or into dense jungle. Ironically, Pablo Meyer crashed down a mountain in his car and his body was never found in the deep crevasse. Erika, his only daughter, by then a married woman and mother of five children, was the one to lose her life in a plane accident in the Andes years later. But before these sad events, Pablo and his Colombian wife, Magola, had become good friends of my parents. They ran the only hotel in town, which was adjacent to the railroad station and thus offered a door to the big world outside.

Only a few blocks separated us from the hotel and Tita would often take me there or Erika stayed with us. Had my parents known how early corruption creeps in, they might have had second thoughts about our visits to the "Grand Hotel." We children loved playing around the little kiosks in the "patio" (back yard) where customers would enjoy cigars and beer while playing "cacho" (dice). We sometimes indulged our curiosity about these men's pastimes by collecting butts and trying to smoke them. Also, dregs of partly empty glasses were not taboo. (Ugh! is all I can say to that now.) We survived very well, however, and our friendship became a close one. For many years, Erika and I were quite inseparable.

In Girardot, and later in Bogota, our circle of acquaintances remained small. My parents appeared ful-

13

filled in each other's company. Social life as we experience it here and now was non-existent. Partying must have been invented later and certainly not in Colombia. "Fiestas" (festivities) celebrated by the population were accompanied by a lot of noise and exploding firecrackers which had no appeal for us. The foreigners of other nationalities associated more with each other than with the local population. The class difference in Colombia was quite noticeable. The living standard of the population in general was often low and different from ours. Colombians maintained a division between the Spanish-Indian mixed and the "old" Spanish families. As a matter of fact we, too were never once asked nor did we set foot in the residence of any of the old families of Spanish origin. Probably, they felt some disdain towards us foreigners. While some were very wealthy, living in unobtrusive elegance, many were plagued by poverty, which they bore with extreme pride. They lived in beautiful Old Spanish mansions with uneven red tile roofs squatting on thick, white adobe walls adorned with an occasional window behind a cast iron balcony. Often clouds of bougainvillea gave the houses a fairy tale appearance.

I learned a bit about the tragic pride of these people a few years later when my father, out of pity, hired a scrawny old secretary who had no knowledge of typing or any other office work but was so destitute that help seemed essential. She spent the time in the office crocheting little handkerchiefs for us. But she never came to our house. She was one of several sisters, all as untrained and destitute as she, and all unmarried. They clung to their home and tradition. This meant that the girls in a family were scantily educated and were carefully chaperoned by their male relatives until marriage or a life of spinsterhood. Their homes were filled with the most exquisite art objects one occasionally heard about. When poverty reached an extreme, they would send someone to the "gringo's" (foreigner's) house with a beautiful hand-hewn old silver object, some dating back to time of the Conquistadors, wrapped in an old scarf. Mother bought a few pieces, also out of pity. We really did not have that much cash to spare ourselves.

My parents occasionally would meet some European adventurers who were trying to explore possibilities of this country so alien to all they knew from old Europe. Sometime during late 1929, they met a young man, Wolfgang Graf Stillfried, and thus the history of our two families merged and we have been trying ever since to sort out the real facts from the many fantasies of how this meeting came about. Since none of the participants are around any more to clarify this, I will try to choose the most likely version. It appears that my father, a spaghetti-thin, six-foot, seven-inches-tall man, with very elegant, useless long fingers, was stymied by trying to repair some damage to his car. Thus Wolfi Stillfried came upon two endlessly long legs stretching out from under the vehicle, futilely stirring up clouds of dust. Being a very practical person of good Christian qualities, Wolfi offered his help. Upon the proposal, proffered in strongly German-tinted Spanish, Father wiggled out from under his vehicle and, with a solid handshake, the two young men bonded in a friendship that was to last to the end of their lives and the consolidation of our families.

Wolfi was the oldest of ten children, of whom Dominik, my future husband, was the youngest. Wolfi had come to Colombia penniless. His father was still too young himself to hand over the administration of their estate, Silbitz, for a good while yet. This must have been the reason for Wolfi to decide to see the world and make his fortune before duty and tradition would take over and demand his presence in Germany again.

My parents also were of very modest means. Even so, Father Harald and Wolfi came up with the most grandiose dreams. My father had no money but possessed an overly optimistic belief that in the long run, he could not protect himself from wealth. Wolfi saw virgin forests, free for the taking for anyone who would conquer the wilderness. He visualized lush fields, green gardens and fat cattle, a Silesia transplanted into the tropical wilderness. The perfect place was found, three days of arduous mule trek up into the high Andes, literally in the middle of nowhere. Some research had disclosed that the planned "Pan-American Highway," which was to connect North and South America from Alaska through Panama to Chile, was scheduled to cut through that jungle promising a value increase in the property some time in the future.

With little money, Papi bought a cleared piece of jungle, by law immediately giving them ownership of much more uncut forest for clearing and Wolfi went to work. With his own hands and perhaps a peon or two, he cleared more land and built himself a three-room house with a veranda running all around it. Everything was made of rough wood. The house was slightly elevated and set on tree trunks. The sliding doors and windows, of course without glass, sported ample cracks to let the fog drift through. The cooking stove was an open wood fire on an adobe base. The smoke drifted up through the rafters. Water was provided by a crystal clear, cold spring behind the house. It was passed through a length of hollow bamboo to an outdoor "alberca" (wooden trough) behind the kitchen. Years later, we placed an outhouse strategically over the water runoff from the house. Voila, thus was created instant flush! Furniture likewise consisted of primitive home construction, bench tables and bedsteads. Is anyone inquiring about electricity and appliances? Candles and a kerosene lamp were great luxury!

This homestead was located on a small open space surrounded by the beginnings of a grassy field studded in a grotesque manner all around and up to the walls of the dense forest by fallen or half burned tree trunks. Nowhere was there a space larger than a few feet without some mammoth obstruction. Thousand year old trees do not burn or rot very well. Planting and plowing had to be done with hand tools. The rich humus soil produced radishes the size of a child's head and other vegetables on a similar scale but they were not always palatable. All of it was now awaiting a woman to take care of the man and his house. By happenstance, it was a lovely young girl all the way back in Silesia in Germany who was just finishing her University studies in Breslau. Her name was Margot Schlenker. Wolfi had met her and fallen in love before his departure to South America.

First Time to Germany

My parents made their first trip back to the old country since their departure after World War I. It was the summer of 1930. My mother (together with me) extended her stay to visit her relatives, my grandparents and a few aunts. We then traveled to Silbitz where we met Margot who joined us on our return trip to Colombia. Silbitz was Wolfi's home. On our visit in 1930, his parents, Count and Countess Stillfried, were gracious hosts to my mother and me.

No actual memories of mine reach back to this event.

17

Fortunately, an old and crumbling letter my mother had written to my father while she was visiting in Silbitz, remains. It contains the highly amusing account of her—and my—experiences. After a game of tennis with "Comtesse" Angela, they were drinking tea in the salon with Countess Stillfried when loud screams from the dragon (a nickname I had somehow acquired) were heard. The mothers ran into the big hall and discovered the wailing monster surrounded by "Bubi" (Dominik) and "Negus" (Ruediger) who were apparently trying to kiss me. Limited to speaking mostly Spanish, my three-year-old's response was understandable. Otherwise, old photographs attest to some good times with the three little ones playing in a boat, or around the fountain, or even enjoying a picnic with the family. Later claims by my future husband that his affection for the "dragon" began at that stage when he was barely five might be taken with a grain of salt! Margot, the young bride-to-be, traveled to Colombia well chaperoned by my mother and me. In those days the steamers took up to five weeks to complete the trip. I wish I could remember those voyages. . . .

After their wedding, Margot embarked on the extraordinary experience of being a pioneer in the jungle. At the time, it took almost three days on muleback from Pinares to the next habitations, the small village of Palermo, located in the hot climate zone. Pinares had to be reached along treacherous "trochas" (trench-paths) and was located near the top of the central "cordillera" (mountain range) of the Andes, in an area named "cielo roto." Literally, this meant "torn sky." It rained copiously during the two rainy seasons.

For the birth of two of her children, Margot had to negotiate the "trocha" for a couple of days to find people who could assist her. It is mind-boggling for us in this day and time to even begin to understand how a young, well-educated person could endure this extremely primitive life of privation and childbearing without medical assistance. Her second son was born in Germany but she was back in Colombia for the birth of the third baby, a daughter. For a while, Wolfi's younger brother, Norbert, came to stay with them and help with the jungle work. He also visited us in Girardot. I remember little of this handsome young man who later, in 1942, was killed in the war in Russia.

Meanwhile the Krogh family would not be outdone. My sister, Christiane, was born in 1932 before I turned five. It was a normal home birth, attended by a midwife. A doctor was an unknown in our house and so were thermometers and all other medical paraphernalia except castor oil and "purgante" (purge) to rid us of unwanted parasites.

We knew of a Doctor Martini in Bogota whose acquaintance I made a few years later. Assisted by his very capable and resolute helper, Schwester Betty, I was manhandled and poked to receive the immunizations, all at once that any respectable child should learn to endure at an earlier age. Dental care was brutal and commonly performed with pliers and a foot pedaled medieval contraption that squeaked and ground loud enough to obliterate the desperate wails of the hapless victim. This all was accomplished without the help of pain suppressants.

Mami became ever more energetic in her home teaching program for me. The educational situation in Girardot was dismal and my parents decided on home schooling. Although Spanish was the language in use with everybody but my parents, I had learned to read quite well in German under my mother's capable tutoring. The books we had available were read over and over again fueling my vivid imagination. German books were not to be had in Girardot, one depended on somebody's trip abroad to furnish new supplies. When I had no book in reach or other activities kept me from reading, I would make up my own stories, a habit I carried with me well into adulthood. Entire novels were dreamt up and "read" in daily installments in my mind over periods of weeks. They mostly included animals and the wilderness. Of course, I would be the heroine rescuing some creature or other and fleeing with them to secure places where we all lived together happily ever after. Tarzan-like adventures supplied the main subjects of my early stories although I cannot remember ever having read anything about this jungle hero. Later on, adventure and romance also became part of my stories that became more elaborate but no less fantastic, as I grew older. I have never known a moment of boredom. As soon as I was deemed old enough to read an entire book, my parents got me Selma Lagerlöf's great book about Nils Holgerson's travels with the wild geese. My fascination with this saga certainly indicated an early predilection for air transport!

In the Shadow of the Andes

Recollections of our first trip to our farm in the jungle, Pinares, probably in 1933, are firmly embedded in my mind. Mami needed to go to Germany for medical reasons. Tita and I with baby Christiane, then a little over a year old, made the trek up to Pinares in classic style. Papi accompanied us by train in five or six hours from Girardot to Neiva. The heat was brutal even though the windows were always open. The smoke from the engine drifted through freely, with dust, bugs and whatever else, airborne. I loved the exciting trip and the stay in a "hotel" that nowadays would defy description. I remember the huge cockroaches flying through the window grill as not being unusual, and also the dirt which obviously had not been touched by a broom. I remember most the thrill of very loud music or some such cacophony that barely let us sleep all night long.

With anticipation and excitement we got up again at two in the morning, in the dark, to be hoisted onto an old "camion" (truck) for the drive to Palermo. These vehicles were haphazardly loaded with chickens, pigs, goats, and sacks of feed, sugar, fertilizer and people of all ages who exuded odors akin to that of the livestock. The "chiva" (decrepit vehicle) was quite rickety and the ride so bumpy we were frequently alarmed by loud shrieks and calls when someone or something had gone overboard. The two-hour drive left us mangled, before the day had actually begun.

In Palermo, Papi handed us over to Wolfi, who with a chain of perhaps fifteen mules met us for the arduous two-day ride up the mountains. There was little to enjoy. I soon experienced sheer tortuous misery on my earliest trip up there. I had been secured onto a mule so I would not slip off. I still feel the splashing of water on my legs as we forded a wide river in pitch dark, before daylight. I recall the weird sensation I felt as if the mule was going backward instead of forward and my fear of not hearing the other animals in the caravan. Had I been left alone? Then, after what seemed an eternity, the beast clambered up on the embankment of the opposite shore. There was the incomprehensible fussing, yelling, and whipping of mules. Wolfi's bad temper was unmistakable. But he was in charge of at least fifteen animals loaded with people as well as a heavy cargo of supplies. The "arrieros" (mule-drivers) on foot had a hard time keeping the mule

21

train in marching order but on went the trek. Our wet clothing helped to keep us cool at first. Even though it was still dark, the merciless tropical heat was always present. The early departure would bring us up the mountain a bit before the sun would rise and make the temperature almost unendurable.

I never will forget the fantastic trails that wind their way up a bare, very steep mountain face. Mules have the strange habit of always walking on the very outside of any path, oblivious to the frightening abyss below them. One knew that, occasionally, some would be literally pushed "overboard" if another mule train should happen to come from the opposite direction and they got their heavy, protruding cargo entangled. While looking down into those precipices fascinated me, I sometimes found myself in need of looking in the other direction, up the naked, steep mountain cliff towering above us to find a sense of safety. The higher we got, the more spectacular was the scenery and, even in those early times, I appreciated its beauty. The distinct nutty smell of the "pasto gordura" (grass) that commonly grows there is unforgettable. Huge titian blue butterflies surrounded us when we forded creeks. The flora was of tropical beauty and always one could hear the call of some strange birds hiding in the canopies of tall trees. The choir of a multitude of birds in these lonelier regions was memorable, where boys of all ages, armed with home made slingshots were not around targeting any living, moving creature. It was a national sport to kill anything in sight.

We had climbed up the mountain into a more endurable climate by afternoon and my tears of exhaustion dried slower. Also, it started to rain. The water cascaded down in buckets. We were so drenched that my sore seat squished on the saddle in the most uncomfortable way. I remember that I now cried in rhythm with the falling rain. At least, Wolfi could no longer hear my fussing and admonish me to stop as he had frequently done before. He had little Christiane on the saddle in front of him and she probably was quite as miserable as I. Tita probably did not dare complain too much.

Finally, as it was getting dark in tropical speed, we saw the flickering light of a kerosene lamp and knew we had reached our destination for the night. By now, we were in unaccustomed cool temperatures after the daylong climb up the mountain and the constant rain. I learned that, in the tropics, temperatures are not dominated by seasons but by the altitude of the terrain. The climatic changes in the equatorial region consist of two rainy spells, interspersed by two dry seasons, during each year. In the evening dusk, under dripping trees and surrounded by mules tied to wooden posts, stood our "posada" (inn, hotel, motel, you name it), a three-room straw-covered "rancho" (hut). One room was a kitchen with an open cooking fire. The other two rooms contained long wooden platforms along the walls for sleeping—that was it. A motley crew of mule drivers was drying themselves in a haze of "aguardiente" (Schnapps) and politely made room for the newcomers in the smoke-filled kitchen.

Not even the enticing smell of the slabs of meat roasting on the fire could remind me of the fact that we had eaten hardly anything all day. I was wet and shivering from cold and so very tired. While the sure-footed mules made them essential on the mountain trails, I defy anyone to try the beasts for comfort. I could offer a comparison of this locomotion to sitting on an unfettered engine running at bumpy speed. Even though we never trotted or even tried a canter, this had been a very long day for us

23

all. We would not have found other "ranchos" or accommodations in this sparsely inhabited region. Now, like it or not, I was ordered to take a gulp of that raw aguardiente, supposedly to warm me up. The damp saddle blankets on top of the wooden pallet were our beds. Others would join us later finding a place on the pallet along the wall. I guess a wet poncho became the cover. Mercifully, I do not remember more.

We now were half way up the mountain. It was cool and our start, after a hearty breakfast of "panela" (raw brown sugar)—water, eggs, meat and arepas (tortillas) was not as early as on the day before. We rode through more densely overgrown areas until finally we reached the real, old growth jungle. I was awestruck by the immense trees, the likes of which I had never seen, with thick undergrowth, and long heavy vines entwining it all. The daylight barely made it through the dense canopy above us. This would be our route for many hours up to our point of destination. The "trocha" is a trail of mud that has been carved out for many years by the hooves of cattle and mules. The animals always trail single file and step into the same holes, thus cutting out deep troughs through which they slurp slowly. They are often up to their bellies in mud since it never dries enough in the dense rain forest.

When a decline has to be negotiated, the animals just slide down the slick mud, while you stretch your legs ahead hoping the beast will not become entangled and topple, catching you under its weight, as happened to me once in later years. Growth is so thick and tangled as to be nearly impassable. Some plants produce huge, plate-size leaves that become useful utensils. One can fold them as drinking cups or use them like paper for a call of nature.

Roots and fallen trees or branches are constant reminders that no road crews are at work. My next disaster was an encounter with such a fallen giant. The mule steadily trudged on and barely made it under the obstructing tree, while the inexperienced little rider, quite unable to control the beast, was swept backward and landed up to her neck in a mud hole, screaming murder. Wolfi was fuming mad because, after extricating me from the mess, he still had to try to catch his prized mule, which merrily trotted on down the narrow path where no overtaking was possible. With a barrage of unkind words, he had to let her go on. He found her hours later at home, munching on her feed. Meanwhile I was plunked onto some other cargo beast to continue our journey. A few hours more brought us to our destination where Margot lovingly greeted us. She seemed glad to have some visitors in this solitude.

Of course, I instantly fell in love with the wildness of it all; the crisp fresh air after the years in our stifling Girardot was so invigorating. The high dense jungle was well cut back to allow for the sun to shine on the lush green of the "Kikujo" grass that Wolfi had sown in every bare spot between the fallen tree-giants. This grass was imported from Africa and was particularly useful in combating the many tree trunks that the grasses' roots would simply pierce and crack open. Later on it was discovered, that the Kikujo did not shy away from a wooden house or any other construction. But for the time being, it produced thick carpets of lush indestructible fodder. Any walk away from the house became an adventure since it meant clambering onto tree trunks and jumping or falling into deep crevasses to get to the next tree. In those early years, when we were still small, we would not have dared venture far anyway. Our legs were just too short and the stories we heard not always comforting.

Trees grow in the jungle that will put you into an eternal sleep if you rest under them and breathe in their fragrant scent. Also, there are many ants that, as we were told, can finish a person off as quickly as piranhas do in the water. Snakes abound, among them the anaconda. The large tapir and the panther are not easily seen but they are fierce. Any venture into the forest, as the lumber cutters undertook daily, was fraught with danger. The "machete" (bush-knife) was the most valuable tool and they always carried it with them attached to their belts. It was used to clear brush, vines, and small trees and to battle dangerous animals or to just plainly use to cut bread or meat at mealtime. Once the large trees had been cut down, years of waiting were necessary to dry some of the brush before it was burned. That is all except the ancient trees, which are probably still slowly rotting away after 70 years.

We had a most spectacular view from the house. From our altitude of 9000 ft, on clear days we could see the distant plains shimmering in tropical heat, at sea level. Not a village or habitation came into view no matter where we looked. The red and yellow hues of large forest fires would sometimes send dark smoke clouds into the blue sky, rising from the distant valleys during the dry summer months. Fire was the most popular means of clearing the land and preparing it for pastures and crops.

It was quite necessary for us to stay close to home with the chickens milling around, and some cattle, mules and dogs that kept us company. However, the rainy season was just beginning and we soon learned to live in a constant state of dampness. Heavy fog drifted through the house most of the time. It actually wafted through the cracks between the wooden boards to envelop and awaken us in the morning with a damp kiss. If we walked

out, we came back wet and muddy. The only place to dry
the clothes and many diapers was in the kitchen over the
smoky fire. There the large pot of our daily "guarruz"
(corn gruel) was simmering underneath the lines of clothing. For nearly three months, we were never really dry.
And we, Christiane and I, stayed there that long, until
Mami's return from Germany. Margot, even with all the
hardship she endured, was loving and uncomplaining,
and Wolfi, though stern, took us in like a father.

The hardest to get used to was the food. Corn was the
staple. Breakfast consisted of corn tortillas and "agua de
panela." Corn mush slowly cooked in a large pot with
pieces of air-dried, often rotten smelling meat. I can still
remember it as disgusting. With a few peas or carrots and
green plantains if available, thrown into the pot, this
thick gruel was our noonday meal as well as supper every
day without change. Rarely, a mule trip to market two
travel days away would bring some newly butchered and
salted meat, but lacking refrigeration, it was no longer
fresh. The occasional egg and milk with the agua de
panela was a treat. The indigenous woman who did the
cooking would not have been able to prepare anything
else anyway, as there was nothing else available to cook.
However, her knowledge of herbs and the ways of nature
were priceless!

Not many weeks after our arrival, it was discovered
that I had blood in my urine. Margot was quite concerned
but our cook told the "senora" that she could clear the
problem and heal "la nina." There was little else one could
do but believe her and submit to her medication. For days
I was made to drink an infusion produced by boiling the
silk of cornhusks. I actually remember the sensation of almost drowning in that stuff and I seemed to be glued to
the potty all the time as it washed through me. After a

few days, the coloring turned from red to pink and back to normal. It was an amazing feat! I had been totally cured from a kidney infection without the help of doctors or chemicals.

Years later in Bogota, when I was twelve years old, I suffered a similar infection and, remembering the good old Indian woman's medicine, my mother cured me again the same way even though we had a doctor available. When I contracted mumps, the smelly Indian remedy was a thick pad of filthy sheep's wool, cut from the juiciest section of an old ram's anatomy, between his hind legs. In bed for weeks with that horrid stuff around my neck, and in such close proximity to my delicate nose, was almost too much to bear but I survived the mumps, the wool, and all the bad memories, too.

These Indian "campesinos" (peasants) lived a very primitive life seemingly oblivious to hardships. During one of our stays in Pinares, there was a crew of lumbermen clearing the forest. Their woman cooked for about eight men in an open "rancho" (hut) with just a cooking and sleeping area. When I walked down to get some eggs, I discovered a new baby slung on her back. She had just given birth on the bare dirt floor, unassisted, and now was back to cooking the meal for the men. Not many words were ever lost over such ordinary events. When a job was finished, the women packed everything they had, pots, clothing and the latest baby on their backs and marched behind the men to the next job, often days away. How utterly luxurious our lifestyle seemed in comparison! Perhaps it dawned on me then how much life depends on one's resourcefulness and acceptance of situations, as well as utilizing given opportunities.

Our stay in Pinares was over when Mami came back to collect us. Under Wolfi's expert guidance, we headed for Palermo again. From this trip, I recall seeing Wolfi, with little Christiane on the saddle in front of him, way ahead of us disappearing from sight through the thick brush. It was afternoon and already quite warm. Of course we were very tired. Suddenly, I experienced a slow motion slide of my saddle into a precarious tilt to the side. While the saddle slid down to end at the mount's belly, I luckily extricated one foot from a stirrup, and hanging there with the other, I landed on the ground. As mules do, mine had deflated enough so the girth gave way. No matter that the heavy, western style saddles called "silla" (chair) were well secured under the neck and tail of the animals, the girth around the round belly also had to be tight. Mami and Tita both had no idea how to fix the problem. When they saw Wolfi looking back at them from a great distance away, they gestured to him for help, but he must not have seen them. He continued trotting out of sight around the next bend of the mountain. Wolfi was gone and we were totally alone. Somehow, the two women finally managed to push the saddle upright and, admonishing me not to let it slide again, we went on our way. We never saw Wolfi again that afternoon, nor any other human being. There were no habitations and seldom other trails in those areas but we had managed somewhere to take a wrong turn.

Night was descending with tropical speed. Millions of fireflies were the only comforting presence we perceived. At last, we came to a small rancho but the old woman inside was quite unable to tell us where we were and where we should be heading. Neither would she let us in. We must have looked quite frightening to her. We turned back and let the animals try to find the direction they wanted to take. It must have been a couple of hours later when we heard many voices calling and saw torches.

Here came Wolfi with several men looking for us! His annoyance was mellowed seeing our exhausted and frightened state and by the fact that he actually had found us. Having deposited little Christiane with some muleteers in the "posada" (inn), he had arranged for the search party. We arrived safely the next day in Palermo, and got on a truck back to Neiva, where we caught the train to Girardot the next morning.

I know that we made the trip to Pinares at least three times in those years. It was a grueling and strenuous experience but always fascinating. This, even though no matter how hungry or thirsty we would get when on the road, Father's admonition was, *"Nimm Dich zusammen"* (control yourself). There was no way we could buy some of the lush "arepas" (corn tortillas), chicken or other goodies sold by market women. They walked by the train with huge baskets displaying their wares on fresh banana leaves. Perhaps Papi saved us from catching nasty intestinal bugs this way. We just had to control our appetites and our desire for Coca-Cola. To this day I have no problem going without sustenance on long hikes, saving me from cumbersome baggage to carry along. It speaks of the perversity of human nature that I cherish the memories and would be glad to do it again.

Endurance of discomfort and hardship was part of the system that my parents and the Stillfrieds, were brought up in. We were well protected but never pampered. We learned to use our independence in caring for ourselves as well as those we were responsible for. Many of the current teachings on child rearing would have been a wasted effort in our upbringing, which was based on discipline. That prepared us well for the upheavals and hardship in store for us in life. The discomforts we experienced were caused by the primitive situations we had to

30

master and were often much like those endured by pioneers and early settlers. It is good to remember that we lived in a still relatively underdeveloped country.

Call to Civilization

It was apparent that further schooling would become necessary for me. Girardot had no qualified school to teach me more than Mami had already taught me. Mami was again pregnant and, in 1935 when Christiane was three years old, our brother, Harald, made his appearance. Papi was travelling often for his coffee in-and-export firm. The talk was now about moving us all to the capital, Bogota, five train hours away at the top of the central Andean "cordillera" (mountain range). The cooler, healthier climate there was an extra incentive.

The Stillfrieds had returned to Germany for good, as Wolfi's presence became necessary to run the family estate and where they would be in a better position to raise their ever-expanding progeny. In 1936, my parents tackled the transfer of our family to Bogota. I do not remember many details about the move but what stands out is my introduction to a regular school full of children.

Having grown up in virtual isolation with my only playmates Erika and Nini, I'd never had any association with boys of my age and I was painfully shy. My first day in the "Colegio Aleman" (German school), I was tentatively placed in the second grade and the teacher introduced me to a mixed group of about fifteen or twenty curious children who stared at me. But I survived the rest of the first day, mercifully ignored. As I entered the classroom on the second day, I had gotten the signals mixed. We had to file in to shake hands with the teacher and bow

31

or curtsy according to gender. I bowed as I had seen the boys do the previous day and thus started a barrage of laughter, "Not only does her name end with an 'o' like a boy's, but she also bows like a boy." Somehow I survived the first few weeks. Although it took me years to overcome a bad case of blushing when anybody addressed me, I slowly loosened up.

To my great surprise, I was soon advanced to the third grade. Apparently Mother's tutoring had been excellent. The school was good, too. A ratio of one-third German to two-thirds Colombian students and teachers meant that our classes were conducted some in German and some in Spanish. English was added to the curriculum in the third grade and I enjoyed it. French came in the fourth, but I disliked this language from the start. Finally, with a special exception, I was permitted to drop French from my curriculum. Unfortunately, this cost me an extra language. Latin was to be added later. A school bus collected us in the morning. A blond boy from my class sat on the bench in back. Hans was shy and nice and he waved me back to where he had saved me a seat next to him and then did so every morning. I experienced the novelty of the tender sensations a young child feels when first exposed to the boy-girl situation. Since Hans was popular, not even the older children, who usually were quite expert in teasing raised a fuss.

Meanwhile, my parents had found a more suitable house in a very nice location on the outskirts of town close to the American Country Club. They joined the club so my father could start playing golf. We had a nice big yard and garden with the house. I acquired my first menagerie of assorted small animals and started to raise guinea pigs. We had wonderful playing areas behind the house in a small forest of huge eucalyptus trees. School friends would join us often and we built a tree house. In a short time, it appeared that my life as a school child would begin a normal course. The old tradition of taking car rides into the countryside, on weekends, visiting lovely "fincas" (country homes) of friends or spending boring days at the Country Club would alternate. Occasionally I was permitted to go along with Papi on the golf course where only whispers were permitted lest I disrupt the men's concentration. There was one swing and one gray wall on which to practice tennis. Otherwise, it meant a day of "behave yourself" at its worst. My allowance of one nickel a weekend was soon used up on a few consoling lollypops or other sweets. During the noon ritual, while the adults sipped their Amer Picon on ice, we were not allowed to talk much, just sit. It was a hard feat, particularly for the tomboy, Christiane.

Mami enrolled me in the riding school of Herr Sachs. If ever there was an unpleasant personality, he had most of the attributes of it. His foul language was something I had not been previously exposed to and his long whip, expertly applied to the horse's rump, kept us all literally hopping. His methods were obviously experienced and professional. The most memorable one was to make us ride on saddle blankets only, mounted facing forward or backward, without saddle or stirrups. He spent long sessions teaching us how to fall off a horse. He soon had me jumping over hurdles. The day of the school fair and festival a rider from his advanced class cancelled and I was called to take his place. Of course, stealing the show was no big deal for a little blond girl in a ponytail riding and jumping on a white horse with only a blanket and last in the line of much older pupils! I won the jumping competition, then ran and hid bashfully behind my mother. Horseback riding became my great joy from then on, even though the chances to indulge were always scant. During our school breaks, we would spend a few days in "tierra templada" (temperate climate) on some friend's "finca" (country estate). The warmer climate was only a few hours train or car ride down the mountains. There we entered an entirely different atmosphere with the exotic fauna and flora so spectacular in these Andean mountain ranges, particularly in the coffee and banana plantation belt. Here riding and swimming were daily events.

2

A Mother's Travail, Germany 1937

Early in 1937, before I was ten years old, and just as life settled into this (for us) almost luxurious routine, black clouds of worry overtook the family. The baby, Harald, barely 18 months old, became critically ill. He was suffering from severe diarrhea and constant vomiting and no doctor could diagnose the problem or find help. Papi was again in Europe on business and Mami was quite desperate. She made the difficult trip to Barranquilla with Harald to see the well-known Dr. Rehbein. He urged Mother to immediately travel to Germany with the baby who could not have survived much longer in the tropics.

Traveling in those days was a major undertaking, and doing so with three children, one of them so ill, must have been a terrible ordeal for Mother. She had to close up the house in a matter of days. I do not remember what arrangements she made for it. Travel documents and passage on a steamer had to be secured, as well as all the packing for the family attended to. A five-hour train ride took us to Girardot where we boarded a flight to Barranquilla on a small aquatic plane touching down on the muddy waters at every Indian village along the Magdalena River. It caused us all agonizing ear pain when we descended into the tropical steam bath at river level. I found this sort of flying much less enjoyable than my recurring dreams as a very young child, when I would fly, without engine, or angel wings, at house level around

Girardot! The novel flight in one of the earliest passenger transports did save us precious days. The trip by riverboat to reach the coast of the Caribbean port of Barranquilla would have taken weeks and been extremely hot and uncomfortable.

Once we were luxuriously settled in our first class cabin on the HAPAG ship, *Cordillera*, for the almost four-week passage to Germany, things eased up some for Mother. We had embarked in tropical splendor with the portholes open. A flying fish once landed on my berth. Looking out on the waves that shimmered like diamonds in the sun, we saw schools of porpoises playing alongside the ship's hull. As night fell, I could not get enough of watching the magnificent phosphorescent glow in the waves. When we reached the more northern regions, the spouting of whales could be seen.

It became colder as we approached Europe and wintry weather. The luxury and elegance of the ship were not lost on me. I loved the soft music played at tea-time and appreciated the magnificent menus and service at the captain's table where our family usually sat during dinner. My father was well acquainted with the owners of some shipping lines, so my mother and baby Harald received all the help and consideration possible during this ordeal, being treated as a "VIP." What a change from our rather Spartan lifestyle this was! The first night on board, I pigged out and ate of the entire menu, then got seasick and lost it on the stairs when I tried to make it to the railing. At the steward's urging, I sat down and again went through the whole offering—and this time it stayed with me. I never had the problem again.

Christiane was ensconced daily in the nursery. Between helping Mami some and watching Christiane at times, I was pretty much on my own and quietly read or played alone in some corner on deck since there were no other ten-year-olds on board. This caused much chagrin to an old British Lord. He demanded of the deck steward, "Impossible situation! I say. Remove that child to the nursery at once, Steward." Children were not wanted on deck. My mother angrily told him off and not much happened to me.

There was much compassion and understanding for my mother's plight. Some nice crew members began entertaining me, showing me the ship and permitting me on decks not open to the general public. It happened that one day I was standing next to the chief steward watching the cranes unload cargo at a French port. Suddenly, we heard a piercing scream and saw a sailor lose his footing on the high mast. He hurtled down and fell with a horrible thud at our feet. The steward whisked me away in a hurry. It was a horrible experience. I heard later that the poor fellow lost his leg and was also badly hurt otherwise.

Mami had an occasional reprieve from her maternal nursing cares when the ship's nurse sat with Harald so Mami could go to dinner. Otherwise she went through sheer torture!

But Harald was failing rapidly. He was literally starving to death. His little body consisted of skin and bones, a balloon-like bloated stomach and a large head with huge cavernous eyes. The poor boy wailed with hunger; although they brought him delicious meals, he just could not keep anything down. The steward would bring broth, then Cream of Wheat, pudding, or anything my mother wanted but the child just could not eat or drink. He was obviously severely dehydrated. I saw Mother sitting in front of her son with tears of pain running down her cheeks as she would plead with him to try just one spoonful. Then we heard the desperate scream of the boy as he tried to prevent them from taking the food away again while he reached out with his skinny arms to hold the dish. I remember wishing that Papi would be with us. But he was far away in Germany and would meet us there. I was accustomed to the fact that Father never was there when a child was born or for any other momentous family affair. Mothers took care of such "domestic trivia." Also, in the 1930s, such separations were still major obstacles before transatlantic flights and rapid ocean crossings were possible. Any business trip meant months of separation with only scant communication.

When we arrived in Hamburg, our worried father met us at the ship and Harald was whisked away to the Eppendorfer Hospital where he was immediately put on a newly developed kind of "IV" to get fluids and some nourishment into him. He was in the hospital for many months, mostly under intensive care.

In the meantime, Christiane and I were farmed out to relatives and friends. Little "Geng," as Christiane was nicknamed, had switched in mid-ocean from her Spanish only, to some acceptable German. Otherwise, she was the same tomboy; nothing was safe in her proximity. I believe Christiane and I first spent some time in Berlin with our grandparents, Riess. Mami's parents lived in a very modest apartment in Berlin-Schoeneberg. Much later I began to question why Grandmother, in the manner of a housekeeper, occupied a tiny room next to the kitchen, while Grandfather inhabited the small living/dining/library/room, where he slept on a pullout bed. Their relationship was obviously not a warm one.

We children spent countless hours with Grandfather, never experiencing a dull moment. He knew so many wonderful stories about plants, animals, and nature and had books and pictures to illustrate his fabulous tales.

Using his fantastic imagination, he fabricated events and exciting stories out of anything in sight. Our greatest joy was trips to the Zoo where we spent the whole day, nibbling on raisins and nuts that we had bought to feed to some select animals. At other times, he took us on day trips to the Grunewald, a large forest around Berlin. There we hiked and rapturously listened as Grandfather introduced us to an exciting new world. We fed wild swans and learned about the fascinating insects, beautiful flowers, tiny ferns and all the wonders of the forest. Alas, these events were much too few and the time so limited, but I truly believe that Grandfather promoted our lifelong love and attachment to nature.

I learned then to find some beauty and happiness even in the most dismal situations as they were in store for us in the future. Did we not see in Colombia, how the dreariest, poverty-ridden huts would display flowering plants in old tin cans outside their dusty entrance? Even amongst the ruins of a burned-out building, there would be the bloom of a small weed. Accustomed to the abundance of the lush tropical nature, we had not learned to look for the perfection to be found in the small wonders surrounding us at all times. During and after the war, when plagued by hunger, one could find acorns or nettles growing along the roadside, to boil up for a meal. We recognized that many weeds are useful as well as pretty. In the saddest moments a sunray will shine through leaves or a rain puddle will offer the silvery glimmer of a reflection when a bug paddles around in the water. Grandfather pointed out much of this; he also had collected tree bark and carved a set of beautiful sailboats for us, of which one or two have survived to this day.

After an exciting "S-bahn" (rapid transit rail) trip back, Grandmother would serve us an excellent supper.

Again, she ate in the kitchen and not with us. We did not question the arrangement. Then we slept in the cold splendor of the "Gute Stube" (the fine room), with its heavy, musty furniture piled in so tight it was hard to move around in it. But it contained a huge bed, plenty of space for the two of us. The room appeared otherwise unused except for storage. Was it waiting for the daughter and grandchildren who came from overseas only this once?

Grandmother took us shopping with her occasionally, once to a small toyshop that I will never forget. Aside from the beautiful dollhouse and other toys that Mami had crafted, I had never seen such wonderful toys. For birthdays or Christmas we had occasionally received such beautiful things brought from Germany. While we enjoyed Grandmother's good food and care, we never warmed up to this reserved, rather stern old woman who was our "Grossmami." She obviously had a heart of gold, which we children could not recognize, and she must have suffered under the rather harsh and unfriendly treatment she received from Grandfather. He with his engineering degree probably suffered due to an unfulfilled career but still felt himself superior.

After the short Berlin visit, we went to the country estate of Father's von Krogh family. Gross Weeden was an old mansion surrounded by a beautifully tended park. What impressed me most was the meticulously kept house where a "Mamsell" (female butler) with a huge collection of keys dangling from her belt, was in charge of all this perfection. She supervised a large staff in the kitchens that not only served us delicious meals, but also were very busy preparing and canning vast amounts of fruits and vegetables for the winter. A field-like garden provided these. I was allowed to help in gathering produce, often letting the best berries vanish into my mouth, an unaccustomed delight. Most of these fruits were unknown in the tropics, while we certainly did not lack a large variety of delicious tropical fruit, which were available all year round in Colombia.

The nanny in charge of my four cousins took care of Geng. Years later it amused me to realize that I had determined then that I would some day be a "Gutsbesitzer's Frau" (estate lady). I would host a large estate like our Aunt Emma and Uncle Emil's, assisted by a "Mamsell" with keys dangling from her belt, who would supervise the maids, cook, and gardeners. I visualized having a chicken house to supply eggs and poultry and a dairy barn to produce wonderful cream and milk. And, of course, a stable with elegant horses and carriages for rides around the fields, all well cared for by a jolly coachman. Well, I did eventually get it all, even though not quite as lavish and minus the Mamsell with the keys, the gardeners, cook, nanny, and coachman. But I had my own chicken coop, entirely in my charge and the dairy where I often helped to milk cows. I also had my horses and I cleaned, saddled, and mucked the stalls by myself. And I thought ours was the most beautiful, vast estate one could wish for. And for us it was so special because we did not inherit it, we had to work for it.

When we left Gross Weeden, we visited Uncle Bruno and Aunt Frieda, my grandmother's sister on Mother's side. She was married to a very dignified old gentleman who was Administrator of the vast forests around Malmitz in Schlesien (Silesia). We loved to walk with our aunt under the enormous canopies of trees in search of mushrooms and berries. It was such a different experience from looking at walls of impenetrable virgin jungle. We were able to walk silently and safely on heavy moss amongst the cathedral-like giants of the well-tended forest. We were only there a few days. Then Mami took Christiane and me to Silbitz for a stay with the Stillfrieds while she rushed back to be near Harald. He was still in the Eppendorf Hospital in Hamburg where he was very slowly being brought back to life. Papi had returned to his business in Colombia.

Christiane and I stayed for some time with Margot and Wolfi and their growing family, living with them in the Manager's house. Silbitz was the estate of the Stillfrieds. The family had owned it and resided there since 1849 when, through marriage, the old castle had become part of the Count Stillfried and Rattonitz estates. The oldest son and heir of the estate would thereafter carry the name "Mettich" after Stillfried. The Stillfried and Rattonitz family traced back several centuries, always living in the region. This province had been part of the Austro-Hungarian Empire. Silesia and one branch of the family were taken over by Frederick the Great in 1740 and incorporated into Prussia. By the early 1900s the heir to the estates was Rudolph, a dashing young cavalry officer. Due to his heavy gambling losses, he had been bailed out twice by his father and consequently forfeited his rights to the inheritance. Rudolph's younger brother, Franz, became the legal heir of the two family estates, Buchwald and Silbitz. Franz, an active naval officer since before World War I, convinced his father to let his brother, Rudolph, keep the Buchwald estate. He took over Silbitz and married the beautiful, vivacious Countess Maria Strachwitz in 1904. Rudolph died in Berlin in 1918, during the battle against Communism. Buchwald was returned to Franz. By then it was heavily indebted and run down. Wolfi was the oldest of Franz's ten children. He was now the future heir of the family estates according to tradition. My husband, Dominik, is the youngest in that family.

Wolfi's parents, the senior Stillfrieds, inhabited the old "Schloss" (castle). It was located in a beautiful park with ancient trees. The front faced a drive around a fountain and a rose bed and the sides and back bordered the remains of a moat. Its waters lapped up to the stone walls of the old building which was covered by vines that turned burgundy red in fall. The "Schloss" was originally built in the early 1700s and was remodeled from a water-fortress to more appropriate elegance around 1850. A large chapel had been built on a high point in the park. The farm buildings and stables were located across from the park, adjacent to the village of Silbitz.

Father Franz had taken over Silbitz and Buchwald also following Rudolph's early death. It had actually been in the Stillfried family longer. Buchwald was in a sad condition, when his father offered young Wolfi the opportunity to take over Buchwald, he refused and choose to go to Colombia instead. Silbitz had to be heavily indebted to save Buchald, but the family held onto the two estates throughout the periods of inflation and Depression. Agricultural conditions in Germany deteriorated in the 1920s. Many estates came close to bankruptcy and had to be sold or were heavily indebted. During the early Nazi years, the situation for agriculture improved. The new regime implemented drastic debt reductions and set the economy onto a robust rebuilding program. The Autobahn construction was one of the projects. The general upturn much helped the indebted farmers. Silbitz and Buchwald remained in the family after going through very difficult times. They struggled through many hardships, never losing their strong faith or failing to give their many children a warm and happy childhood.

Mama Stillfried underwent a remarkable transformation. She had grown up, and spent many years in Silbitz pampered and attended to by a well-trained staff, including a personal chambermaid to help with the care and styling of her gorgeous knee length hair. During the many years of hardship, by then with only the younger children still at home, she uncomplainingly coped. She ran the large house almost single-handed. She daily carried buckets full of coal up a spiral staircase to keep the stoves in the upstairs rooms warm. While they never went hungry, Mama Stillfried herself cooked simple meals for her family. Dominik recalls how much they enjoyed the white roll they only ate at Sunday breakfast. Otherwise the daily breakfast was slices of rye bread, cottage cheese and molasses. (We kept the custom of white rolls for Sunday breakfast to this day!) As the situation improved, the habit of frugality in that household, as in many other country estates remained—to nobody's detriment.

After his return to Germany from Colombia, Wolfi had capably taken over the administration of Silbitz. The estate of Buchwald had been handed over to very young and overly optimistic Franz Jr., the second son, some years before. He had to struggle through all the difficulties for several years, to keep the very run-down estate, lacking much needed funds. He married and raised his family there until they also were expatriated with the rest of the family after the Second World War. Their sister, Pia, third of the children, married in 1937 and moved to Oppeln, also in Silesia. The next two brothers, Gebhard and Nicolaus, studied to become Jesuit priests, but Nicolaus died while still in the seminary. The sixth boy, Sixtus, had died in an accident as a baby. Angela, the seventh child, enjoyed a few years of happy Grand Balls, hunts, and travels before she married into an estate in Bohemia. Norbert, the eighth, battled through school, not much appreciating the experience. After his stay in Colombia, he joined the military.

This was the family and home of my playmates. The two youngest, Ruediger and Dominik, with their parents and a charming old couple inhabited the Schloss (castle). Herr Bartels and his wife, the old couple, were comfortably located in a downstairs apartment. He was the private tutor for the boys and I was invited to participate in the daily lessons. I enjoyed the classes but they were constantly disrupted by the inattention of the two brothers, who had anything but learning on their minds! Not a day went by without our thinking up some games to play among the huge old trees and hiking paths in the park with its creeks and fields full of wildflowers. Of special interest to us, but actually off limits, was the huge straw and hay barn, the most exciting playground one can imagine. After climbing up the steep mountains of straw, we plunged down from the lofty summit into the soft piles below. Hide and seek games were fascinating because one could quietly snuggle into some hole and comfortably wait to be found. Roughhousing was quite common and the boys showed no inclination to treat us girls gently.

Wolfi's older children were almost our age. Often cousins were visiting, as well as neighborhood children. We were careful around the Schloss, however, where (grandfather to Wolfi's children, and father to Dominik and Ruediger) Stillfried would thunder his commands out of the window of his office when there was too much commotion or noise. A favorite entertainment for Dominik and Ruediger, was shooting their "b-b" guns. It was an activity that I never enjoyed. I was the Indian squaw and was ordered by the braves to sit in the hut that

45

we had constructed while they went off squirrel hunting. The whole thing seemed so stupid to me that I took off and apparently spoiled the game.

One day Dominik and his friend, Wolfgang, were teaching me how to ride a bicycle on a lovely flat, wide road in the park. There was no obstacle in sight until the white-clad form of Pia's children's nanny with her charges, Dominik's nephew and niece, appeared around the corner. Seeing the grim face of the much-feared old "Muecke," I knew, instinctively, that I could not miss her and, frozen in terror, I sailed right into her. My two brave companions dodged behind some bushes! I forget what happened next but it cannot have been pleasant.

We also loved to play hide and seek in the dark attic of Margot's house or romp around upstairs in bad weather. One evening after cavorting around and throwing ourselves into the thick featherbeds to soften the jump, we heard Margot calling us for supper. As I started straightening up the beds and moving things back where they belonged, Dominik stood watching me and complimented me with the words, "Such a good housewife I would like to have some day." This was one of the first times when I blushed and felt a strange tingling within because I suddenly noticed that Dominik was looking at me with his beautiful, warm brown eyes. I hastily ran downstairs. Of course, the implication of the importance of a "good housewife" dawned on me much later in life, with the advent of Women's Lib!

Splendid sunshine greeted us on the following Easter Sunday. We all went to church in the private chapel in the park. Even though I had no religious training, I liked to go along with the rest of the family. Dominik was one of the acolytes and while he was swinging the incense burner, the priest intoned his "Dominus vobiscum." To my untrained ears it sounded like "Dominik wo bist Du" (where are you?) and I almost called out, "He is right in front of you."

The ceremony impressed me a lot. I always was elated and mystified by what went on in the churches I seldom visited. I had begun to ask about being baptized. Having lived in a totally Catholic country, my Lutheran parents had no church affiliation and none of us children had been baptized. When I became insistent, Mami did not oppose my wishes although she herself did not believe in the need for it. She made plans and arranged for a ceremony later on. She knew that I took life rather seriously and had developed my own opinion about values. My judgment was not that usually attributed to a ten-year-old. She also knew the rather headstrong determination her eldest daughter could develop.

But on this Easter Sunday in Silbitz, we had fun on our minds and a big celebration. After the service we all were quite hungry, not having eaten any breakfast. We ran down the chapel mountain to the Schloss where the culinary delights of Mama-Grossmama's (Grandmother) famous buffet awaited us. I admired the endless expanse of a table set up in the big dining room. We children (and there were plenty of us), sat at the lower end and thus had a marvelous time. I was introduced to egg-cracking and other table games and competitions, like who would eat the most hardboiled eggs. Ruediger or his nephew, Christoph, usually accomplished that feat. Easter breakfast was quite an event and much appreciated by all family members in this usually very frugal household. Of course, somewhat later, the big Easter egg hunt in the park took place.

After the holidays, the school routine began again. Dominik was to attend a boarding school in Sagan for a few years. On weekends, he would find a second home visiting his brother, Franz, in beautiful near-by Buchwald. Meanwhile, time for our departure neared with the inevitable good-byes. I had developed a preference for the company of the kinder, gentler Dominik so I was sad to leave.

We were now off to a summer stay on the island of Foehr in the North Sea. Harald was supposed to join us there after being discharged from the hospital. A cousin of Mother's owned a "Kinderheim" (summer vacation camp) where we were deposited for the next few months. We slept in dormitories, grouped by age and sex. We had daily classes and spent a lot of time on the wonderful beach. Foehr is one of the larger islands in a chain that runs along the coast of North Germany. There are only a few villages on Foehr. Wyk, where we stayed, was the largest of them. The Friesians had built their quaint, stout red brick houses in the protective embrace of a huge dike. Covered with thick reed roofs, they seemed to crouch behind the dike for protection from the hefty storms that battered the area in winter. On the smaller islands, called "Hallig," the buildings were built on large mounds of earth, in the hope of keeping them above the high floods that wash over the islands in the winter storms.

Many Friesians have lost their lives to the sea in the centuries that they have clung to their islands. They are fishermen and used to hardship. They also are beautiful people. The tall, stately women wear their black "Trachten" (national costume) and high headgear, decorated with silver-filigree jewelry, with impressive dignity. The Friesians are not an outgoing people. They talk little, even less to strangers, but I admired them even then and read what I could about their folklore. Someone gave me a book by the 19th century writer Theodor

48

Storm. I was deeply impressed with the novel *Der Schimmelreiter* (the rider on a white horse) among others. When the heavy fog rolled in from the ocean and engulfed the island, my busy imagination detected the ghostly figure on his white mount cantering along the dike. Never again did I feel so akin to a people as I did to the Friesians. I became convinced that the Nordic branch of father's family came from this stock. I later found this to be true to some extent.

It seemed quite fitting when Harald's, Christiane's and my baptisms were scheduled to take place in the historic oldest church. It stood on top of some Viking ruins at the far end of the island. Grandfather actually gathered the water for the ceremony from the nearby Viking cliffs, using a very old bronze church vessel. We were baptized on a beautiful sunny day in the presence of our godparents and a few other relatives. My Godfather, Eric Klaussmann could not come all the way from New York. Of course I insisted on being baptized by the name of Elke, a girl's name I had recently heard several times. No more "o" (as in Elko) for me! It was a very meaningful ceremony. The repeat baptism years later, when the Catholic Church did not recognize my Lutheran baptism as I converted to Catholicism did not match the early experience.

Our stay in Wyk was extended into early autumn since little Harald was with us now and seemed to benefit from the invigorating ocean air. The waves washing in at rising tide produced music of their own. The smell of the "Watten" (shallows) was a special blend of salt, fish, and some decay. We could wade out a long way in search of abundant seashells, stars, and urchins, but had to be very much aware of the rapidly incoming tide of the North Sea. Every season has its beauty. Ever since, I have remembered the smell of the sun-baked pine nurseries in air heavy with salt spray. One of the most memorable experiences for me was the discovery of a small, blue bellflower that bloomed in the fields and meadows, the "Glockenblume." Many times in later years, during often dark and fearful hours, I had a vision of that sun-baked meadow and the little bluebells beckoning in the breeze. I could almost taste the salt spray, feel the soothing sun-rays, and hear the distant call of the seagulls.

Now most of our good friends and playmates had returned to their homes. So did my very special friend, Fritz Klimpsch, a boy who shared my enthusiasm for all the beauty around us. Later we corresponded a few times, until he was swallowed by the cataclysm of war. Harald's health had improved a little, but it was quite obvious that he was, by no means, well. Mother had to make the very difficult decision to place him in a nursery run by a cousin who cared for two other children who were afflicted by a similar "Tropical Sprue."

Harald was diagnosed to be suffering from this little known illness with no known cure, perhaps triggered by the water or not properly pasteurized milk. No one really knew much about this rare condition, only that children affected with it should perhaps avoid returning to the tropics where a relapse might be likely. Life in tropical Colombia seemed impossible for him and the prompt medical attention essential to him was not available there.

After a brief good-bye from our grandparents in Berlin, we had to return to Colombia at the end of September 1937. Berlin was in upheaval due to a visit by Italy's Prime Minister Benito Mussolini. The German Chancellor Adolph Hitler lavishly hosted "Il Duce."

Miami took us to a place with crowded bleachers

where we could watch our first parade. The number of people and the loud cheering horrified me, but I loved the marching music, the singing, and the parade of uniformed young soldiers marching by in great precision. Right in front of us, some children handed bouquets of flowers to Hitler and Il Duce before they drove on, raising their arms in salute as most of the multitude of people there also did. Little could we guess, or care then, that this was a prelude to things to come in a few years.

We were booked on a nice freighter, the *H.C. Horn.* It was now late in the season, and the trip was not smooth, but we loved it. We were among fourteen children of various ages on board. Since this was not a luxury liner, a nursery was not available so we had the run of the ship. Christiane and others romped with the crew members. Being older, with all of my eleven years, I felt I could not join them so I just watched the roughhousing with some envy. In bad weather, we played games in a corner of the salon. This infuriated some of the older passengers. Once a fussy old couple marched in and swept our cards and checkers to the floor to try to make us leave.

Christiane had switched to Spanish only, sometime during mid-trip. I took back with me an ever-present sense of homesickness for Germany from then on. Colombia somehow never was the same again for me; I had lost my sense of belonging only there. The sameness and lack of the seasons was the most noticeable. While I loved the loose integration of nature into everyday life in the tropics, I often missed its counterpart in the orderliness of the European landscape.

3

Home to Colombia

We returned to Girardot again where my father was now stationed as manager of the American coffee-export firm, Schaefer-Klaussmann. We rented a nice house in a new development next to the swim club. The opposite side faced only a field separating us from the jail. We could observe all comings and goings from our windows. The weekends were always turned into gaudy events, with music from uncontrolled loudspeakers testing our nerves as we were "entertained" by both our neighbors. Of course, activities at the jail entrance, with all the visitors, vendors, and all sorts of fiestas stirred our special interest. Christiane soon acquired several pets; she was very good with animals. We all enjoyed the antics of a toucan and a parrot. These and other pets could easily be obtained at the market and they were usually in dire need of rescue from cruel treatment by unfeeling owners.

Now the problem of my schooling arose again. I was desperate when I learned that I was destined to board, together with eight other children, in the only available private establishment, in order to attend our "Colegio Aleman" (German school) in Bogota, six hours away from Girardot. Frau Hugentobler, with her grown son and daughter, ran the boardinghouse. There we were fed what might have been a sort of Hitler indoctrination and meals of unrefined oatmeal and often "Eintopf" (stew) in a sterile atmosphere of super-clean floors and occasional nasty punishments. In the evenings, Frau Hugentobler read to us while we had the task of knitting socks and baby clothes for the "winter help" in Germany. I understood this to be a sort of Salvation Army to alleviate some of the misery that also was prevalent in Europe. The once weekly meal of a one-pot-stew to save pennies for the "winter help" and some more such practices certainly did not make any sense to us. Living in the tropics, we knew nothing about winters. But we were kept busy and our free time was well regulated and controlled. Neither did the glorification of "Mein Fuehrer," some character far away across the ocean, pose any meaning for us. None of us was interested in politics. Otherwise I enjoyed the companionship with the other boys and girls. Ballgames, hikes and small theatrical performances also kept us busy, besides the rigorous school demands.

Soon a Youth Group was formed and we wore a kind of uniform to these gatherings. It functioned much like a scouting troop, which took us on sometimes extended hiking and camping trips. Swimming in wild rivers and diving into whitewater were two of the tests expected from us to prove our "bravery and worth." I often smarted from the teasing because I was the youngest, barely eleven years old. On one occasion I was glad to have been excused because of my age from the cruel test of courage. Two of the older boys almost lost their lives in the foolhardy endeavor. They had to dive and swim the wild rapids of a river. We never questioned the fact that our "leaders," the Hugentoblers, never took part in these demonstrations of bravery.

To my parents' great astonishment, they read in the newspaper in Girardot some days later, that the "German Youth" in Bogota were being instructed to throw bombs and grenades. The bulky baggage we carried apparently provoked this ridiculous notice. The large balls and other sports equipment had raised suspicion when we boarded the bus to take us to our destination. After all, on these occasions we were all "gringos" (foreigners); our Colombian school friends were not included on these trips because they were not members of the German Youth Group.

Otherwise, these hiking and camping trips were quite exciting and a lot of fun. We would travel from frigid Bogota down the mountain into a deliciously mild climate. We usually stayed in a hacienda and supervision was mostly self imposed. That is, the older ones looked after the younger members. I remember the thrill of a nightly drive home in a school bus. We were exhausted after a long hike and stretched out on the floor of the crowded bus to sleep. I got permission to lay my head on Juergen's stomach, he happened to be sleeping close by. Of course, he did not know and until then, neither did I, that he was my hero, one of the wildest and bravest on all the tough assignments.

There was also school—and that was no picnic. Demands were very high as the curriculum had to encompass both the German and Colombian school plans. I had been set back one year since I had missed so much during the year in Germany, and I never again achieved the high rating I had had before. Frau Hugentobler strictly enforced supervised homework. Disobedience was harshly punished, for instance, by forcing a culprit to swallow a spoonful or two of horrible tasting unpurified castor oil. I can still hear Roland screaming through the upstairs window for all to hear, *"Auxilio que la vieja me mata!"* (Help, the old witch is killing me!) Every morning poor little Hildegard sat in front of a huge plate of porridge cooked of poorly peeled oats that stuck to the gullet. She

54

just could not get it down and invariably would throw up and have to eat the results again.

Our only real escape was on Sundays when the house-family, glad to be rid of us for a while, would dismiss us for a walk in the mountains that surrounded Bogota. We hiked, we played, and we wrestled. Once things really became exciting when the cow pies we used as missiles against each other had hardened due to a drought. Inez was smacked right on an eye and furiously went after her adversary. (Of course, we had some serious questions to answer when we got home bruised and filthy.)

The weekend gatherings at the German Club were fun for us youngsters. There were games of hide and seek in the park, ball games and much other entertainment offered. Occasionally, we could participate in dances and partying organized by the adult club members. On one such occasion, Alfredo discovered, the bartender was storing in an unused bathroom a tub filled with pineapple punch. Much of the good liquid had been used, but the delicious fruit, well steeped in alcohol, was floating in a residue of wine there for our enjoyment. We youngsters made many secret trips to that bathroom. Some of the older boys imbibed too much and began to behave strangely and we were all sent home. When Frau Hugentobler returned to check on us, Alfredo was nowhere to be found. A real search was initiated through much of the night. Finally, somebody found him curled up on a pile of clothing in the corner of a closet. He was in a totally hazy and oblivious state, claiming that his plane had just hit a mountain and he could not go on.

But even these Club gatherings had some purpose, like the collections for the German "winter-help." I also enjoyed the hours we spent crafting small pins and figurines cut out of plywood and painted during handicraft classes. We sold these items at the bazaar for the same cause. I suppose there must have been many pep talks during these activities but I do not remember much because, these things did not seem to concern or interest me. Neither did they interest any of my friends there.

Vacation was approaching and time for us to go home—in my case to Girardot and the family. The swimming pool, with its Olympic-height diving board, was a big attraction. Unfortunately, it soon became a bone of contention for me. Papi displayed little Christiane's valor with great pride. That little thing in her red bathing suit clambered up to the top tier and, without hesitation, she would dive down. Papi collected her after she surfaced much enjoying the shouts and accolades of the many onlookers. She had not even learned how to swim properly, but she appreciated the value of the fifty cents she was awarded after every dive. I was asked to imitate the feat, but I went up and chickened out. What a disgrace! I crawled down the ladder again to dive only from the nine-foot board! Of course, I heard no end, about my cowardice, compared to Christiane's bravery. After all, she was only six years old, and I was eleven! Well, my timid reminder that probably I was more aware of the bad consequences, since I was older, brought me only ridicule. It seems that Papi, as a young orphan in the "cadet academy," had had to perform similar tests of courage.

My swimming holidays were thoroughly ruined. Even more so, when I surfaced from a dive with one side of my white-blond hair tinted totally green from chemicals in the pool. It stayed like that until it grew out again. It was little consolation to me when, just a few days later, Christiane hit the water in a bad way and then refused to repeat her stunt. Christiane was brave to the point of foolhardiness. Once a band of rowdy street boys came along throwing rocks at some object with much noise and ugly screams. Christiane suddenly ran into the road to rescue a half-dead lizard that she carried home. She seemed oblivious to the barrage of abuse and stones that luckily missed her. The lizard stayed all day on Christiane's arm. When she tried to set it down, it would immediately crawl back up as if for safety.

Soon, the vacation was over and I had to take the train for my return to Frau Hugentobler and school in Bogota. I was absolutely miserable about the prospect until Mami told me the big news that she was pregnant again. The baby was due in March and it was being considered, that the family should move back to Bogota. But meanwhile I was able to continue on with my school routine with a much lighter heart, for a few more months at Frau Hugentobler's.

"Calle 69" (69th Street) in Bogota, 1939, marked a year of momentous changes in my life of complacent schooling and growing into the teen years expecting the entitlements deemed due at such an age. I would turn twelve in May, not yet old enough to wonder about adversity and the meaning of unexpected happenings that can so disrupt an orderly life. The road ahead veered in an entirely different direction that would change my life placing the first unusual responsibilities on me. Perhaps it was time to ask more defined questions about where we were going. I was still somewhat a non-person, not accustomed to questioning adults. We were raised in the old mode of "Children should be seen but not heard." Respect for others and of our elders was instilled early on. That was the way my parents were brought up and so was everyone else we knew. We were raised to become little shadows, the emerging duplicates of doting parents, the budding next generation. Or so it was perceived to be. But then I began to sense that this was not so really my mother's philosophy. She was of a rebellious nature and did not see fit to bridle my personality much anymore. The more responsibility she allowed me to take, the more I felt obliged to be responsible. I took deep pride in the trust placed in me and tried not to disappoint.

I had an overzealous sense of truth and pride, some gathered from literature. I read, in German translation, the books of the Norwegian writer Trygve Gulbransen, the "Bjoerndal Family" saga. I was much impressed by Father Dag's admonition: *"Aber das Leben zerbricht unseren Stolz, und wir verstehen das Leben am besten, wenn er zerbrochen ist"* (But life breaks our pride and we learn to understand life best when it {pride} has been broken).

It took me years to accept this wisdom. We grew up with little religious guidance since my parents were not church affiliated. While I often felt I was missing out on something, I also was very critical of the hypocrisy I encountered in connection with religion. This was particularly true among close friends who seemed to think themselves superior because of their religious affiliations. What caused me many problems was the realization that this was a man's world, a man's religion; in a world where priority was always given to the male. Was I not worth just as much, and was I not more capable than many a man I knew could be?

However, we received strict moral directions, simple and clear-cut, from our parents. I grew up knowing (with pride as Papi would point out) exactly what a Krogh did or did not do. One never took anybody else's possessions, no matter how much coveted. One respected other people, not accepting abuse oneself. One spoke the truth, did not cry or complain, even in discomfort or pain; and did not question authority—or did we? Of course, later in life, I had to accept that such pride in one's own creed is fraught with misconceptions, sometimes even with prejudice—and easily subject to failure. Life presented many occasions when I felt extremely grateful for the strict discipline that we grew up with. Later, survival often depended on it and we were well prepared to endure adversity. Of course a good dose of luck and, often unrecognized, guidance is essential to lead us around multiple chasms.

Our family bond was strong, more so since we lived such an isolated life, mingling little with other people whose interests we did not share. The selection of friends in school was limited. It appeared a strange phenomenon that we Nordic girls were far behind in physical development compared to our Colombian friends. Those girls were showing obvious signs of becoming lovely senoritas while my friends and I were gangly, uncoordinated teens. Disgusted by time spent on inane hair-do's, fingernail painting, and talk of boys, I considered boys to be fair targets for silly pranks. Consequently, I suffered some roughing up of the meaner type.

Now my concern was that my days at Frau Hugentobler would soon be over and the family moving to Bogota again. This was prudent on account of our schooling and particularly since Papi was to bring back little Harald. He seemed sufficiently recovered, and the Bogota climate and relative comforts were especially important for him.

Father was in Europe again on a business trip. These trips were still cumbersome and took months since the boats were slow. My very pregnant mother undertook the move from Girardot to Bogota alone. When the big day came, Mother and Christiane arrived by train ahead of an old "camion" (truck) with all of our belongings tied precariously on it. With her proverbial ingenuity, Mother had instructed a carpenter to cut clear through two large wardrobes and other pieces that did not fit through doors or onto the truck. They were later reassembled on location with screws. Thus they were now always ready for any future moves.

The rainy season was not quite over. The "derrumbe," an avalanche of mud and debris that had cascaded onto our possessions was not part of the plan. Luckily, heavy rains and subsequent sunshine had taken care of part of the cleaning, but not much of the damage. Mother had never invested in much of great value so no tears were shed. Somehow, in spite of her very advanced pregnancy and Father's absence, Mother had soon established us in a nice home where we each had our own room. The house was surrounded by a garden, which she lovingly cared for. There also was ample space in the back for our ever-growing menagerie.

First priority was to move the midwife in. It was still Adelina. Our nice Theodolinda from Girardot, and another girl took care of the housework and the cooking.

We were barely settled when Heide-Betsy was born, March 3rd 1939, just four days before we expected Papi who had collected Harald from Germany. It was to be a "finally the family is together" wonderful event. However, after one look at little Harald, the midwife, Adelina, whisked him into a separate room. Soon I was pushed in after him with strict orders not to come out at all. Food, and other needs would be supplied through an otherwise locked door. Harald had contracted whooping cough on the ship! He was still barking violently and, from this tremendous effort, blood vessels had burst in and around his eyes. The little fellow looked as if he had just survived a boxing match. His eyes and their surroundings were blue-black. He was not yet four years old, and hardly knew me. Neither did I feel any filial affection towards this virtual stranger. Yet, here we were forced together out of the necessity to quarantine him away from the newborn baby. I had had whooping cough and was thus considered the only immune person available. My tender age and total lack of experience with small children could not be taken into consideration. We had always had nannies to take care of us children.

I vaguely remember that despite the pep talk my mother gave me through closed doors, with such fine-sounding admonitions of great responsibility, big girl etc., I really did not cherish those two or three weeks in confinement. The chores of cleaning, washing, changing, feeding and entertaining a little child were entirely new to me. Meanwhile I could not visit school.

Above all, I was quite cross about not being able to see or touch the new baby, my godchild, a privilege I had been promised in return for my help. I bargained for naming her Heide, since Mami's name was Adelheid. Eventually even this travail passed and Harald survived my care. However, a few weeks later, probably weakened by the whooping cough, a recurrence of his old affliction manifested itself. Big worries again befell our parents since his health deteriorated rather rapidly.

Adventures in Travel

My parents knew better than to wait for improvement and immediately prepared to return Harald to the hospital in Germany. A good friend offered to help. She had several children, one Heide's age, and a nanny who took care of the little ones. Heide was taken over to their beautiful house and Mami was able to get a flight to New York, on a recently established air service. From there, she got passage on a fast steamer across the Atlantic, and Harald was back in the Eppendorf Hospital just in the nick of time. Mami stayed on for a few months to see him installed again at Frau Gertrud Schroeder's Kinderheim (nursing home). She then boarded the freighter, *Frieda Horn,* to rush home to Bogota.

Little did I understand the gathering political storm clouds. My concerns were about our little family and the need to be together. Reading was my greatest joy. Gustav Freitag's major epic *Die Ahnen* (The Ancestors) and generations to follow, which I believe began with *Ingo und Ingraban,* particularly fascinated my romantic inclination.

Meanwhile, I had again been left in charge, now of a house with little sister Christiane and an undomesticated father, plus several pets and two maids of rather recent employ. Of course this was all besides our regular school schedule. My first problem arose when I noticed that the money given the cook for the market seemed to evaporate in her hands. Our meals became skimpier and worse by the day. Father admonished me not to rock the boat; we should try to endure until Mami's return. I would have left it at that, but the cook herself vanished a few days later. Papi had immediately fired her when he discovered that his whisky had acquired a very watery light color and flavor. No joking with such important matters! Teodolinda, who had taken a different position in the neighborhood, came over occasionally to help out. Somehow we muddled through. Papi most certainly was quite useless around the house and so was I.

After school, I would tie on my roller skates and visit

the Smith's nice house hoping to get a glimpse of my baby sister and deliver her laundry, which was done at our house. However, I did not often succeed. The baby was kept well guarded by an unfriendly nanny who saw no need for my coming into the nursery. Otherwise, I had a seemingly permanent attachment in my sister, Christiane, who had acquired an infuriating habit. No matter what I wanted to do, she would say, "Ich auch" (me, too), and invariably I had to take her along. This was particularly vexing when a new boy, with the most astounding dreamy, blue eyes arrived in school and my girlfriends and I started drooling over him and vying for his attention (of course, without success). On weekends, we accompanied Papi to the Country Club and simply hated it. The small group of international friends that gathered for a Sunday game of golf never seemed to have children our age.

Finally, we received the news that the *Frieda Horn* was to anchor in Cartagena in two days. We were unbelievably happy! It was now the end of August and Mami had been away for four months. The ugly clouds of war were descending on the western world, so Mami had not been able to get passage on an earlier, faster ship. I received permission from Mrs. Smith to bake a welcome cake in her kitchen with the help of her cook, since we were still without kitchen assistants. I made a beautiful pound cake and excitedly rushed home with it. There was Papi with a very long face and an ominous looking telegram in his hand. The *Frieda Horn* had disappeared just hours before landfall. From then on, rumors abounded, but no news. The war had started and the family was split up on different continents! I will relate here a short account of Mami's experiences, taken from her written report:

The *Frieda Horn,* a slow, sturdy 3184 BRT freighter, had sailed from Hamburg on August 5, 1939. The trip was uneventful until they reached Trinidad on August 25. Despite war rumors, the Captain felt they could make it to La Guaira in Venezuela, perhaps for Mother to disembark there and continue by land to Colombia. There were only eleven passengers. Two "deck passengers" joined them in Trinidad for the short hop over to Venezuela. One of them was a tall, young, black man, who was planning to participate in a bicycle race. Just before departure from Trinidad, Captain Struebig got orders to fill his tanks up with fuel, which he normally would have done twenty-four hours later in La Guaira. Initially, the British authorities tried to impede their departure, but were unsuccessful; they had to let the ship sail on the 25th of August. When they were just two hours out to sea, the German Marine Ministry radioed all ships to immediately return to Germany. Poor Mami, still in happy anticipation of a family reunion, had to take a stiff drink and bear it.

Captain Struebig had contemplated letting off the three passengers who urgently desired to go to South America, if he had encountered a sailing or other vessel, that he could have entrusted them to. No contact with ships was made, however, and in the safety of night they reached the Atlantic, shipping out of the Caribbean between Tobago and Barbados undetected.

There was no shortage of food on board, but water had to be rationed. Everyone was put to work. The ship was camouflaged, a new name painted on, and the three women on board were put in charge of sewing an array of flags for changes according to need. They traveled first as Norwegians, then as Finns. Thus they sailed north along the American coast and passed Newfoundland, Greenland and Iceland on the way to the North Cape, sailing under total blackout and without position lights at night; no foghorn was used in the heavy fogs. Actually, the ship did not even have charts for the northern region, a lack which became critical as they went for days without seeing the sun or stars for navigation. Mami really learned to appreciate the job of a Captain; he often could not even leave the command bridge. As soon as the smoke from a distant smokestack came into view, their ship had to change course. One day they saw four distant ships—at least the tips of their masts.

The passengers did wonder about the zigzag course often taken by the ship. They were also made aware that should they be caught, the ship was made ready to be scuttled. Holes had been drilled and bolts loosened in strategic places and all was ready for this ultimate act. The lifeboats could be lowered at an instant's warning. The *Frieda Horn* was not to fall into British hands! For days they cruised back and forth trying to find the passage through the Norwegian Schaeren (islands). At last they were able to follow another ship at a distance and find the passage. In the meantime the ship had been transformed from a Norwegian to a Finnish vessel by the use of paint and flags.

At Honningsvang, a pilot came on board, who told them about the liner *Bremen,* which was pursued up to Murmansk, as well as another ship that was followed by an English submarine all the way into the Polar Sea. From Honningsvang, they snaked south, hugging the coastline with its many fjords. The sight of the beautiful, lush green landscape was a soothing change, after the 12,000 nautical miles they had traversed in eight weeks on the open sea. They passed several grounded German freighters that had run out of fuel or broken down on some uncompleted odyssey.

At last they reached the open body of water at Skagen. Here they waited several days until a flotilla of ships had assembled and, probably under protection from U-boats, they attempted the crossing into Swedish and Danish waters—still always hugging the shoreline. Finally, with a sigh of relief, they hoisted the German flag. They almost got into heavily mined Danish waters, but a pilot reached them in the nick of time and guided them as they passed a huge explosion and the wrecks of several unfortunate ships. Once they witnessed the torpedoing of a ship and saw the lifeboats being taken in by a fishing vessel. Then they shipped by the flotsam of a torpedoed German ship. On the last day, they passed the white *Wilhelm Gustlof* on her way to Ostpreussen (East Prussia). A few years later, this ship was torpedoed and sunk along with thousands of refugees who were trying to escape from the Russians.

There had been no communication with the family for eight weeks although Papi had repeatedly tried to reach Mami via radio. She heard him, but they could not answer.

Some passengers, who had come aboard in the tropical regions for what they thought was to be only a short cruise to Venezuela and Colombia, were bad off without warm clothing. The poor bicyclist from Trinidad, who had boarded the ship for a quick hop over to La Guaira, was still wearing his white tropical suit. Travelling from what now had become enemy territory, he became one of the early British prisoners of war when they arrived in Germany.

The crew and German passengers were honored with

the "blockade breaker" medal some time later. Now Mami was back in Germany for a happy reunion with little Harald—but no immediate possibility to get back to Colombia. Suddenly after four weeks she was called to Genoa to replace another prospective passenger who could not travel at that time. He opted to change for the next trip for which Mami had secured a berth. The ship was torpedoed and sunk on that later crossing. Mami had a big fright when a French plane turned her ship into harbor in Marseille. All German men on board were taken into custody, but Mami was allowed to continue her trip.

Mami finally arrived home in November. The cake I had baked for her months ago no longer existed. Heide was not an infant anymore but a cute baby. We were so anxious to take her home. My anxieties had multiplied over time and caused me to overlook a principle of etiquette. I excitedly called Mrs. Smith to tell her about Mami's arrival, forgetting the customary polite greeting and forgetting to thank her. When Mami arrived, Mrs. Smith immediately approached her about my lack of manners and I had to go to her and apologize. This seemed the hardest thing I had ever done, since I simply felt no guilt. But Mami's admonitions about our indebtedness to the lady were reason enough so we went to the big house and I babbled my not so sincere apology. Needless to say, my feelings towards that friend cooled forever.

Back to the Ordinary

Our family life normalized again, since the days of being one member short seemed a constant condition. School was now the most important issue for Christiane and me. Mother did not appreciate Christiane's efforts, or lack of them. The most ominous shouts and noises would resound in the house, emanating from Christiane's room, where my mother desperately tried to help her with her homework. It was obviously not a very successful undertaking. Nowadays, one would say that Geng suffered from A.D.D. Mother's hair seemed to whiten considerably in those years. Christiane was more interested in climbing trees than studying. She was the first one up and the highest on any tree, jumping off the swing like a daredevil—on one occasion arriving minus her brand new skirt which got tangled and remained up. She knew how to manipulate any tool, and break things with it. In later years she also became quite proficient in repair work. In short, she was a tomboy and the bane of anyone with the intention of teaching her book-knowledge. I kept my prized possessions in my room secured with a lock on the cabinet. If I forgot to lock things, dolls, horses, etc., would be decapitated, at least, since Geng needed to investigate all the mechanisms that made things move. In my sense of orderliness, I had lined up several large chocolate rabbits that I never ate. They made a beautiful display on their green shredded paper nests, surrounded by colorful jellybeans. I once forgot to lock them up, and found the whole lot smashed that same day. Of course, the culprit was Geng. In spite of all this, she charmed everyone with her blond, curly mop of hair and mischievously freckled little nose.

I did well in school except for my lack of ladylike behavior. That cost me repeated run-ins with the boys and consequent walks to the Headmaster's office for admonitions. The one teacher I disliked most (and I am sure the feeling was mutual), was Herr Hommel, our math and chemistry teacher. He was young, had sharp blue eyes, and we never allowed him a moment's peace once we found out that he had a girlfriend named Elli. Of course, he had no sense of humor. He would often aim at me or some other student with a piece of chalk, which he liked to fire in one's direction with the sharpness of a missile when he presumed inattention. I sat on the last bench and he was particularly interested in whatever I might be doing—drawing, knitting, carving, anything to distract me from his boring class.

I was the "cartographer" in charge of the charts and wall maps needed for the different subjects of the day. A nail in the wall behind me held the supplies for all the lessons. I would hang some gory anatomy or biology map (usually one more than the nail on the wall could hold) before the start of Hommel's class. When he walked back to investigate my activities, he would scan the picture meticulously, then turn around and lean against the map, which would fall down and entangle him. He emerged sputtering and fuming, giving me very unkind looks. The class always broke up in laughter because he did this stupid feat almost every day. During chemistry lessons, he made me sit in the front, right by his desk. Once when Herr Hommel was collecting his missiles to fire at some unsuspecting victim, I could not resist the temptation to slide a small, open inkwell under his hand. It was probably lucky for me that he noticed, in the nick of time, what he had in his hand and gently put it down. A scathingly fierce look at me boded only evil.

The boys did not lack imagination either. They would tie Professor Bejarano's shoelaces (the left to the right) under the desk. Or one would bring in a cigar box with a snake, since Dr. Bejarano always boasted of his fearlessness. It was a sight to observe the round little fellow roll toward the exit door when the harmless little snake fell on the floor. We were children, after all, and full of mischief. In retrospect, I think that we remained childlike so much longer than has been the case in the highly pressured later generations. We were quite oblivious and uninterested in world affairs or in the European war that had begun. It all was so far away and what did war mean anyway? Our parents never discussed these matters with us. As a matter of fact, we were not included in most conversations at the dinner table. Papi's business was of no interest to us. Unnecessary babble from us was unwelcome and table manners were strictly enforced. We had to sit up straight and clean our plates. After lunch, we had to observe the sacred siesta time and be quiet during Father's short nap. Disaster struck on one such occasion. I strapped on my roller skates upstairs and tried to sneak quietly down on the wooden staircase. I lost my balance and tumbled down noisily.

During this time, my parents certainly must have felt deep concern about the political situation and the fact that little Harald was in Germany but they did not discuss matters with us. We had no interest in the scant radio reports we occasionally were able to hear directly from Germany. The newspaper never printed much about the overseas situation. It was all so distant.

One occasion that made me perk up my ears was when, after school, I found my parents intently listening to a German newscast on the noisy little radio. Mami was in tears in a discussion with Papi. Mami's exclamation, *"Du wirst sehen, Harald, das wird sich raechen"* ("You will see, Harald, this will have a bad ending") was serious business. I assumed it had to do with the sudden influx of Jewish immigrants to Colombia. Lately they were often seen on street corners selling notions like shoelaces, etc., but in an astonishingly short time, obviously with someone's help, they worked themselves up and became managers and shop owners. The word "Jew" was sometimes used in talks at our Youth Gatherings in the Club. It was not used in a friendly way, but otherwise it had no meaning for me. Some of our school friends were Jewish. My mother tried to explain that disagreements with Jews had arisen in Germany where they became a successful segment of the population. I understood that some of those problems had simmered since the First World War and were apparently being rectified in this strange fashion.

The year 1940 was an ordinary school year interspersed with holidays and shy attempts at approaches to the few available young German boys who were, however, not interested in us girls. I had turned thirteen. I was awkward and felt very unattractive with my straight, stringy blond hair and a nose that was becoming prominent, far from the little button sported by Shirley Temple. I did have dimples, however! So I whispered to my pets about my romantic inclinations and read novels whenever I could get them. Mami had a good library and I found the "hidden behind" books to be the most interesting to read.

We all enjoyed drives into the beautiful Andean mountains which were slowly being made accessible by the construction of often primitive roads. The flora and fauna was stunningly diverse, as one changed altitudes up or down a mountain range. Mami in particular would be enraptured by the large "silver trees" shimmering through the moist fog of a rain forest. Her favorite region however, was the "paramos." The high altitude mountains above 12,000 ft, were bare of trees. To Papi's chagrin, Mother would scamper off and disappear, camera poised, behind huge boulders shrouded in heavy fog. She simply could not stay away from the "Frailejones," the velvet covered, large plants that stretched into the thin cold air to produce abundant fuzz-covered yellow star-flowers. As the plants aged and became brown and dilapidated they appeared as a field of gnomes, peeking in and out of the fog.

Travelling down the mountain, we would enter the "tierra templada" (Temperate Zone) at about 6,000 feet. The abundant growth in this pleasant climate consisted of coffee, bananas, citrus and many other fruits, all interspersed with lush blooming plants and trees. It was a haven for humming as well as many singing birds. Small straw huts were interspersed among these fields of abundance. Rather poor, dirt floored and overflowing with little brown children who watched the automobile with large astonished eyes. Every climate zone had its peculiarities and beauty of its own.

As to my pets: I had a canary and a "Chau-Chau," a very smart and devoted bird and my favorite. I also raised guinea pigs, chickens, and pigeons and had a turtle crawling around. A cat and my parents' dachshund and a toucan helped to populate the back yard and house. I was in charge of my pets, supplying eggs and an occasional chicken or dove for the kitchen. However, butchering was permitted only while we were in school. Even then it never occurred without certain arguments and a flow of tears.

Chau-Chau and Mike, who were allowed to roam free, would occasionally create havoc among the powders and creams of our maids who lived in an apartment over the garage. Mike, the toucan, visited us during breakfast to receive an offering of butter or liverwurst, which he spread out on furniture and walls. He loved my mother and mistrusted us children intensely. Obviously he had been badly mistreated by children, before my mother rescued him by buying him at the market. Mike's strong beak caused quite a few bruises. He also had an ongoing argument with the dachshund. When I was sick with mumps and later with measles (I had to stay in bed for weeks), I managed to get permission to have Chau-Chau perched on my headboard and occasionally the rabbit and cat next to me in bed, while the canary sang his songs from his cage in the window.

We appeared to be a happy lot but one could not deny that my parents had grave concerns about their little son so far away in Germany. This too, was not discussed in front of us. Mami had started playing bridge again. I never understood what compelled these adults to "play" in silence. This was true of Papi's golf and now the same with Mami's bridge afternoons. We children literally had to float through the house, whispering only.

Once I came from school with an important message for my mother that needed an answer before I returned for afternoon classes. I went into the living room and whispered my needs in her ear. I spoke in German as we always conversed with our parents. I was immediately admonished that we had Colombian guests and I must ask in Spanish. I had never before spoken to my parents in that language although we did so all day long in school and everywhere else. My foolish tongue got crossed and I was unable to repeat my request in such an unaccustomed way. I went back to school facing certain reprimand for failing to bring the needed response.

Christmas approached and the usual setting up of the "pesebre" (Nativity) became a big event. Not to be outdone by anyone else's creativity, even those in the churches, I confiscated an entire room for my construction plans. We began in November to gather masses of small plants, mosses, stones and whatever else struck our imagination. Amazingly, my parents left me to my own devices, and the result was a huge landscape of mountains, rivers and lakes created with mirrors, and roads made with sand. I had a large box with wonderful miniature animals and people, as well as the small town Mother had made for me long ago. Somewhere in this landscape was my version of the Nativity. Mary and Joseph, the kings and the sheep were moved along a bit every day. However, the nightly celebrations with neighbors who visited each other singing, praying and blasting off masses of fire-crackers, was not part of our celebration. We waited until Christmas when the tree and many presents appeared. It was a feverishly anticipated event since gifts were only given at this time or on birthdays. Locally, Christmas trees and Santa Claus were unknown. The celebration at the "pesebre" (Nativity) and, of course, the service in church were the main event. Local children found little presents next to their pillows in the morning.

Our family celebrated the traditional German way with a tree, Christmas music and presents on Christmas Eve. I was in charge of baking, an activity my mother had gladly relinquished, and the trimming of the tree as well. Papi wanted it silver and white only. My taste went to colorful with all sorts of decorations. Somehow I prevailed. But when New Year's Eve came, Father and some "happy friends" had their day. Using a b-b gun they shot off many of the decorations. Mami and we children were shocked at the sacrilege and the wall behind the tree was peppered with holes. Unfortunately, this feat was repeated on the next New Year's celebration. Finally, we purchased small clay figurines in the market to save our glass ones. Such irreverent behavior was not at all like Father. I wondered who had influenced him, of course, allowing for the effect of extra holiday whisky . . .

Deeper concerns about the ongoing war at the other side of the world loomed over us as we went through 1941. There was our little Harald and, on the international radio station my parents sometimes could hear lots of excited shouting and "Heil's" (This was the official salute adopted by the Hitler administration). Father's eyes would shine as he saw himself as a commander of a ship, the thwarted dream of a once young cadet. Mother's shining eyes were due to concern and fear for her son in Germany.

We children in Bogota were being prepared at our weekly Scout-like troop meetings to "take up arms" according to an editorial in *El Tiempo,* the daily newspaper. We never really experienced anything like that! We were quite flattered but unfortunately not very athletic during the sports events. The ball I tried to throw during our daily sports and softball session in school generally did not go far or went in the wrong direction. When climbing the imaginable walls of a "fortress," I barely made it to the height of a mule's back and only if there was something to hold onto. And so it went with all my efforts. However, the public's general uneasiness about the German Youth Group remained. After all, the club served "Eintopf" (a plain one-pot stew) on Wednesdays. No one really knew what this fund raising was for. Expressions such as "soft money" had not yet been coined. And we did a lot of singing, songs of love for The Fatherland, the dying soldier, the mystique of a Fuehrer, interspersed with the usual folk songs the Germans have always been fond of singing. Yes, it might appear to be indoctrination!

Meanwhile, we girls were trading off our affections

for either Karl or Eddie or Hans by sneaking candies or an occasional note into boys' pockets and suffering ridicule for it later. We were young with nothing more thrilling to pass the time. School was a bore and homework kept us from being bored at home. I was (rarely) permitted to go to a movie and only when my parents had carefully checked it out. My old dream of owning and playing an instrument other than the recorder, the unattainable piano, had finally shrunk and materialized in the form of an accordion. I enjoyed playing it but no one could be expected to enjoy listening to my practice sessions except perhaps my little sister Heide-Betsy. She was developing into a cute, cuddly, toddler with long blond curls and, of course, a full measure of mischief.

During the mid-year vacation in 1941, Papi took Christiane and me to Pinares. He had developed an interest in farming, bought cattle, and made arrangements to improve the house. A generator was acquired to produce electricity and the walls were tightened against drafts and fog.

On our return trip I had an accident as I rode my horse, Hansi, down the mountain on our way back to Neiva and Bogota. I had the misfortune of being "sat upon" (actually *rolled over* on), by my horse as he took a long slide down a muddy embankment after losing his footing. Of course there was no doctor or pain medication available anywhere, before we would get home. The rest of the day's ride was agonizing and for many months after, I had some paralyzing effects on one side. However, this mishap was eventually forgotten and it appeared we would be going to Pinares more often now. Still school was our uppermost concern.

When Germany declared war against the United States, it did not come as a surprise. Warlike talk and actions had been taking place from all sides for a while, although we had scant news about the details of it.

Colombia, under guidance and subtle pressure by big brother "U.S.A.," decided to declare war on Germany. Although they never sent one soldier and were never included in acts of war, it did give the Colombians a lever in handling the German population in their country. Confiscation of German businesses and property became profitable. At the beginning it only meant that our mobility was restricted. We could not travel away from Bogota. Papi lost his employment with the American firm, Schaefer Klaussmann, after having managed years of profits for the company derived from the coffee-loving Germans. My parents decided to move us all to Pinares to cut down on living expenses. After a lot of hassle and with the help of good friends, Father was able to get permission to relocate the family. We enjoyed one last Christmas in the way in which we had become accustomed and then poor Mami was again dissolving a household. Most of what we owned went into storage as there was no way to transfer all of it into the jungle. We only got a few books and toys back after the war; all else had been plundered or "confiscated."

My parents also took another German couple in to our very cramped quarters in Pinares. Herr and Frau Striepke had no other place to go. It was a good move. Frau Striepke had been mistress of a small school and was an excellent teacher who soon took charge of our schooling needs. Herr Striepke was a man of all trades. Both were good companions and excellent helpers.

I remember little of our departure from "civilization." I was now fourteen years old and realized we were moving into virtual isolation but I loved Pinares and the free lifestyle there. My only concern was the relocation of our zoo. My mother was firm. If I insisted on taking the pets along, they would be entirely my responsibility. My pet bird, Chau-Chau, had died the previous year and Mike the toucan also was no longer. I do remember our ride on mule-back up to Pinares with a sack holding my cat, Mueschen, hanging down my left leg and a sack with the puppy on the right. The four white doves were packed in another container in front of me on the saddle. My beloved canary was ensconced snuggly in cotton wadding in a small basket with a handle which I often had to carry between my teeth to free a hand for one thing or another. We all survived the grueling trip and even my little canary immediately regained his voice when released into his cage again.

We soon settled into an easy routine and I kept busy helping with the milking of our dairy cows. In order to produce often as little as one pint, we had to separate the calf from his mother for several hours. The cow had to be hobbled; the calf needed to suck a little to release the milk flow and then be taken away from its delicious food source. Using the not so clean cow's tail, we wiped the udder, then tried to hold a bucket between our knees while crouching under the cow's belly to squirt some of the precious stuff into the bucket. Meanwhile, the calf would fight for its right, the cow's tail would freely swat our faces, and the beast expressed her ticklish nature by performing kicks and jumps. Well, if we did not land in the mud and the bucket's contents were intact, we sometimes managed to get half a bucket from the four to six animals we had. Unless of course, it was raining and some water might have increased the bucket's volume, (as well as its coloring) from the runoff from the cow's back. After all, the only available shelter was some weeds or giant fern.

We obviously needed to increase our cattle line, so a handsome "red poll" bull was acquired. The beast was rather gentle and placid, but he showed no interest at all in our cows and heifers. However, he was a real escape artist and no fence or gate could hold him. He was constantly running off, to be found again on someone else's property miles away in the warmer climate from where he had originally come. We tried to stand guard to shy him away from the fences. We tried to hobble him and to build large enclosures with old downed trees—but to no avail. Finally, Papi began standing guard, well concealed, with his gun loaded with salt and a few b-b pellets. Even though the shot obviously hit the bull and the animal turned away, he would escape again a bit further up or down the same fence. At last our Beauty had to be sold and a plain animal took his place with great fervor.

My chicken coop was soon harboring a motley crew of colorful hens and roosters, although we seldom collected an egg. After some observation, we discovered that some very busy-looking hens would rush off in the mornings and later loud cackling could be heard in a distant old tree trunk. No nest was ever found in the masses of ferns and weeds, of course. Here too, I learned the local tricks. We closed the chicken house at night. In the morning we grabbed each hen and proceeded to "tentar" (to feel the egg inside the hen). If one was present, the hen had to stay in the coop, if not she could join the crowd outside. Then we waited and observed until the locked-up victim showed signs of pressure and anxiety. We then would let her loose and carefully sneak after her, sometimes to find her depositing an egg on an already full nest. Hurrah! If we did not do this, she might come back weeks later with a brood of little chicks. Or, more likely, she never returned, having become dinner for some wild animal. Besides chickens and the geese, we also had mules and horses. On weekends, it was nice to ride them to the closest market, a full day's expedition.

Amenities were now added to the house. Papi had the waterline extended closer to the kitchen and the runoff served as flush off for the out-house. A solid fence kept our diverse livestock out of the yard and house. However, the mule, Machete, soon learned how to open the gate and appear for his breakfast on our porch. Machete also knew how to open any gate anywhere and saw to it that he was never within striking distance of the mule driver's whip. He was always up front to dictate the speed or snack-needs of the caravan.

A tiny room was carved out in the back of the house for the Striepkes, by halving our bedroom. Above all, a generator was installed to give us electricity. At first it ran on gasoline and years later Wolfi converted it to a water-driven system.

The hacienda population had grown since several crews were employed to do the forest cutting. Supplies from the distant pueblo had to be brought weekly. Occasionally, I would go along with the workers to the "chircal" (a field highly overgrown with a shrub called "chirco"). Armed with a machete, I swung it along with the others to help with the clearing. A few hours of this work were quite exhausting. However, I forfeited my job when I swung the blade into the back of my knee causing an ugly wound and barely missing the tendon.

We would often ride or walk along with Papi. On one such hike, we went to a distant part of the farm called "Sorbetana." A small woodcutter's hut stood there, deserted, and, of course, we went in to inspect it. Bad mistake! When we got home, Christiane and I wore britches of moving little critters. The deserted hut was infested with starving fleas that crawled up and clung to us for dear life. A major extermination with kerosene was necessary. Otherwise, we frequently had to use a needle to poke out "niguas" (sand fleas) from under our toenails.

Easter fell on an early date in 1942. A proper Easter egg hunt was duly held among the many rotting old tree trunks that abounded in Pinares. They offered the best of hiding places. The one to benefit most from these nests was our dachshund. He carefully followed our parental "Easter bunnies" and polished off all the unwrapped homemade sweets they had just deposited in the nests.

Meanwhile serious decisions were being made. After much soul searching and debating it seemed quite clear that our situation in Colombia looked rather grim. Papi was not permitted any employment. We were firmly confined to Pinares and no one knew for sure how long this might be. We could only guess at what other restrictions might be placed on us Germans in "enemy country." A barbed-wire-enclosed camp a few hours from Bogota had been constructed and it became obvious that Papi, like the other German men, would be interned there.

Years later it came to light that during the war, many Germans in South America were forced out to be kept in camps in the USA or repatriated to Germany for the remainder of the war, often against their will, by order of the United States. Above all, the need to be reunited with little Harald had become ever more urgent. It was decided to heed the call for repatriation to Germany as the authorities urged us to do. We were to join a "Diplomatic Exchange Program." We had to pack and head to the collecting place immediately. Soon we were on our way to the town of Buenaventura on the Pacific coast. With much heartbreak, I had to leave my beloved cat, Mueschen, and the other pets with the Striepkes. It seemed unlikely that Herr Striepke, an elderly man, would be interned. They promised to take good care of everything and they actually spent all the war years in Pinares while we embarked on our big adventure. Our childhood, as we knew it was over!

4

Off to War, Germany 1942

The *Arcadia* was a drab and uncomfortable troop trans-
porter and the voyage quite a change from the pleasur-
able trips we had experienced before. We, particularly,
found the way we were treated quite different from any
p   ~riences. We had never before been locked in
                                              through the Pan-
                                          e might be spy-
                                     peratures were
                                    sh air in the sti-
                                    vere none of the
                                    voyage. I asked
                                    to be rudely re-
                                    like prisoners of
                                    many and Amer-
                                    us South Ameri-
                                    to New Orleans.
                                    ight when we and
                                    peen assembled in
                                    ain and a long trip

                                    he first snow in my
                                    ve arrived at the
                                    Springs, West Vir-
                                    we suddenly found
                                    VIP guests in this
                                    ant suites. The clos-

ets were so large one could have used them as rooms; each suite had its own huge bathroom. Of course, we "dressed" for dinner and the fabulous menus reminded me of the meals on the Hapag-Lloyd's ship, *Cordillera,* years ago. Several of my parents' friends also had arrived and soon they found themselves enjoying life as guests of a resort that few could ever have visited under normal circumstances; however, we were restricted to a one-mile area around the hotel, and tennis courts and golf were off limits. We were quite embarrassed to hear that some of our compatriots apparently did not know about such rudimentary habits as the use of a toilet or other sanitary necessities. This was the case of the large family of one young German. He was married to an Ecuadorian Indian girl who appeared most out of place with her rather grimy brood.

One morning we were alarmed when all the bachelors and unmarried women had vanished. Years later we heard that they were taken to some particularly primitive camps, in Texas and New Mexico, where some of them spent years in rather dismal conditions. A load of about five hundred Japanese—men, women, and children—replaced them.

On another day all the German men between fourteen and sixty years of age were summoned to a conference and returned rather shaken by the event. They all had to swear an oath never to take up arms against the USA. We heard that this was a retaliatory measure precipitated by a similar event on the other side of the ocean where Hitler had demanded this act of American citizens who were to be repatriated in exchange for us.

Somehow the mention of my American nationality came up. Of course, we had never given that any thought. According to German rules a child is part of her family, so that made me a German. The thought of leaving this young American citizen behind was barely approached, then brushed aside. Because of Harald we already had had ample experience with family separations and so the subject was immediately dropped. What would I have done in this strange country without relatives, not speaking its language, and not yet fifteen years old?

Meanwhile we children were enjoying ourselves tremendously. Although we could not venture beyond the prescribed mile surrounding the hotel (and posted guards saw to our compliance), there was plenty to do in this realm. Roller-skating was fun even under the supervision of those good-looking soldiers with stern faces. One rule was soon established. That huge, slick ballroom floor was not there for us to slide on with our shoes. The waiters and other hotel employees scolded us immediately.

The hotel offered a large underground shopping area with luxurious stores displaying fabulous gift objects. Mami splurged and bought beautiful cotton skirts printed with large flowers—red poppies, bright blue bells and yellow sunshine—for my birthday. They were gorgeous, a prized possession in the grim, gray years that lay ahead for us during the war years. (Of course, the climate in Germany and even more the drab conditions then allowed me only to look at the skirt while living there, I hardly ever wore it.) The well tended park at The Greenbriar and the spring finery of nature surrounding it made a deep impression on me. It was all so different from our lush, wild tropics. Little did I guess that these Virginia–West Virginia Appalachian Mountains would later become my beloved home. We were so near and yet so much lay between the closing of this circle.

At last, after four weeks of luxury, we found ourselves hustled onto a train once more for a trip east. We were deposited on a large white vessel with a huge red cross painted on its top deck and sides. The Swedish ship, *Drottningholm,* had been converted into a transport. It soon became obvious that the waters around us were not safe. Or were we being guarded by U-boats? We made it to Lisbon in a relatively short time and once more were ensconced in a luxurious hotel. The Palacio Estoril featured all the amenities of European elegance and a big casino on the other side of the plaza. Unfortunately, the inviting beach nearby offered only bitterly cold waters.

Our stay in Estoril was rather brief. Again, after a few days, we were on a train that carried us across Spain to the Pyrenees and into the arms of our German compatriots who by then had overthrown France. We were greeted by impressively loud marching music at a railroad station festooned with lots of flags, garlands, and flowers. German efficiency took over. Women with loud commando voices and dressed in white nurses' outfits offered platters with "Streusselkuchen" (crumb cake), plus wanted and unwanted advice. Meanwhile, a cheerful exchange took place between us and the passengers on the train on the opposite track that carried the exchanged Americans in the direction from which we had just come. Briefly the thought struck me that I was one American heading in the wrong direction. A cheerful inquiry ensued, "How were you treated? How are things over there?" etc, quickly passed between us, before we rumbled on through German-occupied France.

We arrived at a fancy resort hotel in Biarritz, along the Bay of Biscay, for a short stay; I do not remember the reason for this layover. The cold, stormy ocean of the Biscay Bay was gorgeous. The place was otherwise quite deserted, it being off-season and wartime. Finally, we proceeded to our destination and arrived in the German town of Stuttgart. The hotel accommodations were of noticeably decreased comfort and for the first time, we experienced real cold. Heating had become a luxury! The food was drastically changed to—what else—but "Eintopf" (stew), bread, and cake obviously made with many substitute ingredients. But the worst were the three days of indoctrination. We all were obliged to attend them in a large hall and for the entire day. Thundering "Heil Hitlers," martial music, loud talks and commands which I did not grasp the least bit, were the daily fare. Meanwhile, observing our father's downcast expression did not bode well. We witnessed the death of a big dream, the shattering of a fantastic buildup of ideals that only optimistic Nationalists found in remote countries could have fabricated. The reality was dismal and totally different. Maybe Mami reminded him with "I told you so." In her feminine wisdom and some pessimism, she had always had an entirely different picture of the situation.

But now our parents were pleased to be close to their son. Harald would be with us again. So our first step after discharge was to travel north, collect Harald, and accept the kind invitation to settle for a while in Gross Weeden with the Krogh relatives. They had space in the Administrator's house and we moved into an apartment with the barest of necessary furniture. We received our first food stamps, which were an absolute essential for everybody to survive. Rationing was already strictly enforced. One had to learn how to cope with what was available. Also, we were lucky that the Gross Weeden larder would supply us with some farm produce. We were still rich in coffee and cigarettes to use for barter. This made our beginnings much easier. The village school was only sufficient for Harald, so on advice from Tante Gerda, a cousin of Father's, Christiane and I were enrolled in the boarding school that her daughter, Ingrid, attended. This was the Hoffbauer Stiftung, a girls' school of good reputation, located on a peninsula in the Havel River outside of Berlin in Potsdam, several hours by train southeast from Gross Weeden.

First we had summer vacation, visits with grandparents in Berlin and other relatives. Mother found an apartment in a house in Berlin Schlachtensee, a nice neighborhood with lots of open space and trees. It was conveniently located near the U-bahn, or subway. I do not remember how she furnished the place but we were together at least on weekends. We could come by subway from school.

It was becoming quite apparent that Heide-Betsy needed a more settled life. Our poor little sister had been from one place, commotion, and upheaval to the next for a long while now. She had developed the nasty habit of "attacking" anybody who would come too near her. She would go swinging after anybody strange and most people were strangers to her. Heide spent hours just playing with strings and buttons, or "neckes," as she called them. After all we had no toys.

Harald went to some sort of "Kindergarten" since his health had improved enough to live at home. However, from now on, it meant that he needed special foods and plenty of them. The meat ration for the family went mostly to him and any eggs and butter, too. He needed a very high protein diet including lots of liver that he was supposed to eat raw, for instance. I am sure Mami had a very difficult time supplying his needs. Understandably, he was somewhat spoiled which did not make him more attractive to us sisters. He had become a virtual stranger. Again Mami faced these difficult times alone! Our poor, disillusioned Papi had been sent to Belgrade, Yugoslavia, where he managed a department store during all the time we were in Germany. Hitler, for unexplained reasons, honored the oath of not making him fight against the USA. Belgrade, under war conditions, was no place for families and Papi was not permitted to take us along.

Hermanns Werder, Potsdam

Hermanns Werder, originally called, "Die Hoffbauer Stiftung," was a Lutheran institution, a boarding school for girls from middle school to "Abitur" (Junior College). The school was in the process of being secularized, unbeknownst to most of us. Rarely, one would meet one of the "Diaconissen" (deaconesses) walking along the grounds to their building. They no longer had any dealings with their school, but worked in the military hospital that was established on the premises.

Transition to a large boarding school in a strange country is difficult under any circumstances. For me, it almost began with a drama. My first rambunctious act concerned a picture that I did not like, a sort of black etching that adorned a wall in my classroom. I turned this "offense to my aesthetic feelings" to face the wall. I was promptly called to the Headmaster's room for a misdeed that I did not fully understand even after he explained that I had turned the "Fuehrer" against the wall. Actually, the "Dix," as we named the Headmaster, showed remarkable patience in explaining the facts of German life to this unenlightened foreigner. It later turned out that he saved me quite a few times when I was heading into trouble. However, Mother was called in and spent the next weekend trying to explain some facts that she did not fully understand herself. The word Gestapo had no meaning for us! It was not used much among the population either. Many subjects were hushed up during conversations. This was something one had to learn also, without fully understanding why. It would be years before it dawned on me that the Gestapo was more than a simple Police Force.

I was immediately enrolled in a group called BDM, or "Bund Deutscher Maedchen" (Union of German Girls) with a uniform and all the trimmings. If, from resentment or stupidity I do not recall, but I frequently managed to fall out of step when we had to march. I just did not seem to stay in line even after several reprimands by the Dix for my pigheadedness. The situation cleared by itself when I was transferred to another troop where I was in the first row, being one of the taller ones. Following has never been my strong point. I preferred to lead. As far as socializing with the other girls, I did not fit in well at all. I was the only one with such a different background.

Our school consisted of a cluster of rather large, ugly brick buildings, nestled in dense greenery and protected from the outside by the waters of the Havel River. Each building had the name of a tree. I lived first in the Buche (beech tree) and later was moved to the Birke (birch), where we also had the dining hall and many schoolrooms. Each building was supervised by a housemother and contained many large dormitories. As we progressed in seniority, we were assigned to smaller rooms of two beds. The first year, I was moved from the dorm to a room with my cousin, Ingrid. Next Marianne became my roommate and friend. I correspond with both of them to this day. Completing a transition period, the school had decided that I was well ahead of the grade corresponding to the one I had left in Colombia. I was advanced a grade that made Marianne and me the youngest in our class.

Marianne was a very smart student with a sharp and witty grasp of the German language that I admired. My response was slower. Marianne took it upon herself to extricate me from several verbal entanglements. I just did not comprehend the implications of letting my tongue run loose. Both of us almost got into hot water during an especially tedious session of political speeches presented by an assortment of brown-clad Nazi figures. We were sitting in the large auditorium holding our ears shut with our fingers. Marianne, forgetting about her thus limited hearing, trumpeted, "Even with the ears stuffed, one can not tune him out."

Everyone turned to look at us as we blushed and crouched lower in our seats and held our breath in anticipation of serious consequences. Luckily, the moment passed and we survived unscathed.

The next problem I experienced that culminated in a trip to Dix's office was caused by my delight in comparing, as any child would, my present home with the dream world I had left behind. I would rave about trees, mountains, rivers and people in the Americas. "No, Americans are not all small, fat, ugly and nasty, to the contrary. No, America is not poverty-ridden and dirty. No, Colombia was not a savage country."

In fact, I was experiencing a strong case of homesickness and all I could talk about was what had been home for me. This was obviously not a popular viewpoint. If it had not been for Marianne, I would have been terribly lonely and isolated, and quite vulnerable to the verbal attacks of the different groups of girls, who otherwise went their own ways.

A culmination of my misery occurred when I was summoned to the room of Fraulein Hornung, who at that time was our housemother. She was not liked much by

91

anybody and she certainly hated me! Her little, rotund figure was bouncing around her room on heavy-soled shoes. Her face acquired a red-bluish tint and, as she spat her venom at me the stiff bun on the back of her head performed a dance of its own.

I was flabbergasted as to what she really wanted from me until my disbelieving ears heard and pieced together her invectives: We were trash, that Father had brought crawling back to the Fatherland when we became unsuccessful in that horrible country we came from. She found serious fault in my religious endeavor and my insistence on taking confirmation classes as well as my occasional church visits, which apparently offended "Our Beloved Fuehrer." Then she proceeded in her attack on my family because we carry the mini-title, "von," in our name. According to her, this made us a special kind of varmint and Father ought to be kicked out of the country—. So, on and on she went, not noticing a rather unusual transformation in her victim.

In blind fury, I rose from the chair for the first time yelling at an adult: "My father's daughter will not take more of your insults."

I grabbed a large flower vase conveniently placed on the table and smashed it down full force, splattering the miserable Fraulein Hornung from top to bottom.

"Elke, sit down immediately!" she yelled; she followed me as I ran toward the door, which I slammed in her face. In total hysteria, I ran along the long hall toward our room, passing many astonished faces on the way. Once there, I collapsed on my bed, biting into the pillow, actually faint with fury. My persecutor followed, screaming loudly for me to return. She was firmly ushered out again by some of the girls who actually hovered over me, showing signs of understanding and respect from then on. Of course, the affair ended at the Dix's office. For unexplained reasons, Fraulein Hornung vanished a few days later. My intention to change back to "Elko" began then, as I noticed how popular the name "Elke" was now in Germany! Our next housemother, Frau Kairis, was a war widow whose only son had just been killed in battle. She was much loved by all of us.

Our school life went on as normally as possible. I was enrolled in "Haushalts Abteilung" (home economics) for the "Abitur." We had less chemistry, physics, math and languages than the corresponding science-oriented division. Instead, we worked the huge vegetable garden and learned cooking in the school kitchen. Concocting a meal was quite a feat in those days of "Ersatz" (substitutes). We also had classes in baby and childcare and sewing. It was comprehensive training for the ideal future mothers of the "Glorious Reich" and it certainly appealed to me, since I never did take to sciences or math. The stalemate with Herr Hommel in Bogota, had resulted in a poor start in my early school years. All the basics were missing.

Besides academics, we also had a good sports program. Track and field and rowing—this became the only way for the more brazen girls to contact male rowers (very clandestinely, of course). Potsdam was home to a military orphanage as well as a Napola (National Political Training Institution). These were cadet schools with the most dashing young men whom we never were allowed to approach. The rules of the school were strict. There was no fraternizing with members of the opposite sex. Partying and dancing had been banned by decree during the "total" war. But the school decided that part of our education for the future years of glory, would be ballroom dancing. Dance classes were scheduled with the guys from one of the academies. They took place in the huge dining hall of the "Birke." I remember us hanging out of the upstairs windows in giddy anticipation, trying to get a glimpse of who was coming. But no way could we make our own choices.

We were ushered onto one side of the hall where chairs were lined up for us. The young men sat across the room far away. Of course, we were carefully supervised by our respective "guard dogs." As the music began, boys marched up in orderly fashion, bowed in front of the girl sitting opposite and thus secured his partner. After a few classes, things warmed up. The housemothers had a difficult time monitoring what went on behind the huge columns in the dining-hall where brief hidden moments allowed a fast exchange of address. Thus I came by my first "opera date." During a visit in Berlin, Papi had invited me to my first opera, *The Flying Dutchman*. He was pleasantly surprised by my enthusiasm for this performance. At home in Colombia I had generally turned my back and fled when he put on a record, of mostly Bach, Brahms and other serious music. Now he found out that his daughter was not altogether tone-deaf. He soon managed to get two tickets for *Madame Butterfly*. I was asked to find a date for this, since Papi had to leave. These were big events for me! Being escorted by a dashing uniformed good-looker with the most perfect behavior, was a new experience for this shy girl.

Soon after, I asked Dietrich to escort me to a large rally where the Fuehrer regaled us with one of his extraordinary screaming sessions. We were surrounded by masses of waving flags and raised "Heil Hitler" arms in the noisy hall in Potsdam, where we were required to attend. I loved the marching music and songs, but I did not understand the meaning of it all and found the noise excruciating. Fortunately this was a "one time" affair I was destined to experience. The magnetism surrounding the event was spine-tingling, but I have shunned large gatherings and marches ever since.

Otherwise, we never met the boys—or any other males for that matter. I cannot say that this posed a great deprivation in our development. I came to think of this protected time for a fourteen- to fifteen-year-old as being similar to the cocoon stage of a butterfly. Since there was no distraction and no flirtation, we had time to develop in our own sphere, rich with dreams, poetry and friendship. There was no need for fancy dressing, hairdos or such. There were no heartbreaks or spats of jealousy to cope with.

Our teacher of literature, affectionately called "Tante Lu," had a wonderful knack for presenting poetry. Memorizing Rainer Maria Rilke's poem, was a joy:

Der Panther

Sein Blick ist vom Voruebergehn der Staebe
So mued geworden, dass er nichts mehr haelt.
Ihm ist, als ob es tausend Staebe gaebe
Und hinter tausend Staeben keine Welt.

Der weiche Gang geschmeidig starker Schritte,
Der sich im allerkleinsten Kreise dreht,
Ist wie ein Tanz von Kraft um eine Mitte,
In der betaeubt ein grosser Wille steht.

Nur manchmal schiebt der Vorhang der Pupille
Sich lautlos auf. Dann geht ein Bild hinein
Geht durch der Glieder angespannte Stille
Und hoert im Herzen auf zu sein.

My attempt at translating this, one of my favorite poems follows:

The Panther

His gaze has dimmed from passing the iron grates,
It has wearied and no longer holds an image.
To him it is as if there were a thousand bars
And behind those thousand bars no world.

The soft glide of his smooth strong stride
Which circles in the smallest space,
Is like a dance of power around a center
In which a strong spellbound will is held.

Only sometimes the curtain over his pupils
Quietly rises. Then a picture enters
Glides through the tensed silence of his limbs
And in his heart ceases to exist.

Only later did I understand how Tante Lu tried to make us think and find deeper meaning in such poetry that at first I had taken literally, loving that big cat in the Zoo. Gradually, I learned rather to relate it to the trapped spirit within us.

The little poem of the panther has stayed with me. It means as much to me as it did so long ago. Tante Lu had a subtle way of tapping our awakening awareness. She also was very outspoken, not shying away from telling us occasional political jokes that were clandestinely circulated. She suddenly vanished soon after telling us the newest joke about Hitler. We never heard of her again. Much later, I wondered if she had become a victim of her carelessness. At the time, I was unaware that to speak freely was suicidal. Alas, our calm cocoon-stage was rapidly disintegrating and times for dreams and fantasies became ever so scarce. Everything was focused on the grim need for survival.

Vacations brought the family together on ever-scarcer occasions. Our family was invited to spend our first German Christmas with Wolfi, Margot and their family in Silbitz. Wolfi had been released from the front and was at home, running the estate since all his brothers except the youngest, Dominik, were in active service. He was father to seven children by then. With my little sister in tow, we went on our first extended train ride alone, from Berlin east to Silesia. We had received careful instructions about all the particulars, but the train to Breslau got in late. Lucky for us, we had an address where we were supposed to spend the night in such a case. Taking my little sister by the hand and lugging our knapsacks, we headed towards Bahnhofstrasse 9 in the pitch-dark night, without the benefit of any illumination. It was total blackout time! After an interminable search, we finally came to a huge black portal in an old building. Only my sense of responsibility for my sister kept my spirits up. I was actually terrified and it was cold and rainy.

When we at last located # 9 and managed to find a keyhole to open the heavy door, we stood in a dank hallway even darker than the outside, if this was possible. The two of us felt around the wall until we finally found a button to push that produced a dim light revealing a large decrepit stairway. We had to climb up to the fourth floor. We made it only half way up the third when the light went out again. I ran down and found the light switch, then back up to where Christiane waited. Bingo, the light went out again. Repeating this obviously futile endeavor twice more, it finally dawned on us, that there might be another light switch somewhere. After all, we came from "rancho" country where these tricky inventions were not part of our experience. We found another almost invisible button and made it up to the fourth floor where a grouchy person let us in and showed us to a cold room.

It was with great relief that we managed to catch the train to Strehlen the next morning and made the connection with the "Bimmelbahn" (small train with a tinkling bell) to Kurtwitz. This relic out of fairy tales was still huffing and puffing its route through the farm communities, very likely stopping when someone waved to hand over a message for the next village. A horse and buggy met us, the only means of transportation besides the train, as gasoline was strictly rationed for the war effort. The Stillfrieds had lost the right to the use of their automobiles after being caught driving them to church, which was considered nonessential. We never sat in an automobile during our time over there.

The next day, we experienced our first actual snowfall. I will never forget the magic of those soft flakes coming down from the clouds and settling in such gentle fashion on tree branches and fences, soon covering everything in a clean, comfortable blanket. The radio was playing, "Leise rieselt der Schnee" (Quietly the snow falls), a lovely Christmas melody. Through the snow, a young man in a hunting outfit came walking over from the Schloss. His beautiful, chestnut-red hair shone through the snow. My heart seemed to make an extra beat when I recognized Dominik, my old playmate, coming to say hello. Although we had not seen each other for more than five years, we were able to renew our relationship as if no time had elapsed.

Soon it became apparent that this time was different. Dominik, now seventeen years old, was home on Christmas break from his school in Sagan. I was fifteen and had my first vacation from Hermanns Werder. We no longer played Indians or hide and seek. During our short school break, he would fetch me almost daily for walks through the magic world of a deeply snowed-in forest or just to pay a visit. This was first love as it happens in dreams! Conveyed by the touch of a hand, a certain look of the eyes, a careful word—nothing physical, yet the heart could beat wildly. This beautiful experience was marred once when Dominik tried to impress me by shooting a pheasant. When the bird fell in front of my feet and I stroked its iridescent feathers with tears in my eyes, Dominik, having been brought up as a "gentleman hunter," probably thought me rather silly. When I asked, "What will you do when you finish school next year?" his response was, "I will become an officer and try to join the Airforce."

I was not familiar with the military or with it being a way of life. It was also unknown to me that among these families, the oldest son, by tradition, inherited the estate and the following sons would become priests, officers, or an occasional diplomat or lawyer. When Dominik once asked me, "Would you ever consider marrying an officer?" I did not connect that to my future. So far, marriage had never been part of my imagination.

Even so, our happiness was quite subdued. Only weeks before, the dreadful news had been relayed to the family that Dominik's older brother, Norbert, had been killed at the Russian front, somewhere near Ilmen Lake. According to the report related by his comrade, Norbert had tried to help a wounded member of his platoon. While doing so, he was struck down and immediately buried during the heat of battle at that forever-unknown spot. It always saddened me to think how the lives of millions of young men the world over, who are just following their countries' orders, are so unceremoniously snuffed out and soon forgotten. Sometimes no marker or memorial attests to their last resting places.

Norbert had been in Colombia as a teenager. I barely remembered him to be a good-looking nice boy. Margot had sometimes insinuated that this would be an excellent man for me. I did not know more about him except that he was much loved by his siblings. The war did not spare anyone. This was the first war-related blow to the family that had been somewhat protected from its direct consequences by living in the country and so far east of the main hub of events.

We knew nothing about the fact that, all this time, there was much underground dissent fomenting. Several plots against Hitler's life did not materialize and others failed. People disappeared, never to be heard from again. Hushed conversations by the adults were mostly kept from our ears, since children were notorious for repeating things at the most inappropriate time. I learned much of this, years later when we met some of the survivors and learned about the now public accounts of the gruesome happenings.

It took me a long time to even believe any of this to be possible. It then became an obsession with me to read all I could about the history of the underground movements, particularly as I learned that several family members and relatives were involved and lost their lives. Years later, I repeatedly read and heard some utterly nonsensical claims that all Germans "knew" and all Germans were at fault for the catastrophic events. Many Germans did not know—and others just would not believe it. Many of those who knew or guessed that something was dreadfully wrong were afraid and chose to look the other way, exactly as other nations did for a long time. Those who knew and chose confrontation paid with their lives, dragging their families and others with them. Yes, we had learned in history class about "tyrants," some of whom were even glorified as heroes. It had never occurred to me to look for them in modern times—they were now called dictators—and to find them so brutal and involved in mass terrorism.

The Sky is Falling

During these minor battles to adapt to my new life, the real air battles over Berlin had begun and were rapidly accelerating as we went through our school year of 1943. The novelty wore off soon enough and the seriousness of the situation sank in, even for me. One evening, returning to Hermanns Werder from Potsdam later than usual, involving a ride on a ferry and a good twenty-minute walk back to the school, I heard the air raid alarm go off and, simultaneously, the fireworks began. It was awesome to observe this barrage under the open canopy of the clear night sky. At first, the deep rumbling of a hundred heavy bombers overhead (supposedly targeting oil refineries and such, in the population centers) shook the ground under me. Close to a hundred planes, in loose formation, were flying toward Berlin, heavy with deadly bombs. Some were touched and embraced by the spidery arms of searchlights which painted weird designs in the night sky until they found a bomber and were joined by other beams. Next, a spray of antiaircraft guns would explode around the plane. It was a gruesome, picturesque spectacle I could have enjoyed if it had not been so deadly serious. An occasional fighter plane would zero in on the slow bombers and be engaged in battle by the protector fighters. I once actually witnessed the fast spiral descent of a crippled aircraft. I was frightened, thinking about the poor crewmembers and their fate. Had they survived to use their parachutes?

By the time I made it to our bomb cellar, I was quite shaken and out of breath from running. The safety of our bomb cellars was questionable, since they stood half above ground. Also, all the buildings' heating lines and hot water pipes ran just above our heads along the ceiling. Bunk beds in tiers of three were assigned to us. I had a top bunk and used my knitting to pass the time as long as the electricity was still on. During close bombing the entire building often shook and plaster rained on us. We hovered there, gripped by fear, and in silence. While at first we would experience one air raid a night, escalation of the war soon advanced us to three and four and also some in the daytime.

So far, we had not suffered much real damage in our area. Potsdam only lay on the airway to Berlin. But that was to change soon. Apparently the Red Cross marking the white roof of the first school building, the "Linde" (which had been converted into a hospital for severely wounded soldiers), had no meaning. Never mind the Geneva Convention! The building was the first in the area to receive a full hit. While we were usually strictly kept away from any association with the male inhabitants of the Lazarett (field hospital), it was a grim sight, when they were carried and dragged over after that air raid and left for us to look after until other help could be summoned. The boys' deadly pallor was covered with plaster, and new bleeding wounds made them writhe in pain. We were just as shaken and plaster-covered and, unfortunately, totally inadequate to be of much use, not having had any medical training. This had been by far the closest hit. Their building was barely a few yards away from ours. I will never forget the distinct sound of whistling and clattering like that of broken dishes that is made by a bomb hurtling toward you. Neither can I forget the horror of it all!

A newborn nursery was installed in our building. It was part of an orphanage and supplied a "nurses' training" facility for us. Together with some adult nurses, we were in charge of about twenty-five newborn infants. During air raids we had to help, each carrying two babies with us to the basement. When the siren gave the all-clear, it was our job as "fire brigade" to go up to the attic and inspect it for slow burning phosphor. The geniuses in charge of inventing effective killing machines had found it useful to spray the targeted buildings with phosphor before dropping the heavy bombs, so that the dynamited buildings would catch fire once they had collapsed. The phosphor was deadly stuff when it got on the skin, the more one rubbed it the more flammable it became, we were told. Flare bombs that illuminated the sky and all the targets below were referred to as Christmas trees. I often saw this really picturesque sight. Needless to say, most of the windowpanes of the adjacent buildings were shattered during closer bombardments. Cold winter air had free access to the buildings until the panes were replaced.

Cleanup and repair took quite a while, but life went on as usual. It made me wonder, later on, how we could actually feel a bit relieved after we had a third or fourth air raid in a night, meaning school would begin two hours late the next day. Complexly, a few years later, when I was out of Germany and in New York, the noon siren emitting a similar sound as the air raid alarm, set me shivering and into a cold sweat. It is an effect I still experience now, some sixty years after. I have difficulty watching television shows depicting the sounds and sights of those air raids. I also avoid watching shows with shooting, violence and death. The community spirit that became evident in all the misery of war, the lack of complaining and determination to survive, illustrated the fallacy of the theory that a war can be won by demoralizing the civilian population. People become accustomed to the miseries and finally numb to it all.

Back in school the grim news began to trickle through, even to our news- shielded girls' haven. The German 6th Army had been surrounded in Stalingrad, and it seemed they would be sacrificed in this horribly cold winter so far from the home front. I began to wonder about the radio news broadcasts about the "victorious retreat" that the German army was engaged in at different places. The idea of backtracking "gloriously" and still claiming to be winning a war, seemed a total contradiction to my logical mind. My knowledge of European geography was as bad as that of its history. While in Colombia, we had been absolutely stuffed with Simon Bolivar and his glories, which bored me to tears and I forgot every bit of those years of futile lessons. However, we had never learned much about Europe and the rest of the world beyond ancient history.

But even as the news was conveyed to us so carefully screened, we could not ignore the fact that the air raids were intensifying in violence and occurring much more often. Many families had already been evacuated, and my mother accepted the Stillfrieds' invitation to move from Berlin to the safety of distant Silesia. The small apartment in an old building next to the chapel in Silbitz was empty and could be made habitable for Mami and the two younger children. Christiane went to a different school in Silesia now and we both came home only during the vacations. I remained in Hermanns Werder since I was close to graduation, and Potsdam was not yet severely bombarded like Berlin.

Before Mami moved, I accepted an internship in a nursery as part of my training in child-care. There happened to be a very nice orphanage within walking distance of my family's apartment in Berlin. I could live at home and walk daily to my work with the babies; aged newborn to about three years old. I could not help questioning the whereabouts of the parents of so many children. Particularly, since there also were so many in Hermanns Werder. Of course, I never got a real answer. I did overhear a conversation between two nurses that the father of lovely year-old twins was a high ranking SS official. No further information about their mother or family was forthcoming.

The question remained in my mind until a few months later when, amongst much secrecy, we were informed of a special assembly for the older girls who were to attend a lecture given by some high ranking officials. It was also rumored that the school was becoming an "SS Heimschule" (SS boarding school), a fact that would not change anything in our day to day curriculum. Frau Kairis, our beloved housemother, talked to some of us about the nature of the meeting and the lecture. Talks of this sort at a time before "sex" had been "invented and become a general barbecue" were quite difficult. But this sensitive lady knew how to approach her different charges. She insinuated that attendance would be voluntary. She seemed pleased at my reaction and immediate decision not to participate; as soon as I understood the talks were about some kind of "breeding program" for girls who would choose to bear "fine-specimen-children" for the Fuehrer or such drivel. A handful of us were appalled and stayed away, suffering no more than furtive sidelong glances and whispers behind our backs.

At the same time, my confirmation date was drawing near. The ceremony was to be held at the majestic Berlin Cathedral. Already the building, which was later completely demolished, had suffered severely through bomb damage. Mercifully, on the rainy Sunday when a few family members gathered around the altar, no sirens went off. My cousin was also being confirmed, as well as one or two other schoolmates. Mother easily gave in to my request and our little heathen, Heide, was to be baptized right afterward in a side chapel, I was her godmother. She was also named Betsy after her other Godmother, Betsy Schaefer, in New York. Heide-Betsy fidgeted around playing with her fingers along the carvings of the baptismal font. She then piped up in a loud, clear voice, *"Mutti, warum waescht der Onkel mir die Haare?"* (Why is that uncle washing my hair?) Well, at least she did not swing out and hit the pastor.

Dominik was now in a flight school not far from us in Berlin Gatow. He asked me out once for a walk in the Grunewald. Blackened snow still lay on the ground and it was weird to find all the trees decorated with tinsel. Apparently, the bombers would dump tons of this stuff to distract the radar search. I collected quite a bit of it to use as tree decoration for the next Christmas. Otherwise, our walk was a disappointment. No real conversation came up; to me it appeared obvious he was only fulfilling someone's wish to look me up once. I was smarting from the fact that even though he was near Potsdam, he had never before or after made an attempt to see me. Dominik had finished his school in Sagan and, after absolving the mandatory Arbeitsdienst (labor brigade) he had volunteered for the airforce. Dominik told me how he had almost flunked the examination for acceptance into officers training on account of his poor spelling. His rapid response when questioned, *"Erbliche Belastung Herr Oberst"* (Tainted by an inherited defect Sir.) brought a friendly grin to the faces of the examining officers, "Do you mean tainted by your ancestor, Field Marshal Bluecher?"

"Yes, sir."

The historically known deficiency of his famous progenitor had saved the day for him.

We dragged our wet, cold feet to a snack stall and managed to get a sort of water-ice cone before Dominik escorted me back to school again. I felt let down and lonely.

Never again did I walk in the Grunewald, even with my grandfather. Neither, unfortunately, did I visit my grandparents much. Toward the end of the year, I got the news that an air raid had demolished Berlin-Schoeneberg. Blanket bombing had now been perfected and destroyed entire boroughs. Grandfather was fire warden in their apartment building. He was still robust at age seventy when caught in the air raid. The heat of the fire-storm shriveled this tall man to the size of a baby. The only way my grandfather's corpse, still clutching a fire extinguisher could be identified was by his perfect teeth.

My grandmother had not been home during the air raid, after her loss she found refuge with her sister, Tante Frieda, in Silesia.

Travelling to Berlin after school breaks was traumatic. Although the trains were still running, all the stations were without window glass and most buildings lay in rubble. Their inhabitants rushed about, ghostlike, to find the necessary food to stay alive. The beloved Berlin Zoo was hit one winter night. Horror stories about all the animals that got loose during the bombardment were told. Even the snakes and alligators escaped into the bitter cold and had to be shot like most of the other animals. Now Potsdam was also being singled out for air attacks, as were all the other cities.

Our classes continued, even though most of the capable teachers had been called away. Their substitutes were very old, not always well trained women. A general sense of school being only a secondary aim had spread, but we were obliged to attend. We older girls were frequently called upon to perform other duties. For several months in the summer, we were shipped to the Warthegau, a region along the Polish border, to help farmers with the harvest. These new settlers were Germans who had been displaced from Russian-held territories and were now settled in this once Polish region. We soon got the feeling that we were not really wanted there. These people instinctively knew that the "new" homelands were not going to be theirs for long. They worked the soil as farmers will always work the land entrusted to them, even under difficult circumstances. It was backbreaking work, hoeing and plucking endless sugar beet rows, chopping weeds and harvesting potatoes by hand. We were totally unaccustomed to this type of work.

Fortunately, we were well fed. The main meal consisted of huge bowls of delicious dumplings floating in rendered pork fat. Each family member or worker only had a spoon to reach out and eat his fill. No individual plates were furnished, of course. In the evenings we girls all gathered for pep talks and walks to the lonely, beautiful lake in the distance for a refreshing dip, before we went back to our barracks.

Back in Potsdam, we had to become accustomed again to our ever-decreasing larder and a steady sensation of not having eaten enough of the not very appetizing meals. Our morning porridge consisted of some kind of flour mush with saccharine sweetened clumps that we ate as dumplings. Strange looking little objects floated among the dumplings, looking very much like the kind of meat ration no one likes to think about, even less to eat. Garden duty was gratifying. One could occasionally snatch a carrot or some berries and, during asparagus season, the kitchen offered us good meals of this delicate produce. The vegetable garden supplied the school with a much-needed supplement to the increasingly shrinking official food rations. We always were hungry. When in town, we could sometimes buy a salt pickle or even a watery ice cone. These were occasionally available without ration stamps. Food rationing was strictly enforced. Visiting the family briefly during a short vacation, of course, was always a highlight. We were then spoiled with occasional farm produced goodies.

I did not see Dominik very often. I believe he was still in the Air Force Academy in Berlin-Gatow. But Wolfi's and Margot's children were close to my age so I did not lack companionship when visiting in Silbitz. We only saw Papi during the Christmas visit and a few times when he had business in Berlin to attend to. He would bring nice things from Belgrade. The best was a real lambskin fur coat for me, which I loved and everybody else envied. Winters were exceptionally cold in Silesia and the heating of the old stone building was very difficult. Mother had a wood burning stove for cooking and heating one room. Of course, a flush toilet and hot water were things of distant dreams. As always, with little choice even though complaining Mami struggled through the hard times doing what she could to feed her family, in particular, Harald. But Heide also had grown into a gangling schoolchild. Both children gave poor Mami considerable discipline problems. The days when I came home on a break, she was glad to put me in charge, particularly of the kitchen. After all, I was supposedly learning all about cooking. But there also was all the laundry to be done with scant soap supplies and in ice-cold water, using one old tub and a washboard.

When Papi came to visit, all attention went to him. He spent much of his time in the more comfortable house of his friend, Wolfi, and charming Margot. I sensed the sadness this caused my mother who lacked the comfortable facilities. Her cold little apartment consisted only of a bedroom and a kitchen. I urged Mami to go and join Papi and the others, while I stayed with the little ones. One day, after hearing the stream of complaints Mother voiced about the children, my father decided that both children were due for a disciplining session, which he had a parental duty to perform during his short visit. As was his way, not having any pedagogic knowledge, he picked on the first infraction to punish them.

It was five in the evening when he and Mami were going down to dinner with Wolfi and Margot. The children who had been playing with others in the "Hof" (farmyard) were late coming home. Father accosted them and administered a good spanking in front of the other children, sending ours home with orders that I was not to give them supper but put them straight to bed. Both arrived howling and I was overcome with "righteous indignation," and furious with Father. Against his orders, I fed

110

them their supper. Then I marched down resolutely like a big avenger and actually, for the first time, stood up to my stern father. I gave him my opinion about his injustice, and announced that I had fed supper to the children. My bravado was beginning to shake, as Father was staring at me! I was absolutely astonished and stupefied when he only looked sideways at my mother and said, "*Ist die verrueckt geworden, Ada?*" (Has she lost her mind, Ada?) He subsequently turned to Wolfi to continue his conversation. I ran home to my poor siblings, not at all sure if this had been a victory or a defeat. After all, I really idolized my father, as unapproachable as he often seemed.

A great event on the farms was the "Schlachttag." Hog butchering was always made into a feast and many were invited to participate. This was a special treat during these hard times! At Margot's place, the maids had cleared the washhouse and huge kettles were heated, soon emanating the delicious smell of pork broth. The kettles simmered the entire day, boiling up meats and sausages for canning and eating. Fatback was rendered and made into "Schmaltz" (lard with browned onions and pieces of apple); it all was delicious and a small Schnapps, if available, helped digest the heavy meal.

Another traditional event was the "Treibjagd," or hunt. The village population and all the children would walk around the fields flushing out hares, foxes and pheasants for the hunters to shoot. I happened to be there during one of these hunts and was invited to attend. Wolfi asked Christiane and me to hover behind a mound of earth, probably to keep us out of the way. I was horrified as I witnessed the shooting, and saw a wounded hare clobbered to death with a stick while it was screaming like a baby. Two deer that did not see us jumped right over us in flight. I had had enough and took off for home!

At Dominik's next visit he shot a cat and that really did it for me. We had a serious disagreement over this. I simply would not accept the reasoning that cats damaged the crop of young hares and pheasants, which needed some protection from such predators, as cats were. Battles between environmental and practical reasoning have always been blurred. We saw each other less frequently now, even though Mama Stillfried would, on occasion, invite me over to have some cake with Dominik. On one of his last visits, before he left for flight school we had a serious talk, which I understood to be of concern to both of us. He mentioned that he could never marry a girl who was not Catholic! Well, I always seemed to be on the wrong side as far as religion was concerned. It was just as well that I was not contemplating marriage to anyone at all at that time.

Instead, it pleased me that on my first and only attempt to fire a handgun which Dominik brought for target practice, I hit a bull's-eye, better than anyone else. However, my dislike for the weapon intensified. It was noisy and hard on the arm so never again. Sophy Kowollik, the jolly, fat family secretary with masculine behavior and loud vocal prowess, teased me again, mercilessly, for being a sissy. But I was used to it by then. She targeted me frequently and I preferred to avoid her if possible.

Occasionally, we would visit the neighbors. Our playmate, Wolfgang, of bicycling days, was now a good looking soldier in uniform. He sometimes had a way of looking at me, that made me feel uncomfortable, even though I did not understand why. After his visit at Margot's house, I got permission to drive him home with the horse and buggy, quite a treat for me. Wolfi sternly demanded that little Mechthild ride along with us. I felt embarrassed and quite bothered by her giggly insinuations and re-marks as she sat between us. The little imp sensed much more than I, why her father had been so stern. I liked Wolfgang's younger sister, Rosvita, very much. With hor-ror, we found out a few years later, that the poor girl stayed behind when the Russians came and was brutally murdered, together with her parents. Their older brother had just been killed in the war.

As the year 1944 unfolded, the savage war had to-tally overtaken the civilian population. Increasing air raids spread death all over the country. Food became scarce and all we heard in the news was about the "victo-rious retreat" of the army. One day in summer there was much hushed whispering around us, and as I stood with a group of classmates and a young teacher, I learned that there had been an attempt on Hitler's life. Not many com-ments were forthcoming; someone ventured a worry about the people involved in the "putsch," but immedi-ately was cut short by someone else's, "The traitors should be hung."

We never heard much more about the ensuing wide-spread hunt-down of the conspirators and their families. Thousands of innocent people lost their lives in connec-tion with this event. As I learned later, on that fateful July 20, Dominik's unit was instantaneously mobilized and all the young air-cadets were marched toward Berlin not aware of what was happening. But, just as suddenly everything was called off and they marched back to their flight school. As was then discovered, the assassination attempt on Hitler had failed and he remained very much alive.

While in flight training, Dominik with his instructor was able to take his plane and land near home for a brief visit, a couple of times. On a solo flight he once flew over his home and could not resist buzzing the workers on the field when they did not pay proper attention to his antics. It almost caused him a court-martial, because of the wife of a high ranking airforce official, who unknown to Dominik, lived in Silbitz as a bombed out refugee. She told her husband about this affair. He let it go with a stern reprimand. At night his unit had to man the "flak" (antiaircraft guns). During the day, they were frequently driven to Berlin to perform disaster aid. With little sleep, they were often exhausted. Once on a return flight from Silesia, lazily following the straight railroad tracks toward Berlin, Dominik was overcome by drowsiness and fell asleep. He was awakened by the loud noise emitted by the diving plane in the nick of time to correct his free-fall.

Meanwhile, we heard nothing about the gruesome hunt-down and killing that followed the attempt on Hitler's life. Thousands, many without knowledge of the events that had occurred, were rounded up. During my next visit in Silbitz, I experienced first-hand some of what I later read in so many books. Dominik's oldest sister, Countess Pia Matuschka, and her four children had taken refuge in the downstairs apartment of the Stillfried's home. Following a brutal house search after her husband's disappearance in Breslau, she had to leave her own home. She had no knowledge at all that her husband had been implicated as a collaborator merely by his name appearing on a list as a future minister. These brave men who were involved in the attempt, kept everything from their families in the hope of saving them in just such a case as this failed insurrection. Even this precaution did not save the families from harsh retributions or death.

We seldom saw Pia and, only occasionally, one of the

children. But one day, as I was walking up through the park, some official looking vehicles were parked in front of the "Schloss" and several black-clad, angrily-shouting men commandeered the people around. I saw Pia, dressed in mourning, as I rushed up to our little apartment by the chapel, I realized that something very ugly was going on down there. Later I was told that the Gestapo had ransacked Pia's rooms and taken much with them, leaving her with the ugliest of threats and assuring her that she would never again see her husband alive. At that time, I was unable to connect this event with the Hitler plot. I knew too little about it all.

After completing his flight school and getting his "wings" in August, Dominik was posted for combat training in Wiener Neustadt. The young pilots found their time there poorly utilized. There was little training, and for long spells no flights were scheduled. There were times when they just sat around and no planes seemed to be available. In their minds the question arose, if somebody was sabotaging the flight training plans, or, if they were being held back for unknown reasons. The Silbitz secretary, Sophy Kowollik, tried to coax me into going with her on a visit with Dominik in Wiener Neustadt. But she could not convince me of the need to show that much interest in our young man. She was nice enough however, to carry a small package with cookies I had baked for him, to Dominik, promising not to tell him who had sent them.

School, or what semblance of it still prevailed, resumed on time. We were supposedly getting ready for the "Abitur" (graduation) in the coming spring of 1945, although little book learning took place. After nights of heavy bombing, we were sometimes loaded on trucks and driven to Berlin to help out in the digging process. Actually, these projects were poorly organized and futile.

Even if we had been given tools, like shovels etc., how were we to attack by hand the huge mountains of still smoldering rubble that once were buildings? We were aware that we were looking at vast tombs. Knocking signals could occasionally be heard from the poor people who had been buried alive. Dust, heat and stench were pervasive. The most we could do was help in the outdoor soup kitchens where processions of ghost-like figures assembled to receive a ladle full of thin goulash and a slice of hard bread to keep them going till the next bombardment. We lucky helpers could board the truck back to the relative safety of our school on the Havel Island in the evening.

We were already training for our sports Abitur. I was a poor runner and bad in high jumping but could hold my own in distance jumping. Discus or ball throwing weren't my strength either. In short, I was a general disappointment and probably would have flunked the important sports Abitur had it not been for horseback riding. I had taken it up in an equestrian school in Potsdam where the proverbial gruff instructor showered me with the most unlikely compliments. According to him I sat the horse like an "inspector on a Sunday promenade," or like a "slice of butter on a hot potato." Between these gentle satires, he used the meanest language I had ever heard and never shied away from whacking my horse with his long whip, sending me in high flight from the back of my bucking mount. All of this took place between one air raid and the next. The bombs were crashing around us before we got off the horses. However, I did manage to earn the equestrian bronze medal that saved my sports degree.

Late in fall, our entire class was ordered on a secret mission. We went by train to an area near Landsberg where we were housed in a few rooms of a very run-down castle (the former owners had mysteriously disappeared!) that had become a "Lazarett" (field hospital) for Hitler Youth. We girls from the home economics department were placed under the charge of the kitchen staff and had what appeared to be ample supplies to work with. We inquisitively looked around and discovered that hundreds of young boys were there dismally housed on straw pallets with barely a blanket for cover, in this already very cold fall. They were very sick, many of them dying from infection and fever. The poor fellows would sneak down to the kitchen door to beg some extra food from us. If the supervisors were absent, we would help where we could. We found out that they had been living in dirt tunnels in the area where they were supposedly digging anti-tank trenches, a secret endeavor. There were some thousand youngsters thus engaged, many getting sick and ending up in this Lazarett. They were very young, some not yet fourteen years old. We were puzzled. *What did the anti-tank trenches mean there, in the middle of Germany?*

Back in school, we noticed some general dissipation of the school routine. We were being sent home early with an order to sign up for the Arbeitsdienst (work brigade) in our home place. We were to come back the following year with a certificate to prove that we had absolved the Arbeitsdienst. We would thus be eligible to receive a "Not-Abitur" (auxiliary Diploma) with no other strings attached, no cramming for exams, no sweating or flunking. Gladly, I got myself home to Silesia away from the devastated Berlin area and the much increased bombing over Potsdam.

A cloudless blue sky stretched to the horizon. It was late in the fall of 1944. These last warm days before the brutally cold winter descended on us were a gift from heaven. The Silesian climate resembles that of central

117

Russia. The summers are very hot and the winters very cold. The particular beauty of this day almost erased all thoughts of war, but for the fact we had all been ordered to dig anti-tank trenches. A general call to the village population had assembled every able-bodied soul from six to seventy years old. Except for a few women from the village, we were only children and old people. The men had been away fighting Hitler's war now for several years. So had the older teenagers and younger women who were called to service in factories.

The school had sent us home to do our "stint of duty" by enrolling in the "Arbeitsdienst" (work brigade) in our respective home district. But my mother had wisely balked at the idea. She refused to let me sign up with the other girls from the village. She took a dangerous risk and reminded me that, having been born an American, nobody should have a right to press me into this service. The notion that people had rights was a new one for me. Fortunately, the "Buergermeister" (major) had no time to inquire into the regulations pertaining to a foreigner in so remote a place. If he had, I would have been shipped east with the other girls of the village, thus becoming an early victim of the Russian invasion. None of those girls survived the horrors awaiting them. My nationalistic feelings were not developed one way or the other; even so, I would have liked to join the village girls. However, having been brought up respecting my parents' wishes, I remained in Silbitz to become part of the motley crew of trench diggers.

We had been promised extra rations of cigarettes (I did not smoke, but nobody would decline valuable trading goods) and chocolate rations. We did a little digging and a lot of talking. The old peasant women enjoyed rustic stories, which would have drawn a furious blush from any young uninitiated girl. However, I did not understand their dialect so their jokes passed by my innocent ears. The rest of us, mostly concerned about food and trading for such, did not mention the ongoing war either. One did not talk about it and, if so, then only in positive terms. No one really believed that these trenches we were scraping into the hillside would make the slightest impression on whatever tanks would come. Furthermore, no tanks were coming. After all, Hitler himself was saying so in all those radio talks about the "victorious retreat."

Silesia, one of the most easterly provinces, seemed so far removed from the war. There were no air raids. The occasional Russian planes straying over the area never managed to find their targets with their bombs. One joked about them, while we knew the British and American bombers to be deadly on the mark. As one initiated to the furies of the air raids over Berlin, I could have talked about it. But who wanted to hear about those hour-long waves of bombers that made the ground tremble as they searched out helpless targets to drop their deadly loads onto a population that had barely heard the sirens in time to scuttle into a dismal cellar? That life belonged to the cities. So did the acrid smoke hovering above and obscuring the sun for days, and those eerie drawings dissecting the night sky when the searchlights zeroed in on a plane to bring it down in a barrage of flak. What would become of the pilots if they made it to the ground safely? These questions and many more were with me a lot.

Occasionally, I wondered if all of this was what being young meant. This was no time for adolescent dreaming. Everything was so different from what I had ever read about. My sadness was only dispelled by the knowledge that my own little family was still intact and, presumably, safe. My train of thought was interrupted as some-

119

one cried out, "Hey, do you hear that? It sounds like bombing in the east." I set down my spade to listen and even put an ear to a rock. There it was—unmistakably—the ground was trembling! In the silence, we could hear the distant growling and rumbling. I knew that these were not planes flying from the east to bomb a city. Planes seldom came from the east. These were tanks and cannons, this was artillery, and it was already deep on German soil. Half-heartedly, we proceeded with our idiotic assignment. A few days later, work on the half-finished trenches was quietly given up. Nobody knew why.

As winter set in with full force, one of the coldest in memory, not much activity from the front was noticeable at first. Christmas came along but our spirits were subdued. Nobody knew how close the front really was. One simply did not talk about it. There was a general fear of being accused of subversion. Also, there was the fear of facing a reality that was too hard to comprehend. So we prepared for whatever Christmas we could have. I made candles from scraps and leftovers and scrounged around for acorns to substitute for nuts. Citron could be made out of pumpkin skin. No one knew anymore that marzipan was not made from potatoes. A few handmade gifts allowed the joy of giving, otherwise there was unusual restraint in the celebration. The religious aspect had been curtailed by the Nazi regime. The old traditional Christmas carols like "Silent night, holy night" were blacklisted. However, here in Silbitz, the religious traditions were still observed as the family and the villagers of both religious denominations assembled in the chapel for the midnight celebration.

This was a sad season. Everyone was mourning or missing some family member. Most men were away. We did not know where, or if, they were safe and alive. I was concerned about Dominik, who had not been seen for a while. I hoped that he had received my Christmas package with cookies and a Madonna and Child transparency I had made for him from some cellophane paper strips with strange arrow designs that had been dropped by planes over the Berlin woods.

All the children enjoyed sledding and ice skating on the solidly frozen moat around the Schloss. Sometimes, however, a careless child would break through a thin ice patch and have to be rescued. One of them happened to be my little sister, Heide, whom I managed to fish out of the freezing muck in the nick of time. I was also very busy wiping runny noses and rubbing purple, wet little hands. Otherwise, to the great joy of all the younger children, I spent most of my time on ice on my behind. I never had the chance to really learn—and the opportunity to become proficient in skating or skiing came too late in life for me. Great fun were the few occasions when a horse was harnessed to a large sled and all the younger children were summoned to attach their small wooden sleds in a long dragon's tail behind the big sled. With tinkling bells we would be off for a happy sleigh-ride! The ones hanging on at the end of the long tail would be swung about mercilessly or just thrust into snow banks on either side. It was quite difficult to keep us all in dry, warm clothing and, of course, we were always hungry.

Aside from these minor concerns, it still was impossible for us to comprehend the approaching cataclysm. A year before, when a few of her sons happened to be together, Dominik's mother had suggested they send some of their valuable paintings, furniture and other items west to a safer region. The optimistic men had rebelled. Never would the Russians or anybody else endanger this homeland! This winter again, she made an attempt to bring up the subject of imminent danger. However, all admonitions fell on deaf ears. She shrugged her shoulders and said "I do not need these things, but some day you might regret it." Well, as it turned out, the west of the country, subjected to all the bombing, was not much safer either.

Join the Refugees

Two weeks later, in the early part of January 1945, my mother bundled up the four of us, letting us each carry only one suitcase. We were travelling to a "spa" in Marienbad in Czechoslovakia at the German border. We were going there only for a checkup in the Institute for Tropical Diseases, an expected stay of two weeks. Perhaps there was a need to have Harald's condition checked out again? There seemed no reason to take along any more clothes. Our friend, Margot, joined us for a short break in her busy life, leaving her seven children behind. She also wanted to be sure she was not harboring "amoebas" from her life in Colombia some years back.

We were surprised when the train ride, which would normally have lasted only a few hours, took almost two days. But this did not deter us. Communications were almost totally disrupted and all sort of rumors tumbled around us, but, unbelievable as it sounds, here we were at a spa as if in the best of peace times. Granted, the effects of the war were noticeable here, too. The elegant buildings, in their no longer so well-tended gardens, were advantageously decorated by the picturesque snow which bent the fir tree branches almost to the ground. An atmosphere of quiet elegance still pervaded if one did not look too closely at the strained, harassed faces of the population. Restaurants and casinos were closed, of course, but the cinemas were always filled to capacity.

A week later, the situation on the eastern front became catastrophic and on January 18, Margot had to find her way home but it seemed totally inadvisable for Mami with her four children to go back with her. We realized we had lost what we still had in our apartment in Silbitz and we again became extremely anxious about our future.

Margot barely made it back in time to hurriedly gather up and pack a few necessities on two wagons pulled by a farm tractor that Wolfi, in much secrecy, had hidden in a barn and carefully outfitted. It was considered to be treason for anybody to even think about fleeing. The first wagon, covered by a tarpaulin, became home for Margot and her seven children, two young maids, and her sister-in-law, Pia, with her four children. They headed west one early morning under cover of darkness. They did not know that this was the last time they would see their home. The second wagon was packed with whatever could be gathered up in a hurry, mostly food and some clothing. With the Russian invading forces lapping at their heels, they were carried along in the endless flood of refugees from the northeastern provinces. These people had been clogging all means of transportation and highways in dreadful misery for weeks. Due to the bitter cold, the main concern was to keep the tractor going. A loyal Polish farm helper ably drove it. The original plan had been to travel to the estate of an uncle, also in Silesia. Fortunately, after realizing the desperation and misery of all the refugees, Margot took it upon herself to change this plan and head west.

Wolfi had stayed behind to look after farm, home, and his parents. The elderly parents tried to stay a little longer, defending their beautiful old house from hordes of marauding refugees, as well as from retreating German soldiers. The full extent of the catastrophe had sunk in and lawlessness prevailed among this flood of people with nowhere to go. Apparently, Mama Stillfried's proverbial southern temperament had once gotten the better of her when she came upon a refugee woman ransacking her linen closet. She was the only person left behind from many who had invaded the house the day before to spend the night. This poor soul had to take Mama's wrath in the form of a deftly handled umbrella swung at her backside. Fully aware of the brutal fate awaiting them at the hand of the Russians, the senior Stillfrieds finally packed up some valuables and supplies on a horse-drawn wagon. They had two horses harnessed to their old stagecoach that carried them, for the last time, in feudal splendor.

They traveled toward Hustopech in Czechoslovakia, where their daughter Angela lived with her husband and two infant children on their beautiful estate. The young Baron von Baillou and his family had already departed. The parents caught up with them further on, at the home of other relatives. Together, they all headed west through a chaotic Czechoslovakia. Partisans and crazed mobs of people confronted them. Many places were overflowing with refugees so they had to continue accepting brief accommodations with friends or relatives.

They finally arrived at Charnowitz, close to the German border. Here they were accosted by Czech guerillas, and von Baillou became the victim of an apparent mistaken identity during the wild torture and killing frenzy that surrounded them. It cost Angela's husband his life. He was shot and left to die in his wife's arms. After brutal incarceration and the loss of all their possessions, the parents barely made it across the border into Germany.

Angela and the children were helped across the border by an American unit.

Just weeks before this all happened, we had been taking advantage of the famous spa in Marienbad on the Czech border, quite oblivious of reality since all communication had been virtually cut off. Perhaps we were in a state of denial. Father had discovered our whereabouts and met us there for a brief visit. He was on his way to report at the central office of the department store in Berlin. It was quite obvious to us that we literally had no place to go to after our discharge from the hospital. There were no communications with Silesia but everybody was becoming keenly aware of the many horror stories spreading about what was happening there. We were not residents of Marienbad so there would be no food stamps issued for us. Without coupons, there was no food to be had. We had traveled with little more then a few pajamas for a brief hospital stay, we had not started out as refugees, we had no supplies with us, no bread, salami, potatoes—or anything else, for that matter. My mother was faced with making some fast decisions. The only link we had with our Silesian friends was an address scribbled on a piece of paper by Margot before she had hurriedly left. The place was Syra in Saxonia, to the Northwest. She had promised she would try to send us some message to that address. The conflicting and chaotic news about the Russian advance necessitated an urgent decision from Mother.

At this point, I had become a real hospital case. When the doctor tried to identify the cause of an irregular heartbeat, a tonsillectomy was prescribed. This was carried out in particularly unpleasant fashion due to a lack of proper anesthesia or painkillers. What was swabbed on tasted horrible and did not relieve my suffering. A few days later, the menu of sauerkraut and mashed potatoes had barely grated down my raw throat when my mother came to the hospital room to get me out of bed immediately. We had to leave that same evening, barely a few days after the radical tonsillectomy. I could not yet speak, even less argue or eat sauerkraut with mashed potatoes, the only food available. I was also running a fever, a rather common event in those days without antibiotics. To this day, I am convinced that my tonsils fell victim to the doctor's ambition to show some accomplishment. After the multiple tests had not produced any tropical amoebas, parasites or other strange bugs that an institute for tropical diseases was supposed to detect, something had to give. This had to be my tonsils. The irregular heartbeat, which also did not sound convincing to somebody who never had been seen by doctors of any kind, eventually corrected itself.

We had been in Marienbad enjoying the relative comfort of the hospital for about five weeks, way past the originally planned two-week checkup. We had been dreadfully bored; the only diversion being walks through the rather nice countryside and constant visits to the cinema. Friends from Colombia were also going through examinations there at the time. This gave Mother some companionship, as well as the fact that the chief doctor and administrator and his wife also were friends from South America. Nobody had specifically told us that the Russians were continuing their invasion of Silesia while we were in Marienbad. We had lived without news all this time and rumors were hushed up until they had been evaluated individually. It certainly showed an appalling naiveté on our part, having to join the maelstrom of refugees at the railroad station with only one small suitcase and a bag containing mostly nightclothes. We resembled the other refugees however, inasmuch as we had no place to go to and only a slip of paper with a very vague address scribbled on it.

An avalanche of frantic humanity pulled us along as we were trying to board a train headed west on a cold, mid-February day. The trains were passing only sporadically and were totally full. The wagons were obviously riddled by gun fire. People held on and hung out of windows and doors. Others were holding onto the roof or the ladders. Miraculously, the five of us finally managed to board a train without being separated. At snail's pace, the train inched along for a couple of days. Air attacks interrupted our progress. It was a trip of horrors! Not only did my throat ache terribly but we were also hungry and oh so cold. The gusty winter wind blew clouds of snow through the broken windows of the compartments. Sometimes the train would stop in the middle of nowhere. It meant we all had to dash out and roll down the embankment, and stay prone. Once low-flying planes strafed the train and the huddled masses with machine guns. In sad irony, we seemed consoled that these planes so generously dispensing death were American or British and that we were slowly moving away from the terrifying Russian grip!

At last we arrived in Dresden where we were able to inquire about the address Margot had given us. Dresden was sheer bedlam. This beautiful old town, known for its famous art treasures and Rococo architecture, had not yet been touched much by the war. It had no military installations or factories. But it was a crossroads, and many train tracks met at this busy intersection. The city was already filled to capacity with refugees. The roads in and outside of the city were clogged with horse carts, handcarts and people on foot. And more kept coming. Every train disgorged its load adding to the overflow. The war seemed to be over as far as fighting was concerned, but the invading troops were proceeding rapidly. The uprooted masses had no place to turn to. There was no way for us to stay in town.

Fortunately, we had been able to find out that Margot and her group had traveled through town and they had found refuge only some thirty miles away in Syra, on a country estate. This was one of the few facilities able to assimilate the influx of such a large refugee family. We were overjoyed and, leaving our one suitcase behind for later collection, we started out in the general direction of Syra. We were lucky to catch brief cart-rides to ease the long march. This was particularly hard on my little sister, only five, and my nine-year-old brother who always had been sickly. Sister Christiane, now thirteen, and I at seventeen, managed quite well on the march. My fever had subsided and my throat did not hurt as much anymore. Due to the resiliency of youth, any new situation seemed stimulating to the two of us. We were happy about the prospect of catching up with our friends.

The reunion with the Stillfried clan in Syra, at the estate of the von Einsiedels was a joyful one and we were quickly assimilated. We soon were all sleeping on cots or on straw in a large "salon" that had seen better days—and was never meant to be a dormitory for refugees. The house was bursting at its seams. Other Silesians had arrived before us, and more came later. The owners, understandably, were not overly enthusiastic about this unwanted influx, but we were all beyond caring about propriety. Our sense of priorities had shifted. We settled down to just living from one day to the next as if there had been no past. There was certainly not much of a future to think about.

When Margot left Silbitz, she had quickly looked into our rooms and grabbed one trunk full of things to take along for us. Unfortunately, it turned out to be my school trunk, mostly outgrown clothes, books and other unnecessary items of no value. Wolfi took it on himself to bury the few nice Colombian silver pieces we had taken with us to Silbitz, together with some of his family property. No one, except perhaps the Russians or Poles later on, ever knew where these were to be found again.

Meanwhile, we were looking around for a solution to our scant wardrobe. We each had only one dress, the one we were wearing. We had learned by now to make use of almost anything. There were some interesting looking curtains hanging along the large windows of the "salon," reminiscent of better times. Following some urgent entreaties with the lady of the house, one soon could see six little girls in matching dresses that had been whipped together by the village seamstress. My recollection of what I had used to fashion an outfit for myself fail me at this time.

Air raids on the surrounding cities of Dresden, Chemnitz and Leipzig now occurred constantly, the flak seldom silenced. But we, in our rural setting, felt hopeful no bombs would be wasted on a village! However, on one of our first nights in Syra after a sunny day of promising spring beauty, we heard ominous thundering. It literally shook the old house and alarmed us. On that night as a culmination to the constant bombings, wave after wave of bombers flew over us and, shortly after, the thudding and exploding of not too distant bombs rendered the night into sobs of fear. We were witnessing the death of Dresden!

That night, as we stood at an upstairs window, the light cast by the burning city, a scant 30 miles away, was so intense we could have read by it as if in broad daylight. I vividly remember the book out of my school trunk that I had been reading, *Gone With The Wind*. This, however, was not Atlanta burning, but Dresden! And this was not the 19th but the 20th century. The firestorm caused by the systematic carpet bombing set off a tremendous holocaust, melting even the asphalt of the streets. The refugees on them had no way to escape. One could only pray for a quicker death of suffocation.

The pall of death was carried long distances as the early spring snow turned totally black from the soot and ashes we also had to breathe in with the air. It was like inhaling the last sighs of thousands of people. It was a repeat of the air raids on Berlin where the snow was black all winter long, under dark and menacing clouds. The trains that jammed into the station loaded with people had become funeral pyres.

Some time later, we found out about the devastating fate of the Stillfried's Uncle and Aunt, Count and Countess B. When it became necessary for them to flee from Silesia, their brother took the four youngest children of the deaf couple west, hoping to find safety. The parents, with the two older children, were to follow later. The train carrying Uncle Niko with the four small children was one of those demolished in the Dresden air raid.

Twenty years later, the Red Cross contacted the parents of the four lost children in what was then West Germany with the news that a railroad worker and his wife had found and rescued a baby along the burning tracks whom they had taken in and raised. They had always wondered about the initials and a crown embroidered on the baby's fine shirt and had never given up trying to find his parents. I can imagine the joyful reunion of the B. family with this son, and the new doubts raised about the fate of the other three missing children of whom nothing was ever heard again.

This one of so many tragic stories hit home, because of the family relationship. The horror stories about the bombardment reached us nearly as fast as the smoke and smell of the burning ruins, burning flesh, burning life. Several more bombardments, spaced over the next few days, singled out Leipzig and Chemnitz, the two other cities close by and finished off what had not been accomplished before, and mercifully plowing under whatever still stood in silent protest.

We attempted a hike toward Dresden with the foolish hope of retrieving our stored suitcase—as if it could have survived such events. We were never allowed into the city, however. The air was heavy with the nauseating smell of death and destruction. Waves of refugees again poured into the ruins in hope of making connection with their loved ones. It caused chaos but then gradually subsided. Dresden was no more. No trains were running and the station was destroyed. So were most of the roads and the treks of refugees had to somehow bypass the city.

During the following weeks, the constant air raids that had become part of our existence became less frequent. There was not much left to destroy. Toward the end of March, an eerie silence enveloped the countryside. Time seemed suspended and hung like a big question mark in the blue spring sky and painfully quivered in the lazy sunshine. The guns were silent. Rumors had it that the Russians and the Americans were within reach of a handshake. If there had been German fighting forces anywhere, they appeared to have disintegrated. They certainly had nothing to fight with, or for, anymore. The only thing lively in motion was the "rumor mill."

On one day, the story was that Russians had been

sighted in a neighboring village and on the next day, the sightings were supposed to be of Americans. To the population, never having seen either, it was immaterial. The all-encompassing concern was food. The farmers still hoarded their supplies. Surviving town dwellers, if they had managed to salvage any possessions, roamed the countryside in search of trading opportunities. A "salami" had the value of a painting, a sack of potatoes would go for a piano. At last, the poorer rural population was able to acquire riches they had never owned or dreamt of owning with their meager farm income. Laws against such trading were still intact, but nobody was there to enforce them.

Feeding our two families, Margot, her seven children, and the maids, Elli and Erna, and Mami with us four, was also our main concern. We had discovered a juice bottling plant. It stood deserted, leaving huge numbers of filled bottles scattered around. Soon several hundred bottles of delicious apple, currant and cherry juices were neatly stacked under the cots in the salon. Margot had stocked up well with Silbitz hams, bacon, and sausages and also flour and potatoes, before leaving their well producing farm and home. We were extremely fortunate to have these supplies, but also aware of the danger such ownership posed. So, with the help of the Polish tractor driver who had fled with them, Margot buried these treasures in several places in the yard during a dark night.

Some of the younger children spent days roaming the countryside visiting farms, and they sometimes came back with valuable surprises. Christiane and Johanna, both cute little things were particularly adept in "organizing." They begged and haggled and slowly acquired two rabbits, four hens and a rooster. It was many years later that we found out the truth of how at least one if not two, of these critters were just "found roaming" and given a loving home by adding them to our little flock. We managed to get a small but suitable barn enclosure where we kept the animals. They were carefully pampered by all. Everyone had to "organize" grain and other feed to make our lovely pets produce often three eggs a day. This was greeted with general jubilation.

The baby, Georg Stillfried, benefited much from our joint care as did my brother Harald, who always needed more substantial food than anyone else. Just before the Easter holidays, our menagerie had grown by an entire sheep that was butchered to supply a feast. Being the oldest child in the group, I had become main kitchen helper for the combined family of now sixteen people. I was also in charge and took proud care of our livestock. In between all of this, I was supposed to teach seven children of various ages history and geography. My knowledge in these fields was meager, but I suppose it served the purpose of not letting us all completely rust. Mami and Margot probably taught other subjects to our horde of youngsters.

Aside from the simpler worries of feeding all these hungry mouths, the much greater concern for all of us, particularly for the mothers, was the total lack of communication and news about their husbands, our fathers. We knew that my father was in a very precarious situation in Berlin, which was being annihilated by bombs. Margot's husband, Wolfi, having stayed behind in Silesia, under the "gentle" care of the Russians, would not be heard from for a long time to come. He trustingly clung to the faith that their home had to be kept in working condition for his family to return to eventually. Pia Matuschka, who had found refuge at the neighboring estate Koenigsfeld, had no news at all to give her hope that the horrible threat of her husband, Michael's, execution by the Gestapo had been false. Personally, I worried much about Dominik. A fact nobody was supposed to guess.

I stifled an expression of joy when word reached us that Dominik had arrived in Koenigsfeld to visit his sister, Pia, and her four children. We were excited to hear they had been offered the use of a horse and buggy for a drive over to visit us. I could barely contain my joy at seeing Dominik again. However, that visit became a great disappointment. I soon found out that a beautiful young girl by the name of Inez was also a refugee at Koenigsfeld and Dominik appeared much in a hurry to go back there with his sister, Pia, so my joy was short-lived. How gloriously miserable one can be at seventeen! My day ended with an hour-long soliloquy in the chicken house where a heartbroken teenager looked for privacy and refuge from the teasing barbs the youngsters employed.

Dominik's stay in the area was a short one and quite illegal. His fighter squadron "106" in Schongau Bavaria had been dissolved when they ran out of fuel. Dominik was to accompany a few subordinates; they were to immediately proceed to Berlin to join the fight against the invading forces. He had managed to get separated from the others and simply jumped onto a crowded train on a different track, disregarding danger of detection by the military police. They could have court-martialed and shot him on the spot for desertion from his Luftwaffe unit. He knew where his sister was staying. Much wanting to see his family, he surprised us all and consequently made it back the same way, undetected. We were unable to contact anyone else of the family until all this madness was finally over.

Meanwhile, we did not lose track of events like birthdays. Several were celebrated with all the cheer and happiness that children give to such occasions. Even though the gifts were very homemade, the cakes tasted delicious in spite of being baked with substitutes and much improvisation. I had become chief baker and produced with pride whatever I could with whatever supplies I could find. An old-fashioned village adobe oven helped to produce good results. Games and singing made these very festive occasions.

Being a refugee often means eating humble pie. We had to cook in the house kitchen, borrowing many items, sometimes even a pot. I was always in someone's way. Since I was the youngest and most often in the kitchen doing my work, I had to suffer quite a bit of abuse from the maids as well as the lady of the house. She could erupt in an evil temper and anger over all the unwanted refugees in her house and I was the easiest target for her unfounded (and mostly quite false) accusations. But we learned to bear anything for our beloved large family. Obviously, everybody suffered from the stress and uncertainty. Uppermost, we all sensed the insecurity of not knowing if we would live to see the absent loved ones or even be alive next week. The bombs had given way to an eerie silence. The approach of the Russians and the Americans was imminent. Who would be first, could we trust anyone? Were we all doomed? It did not take a lovesick teenager, to lose hope. Happiness had been replaced by a tenacious will to survive any way possible.

One of my foraging runs caused my first encounter with "enemy" soldiers. They were Americans. Through the grapevine, we had been alerted to the wreck of a plane nearby that had come down the previous night. The fuel tanks were supposedly intact, and collecting empty containers, we rushed to take advantage of this windfall. After all, airplane fuel would be good for something besides flying. I ran right into a column of marching GIs who totally ignored our ragtag band of scavengers. I did understand enough English to tell everybody back "home" that the Americans were coming.

Americans Are Coming

Next morning, the 15th of April 1945, I heard some loud banging on the old front portal and opening it, I found myself staring down some rifle barrels. Three hulking giants stood there holding our little Mechthild by the scruff of her neck. She apparently had cheerfully greeted these nice men with the "Heil Hitler" every child had been taught to use when greeting strangers. She looked quite worried and helpless as the soldiers demanded to know who this brat belonged to. I rushed to call Margot to come and rescue her little girl from this fearful predicament. A house search followed and we were left with orders not to move from the premises. The boys were deeply upset because the efficient and, at this point not very friendly, GIs had taken their cherished bb-guns.

When it became known that an interpreter was needed, my mother volunteered. A Jeep came for her and we all thought we had seen the last of her. But, on the contrary, Mother returned that evening with a friendly officer in tow. Colonel Droste not only was glad to have found a competent interpreter; he came to meet us all and became an immediate friend to this band of involuntary gypsies. We saw a lot of him during the next few days. He took keen interest in our plight. While he enjoyed our company and the family atmosphere, he also was concerned about our immediate future. My mother continued to help as an interpreter and was made temporary

"Burgermeister" (major) of the village. Meanwhile an entire army platoon had pitched their tents in the yard in front of the picture windows of our "salon," and to our dismay, right on top of our buried food supplies.

I was astonished, to find I was becoming a celebrity. It appeared that I was the first "liberated" American on this part of the front. Somehow, I had never quite realized the implication of having been born in San Francisco, CA. This circumstance had made me an instant citizen, even though according to German law, I was a German because of my parents' nationality. We were also made aware of possible benefits to be derived from the fact that my sisters and brother were Colombians by birth. Of course, Mother had known this all along, but it did not seem relevant before.

Colonel Droste revealed to my mother that this entire section of Germany, all of Saxonia and Thuringia included, was going to be turned over to the Russians by General Eisenhower within the next few weeks. He said, "Ada, this is not yet official, but I feel deep concern about letting your seventeen-year-old daughter fall into the hands of the Russians. I can arrange for a Red Cross unit to take her with them to safety." We all had ample knowledge of the fate awaiting any female from age eight to eighty at the hands of the brutal invading forces from the east. However, I flatly refused to leave without my family.

That evening Colonel Droste returned. He said, "I arranged a permit for your brother and sisters, after all they are Colombians and our allies. Also, your mother once had a Brazilian passport. That ought to do." Since we had no means of transportation, loyalty, as well as practical reasoning, sent Droste back to the drawing board. He resurfaced the next day with a beaming face.

"All right, Margot, I really did not like the thought of leaving you here either. You have two children born in Colombia so that gives us a good reason. You can all pack up and leave together at once."

He was not prepared for the next bout, however. Margot expressed her determination not to leave without her sister-in-law, Pia, and her four children who were still in Koenigsfeld. It took two more days and all of the resourcefulness Droste could muster to come back with another permit. It was allowed based on the fact that Pia's husband had been persecuted and likely killed by the Gestapo.

Now Droste had a condition for us. "I discovered a beautiful girl in Koenigsfeld, I want you to make room for her and take her with you, to safety. Thus Inez became part of our group and, in time, my best friend.

Including the Polish tractor driver, we were now twenty people getting ready to leave. The two flatbed wagons had to be carefully loaded again. The first one, covered by a tarpaulin, was to house the mothers and children; the second was loaded with baggage. We were given two days to pack and a three-day permit to travel. We were told to aim for the area around Kassel, which would be beyond the newly designated Russian border.

Leaving was difficult for us. Colonel Elmer Droste and his unit and we had become attached to each other even though we were officially not permitted to "fraternize." We also had felt more secure than we had in a long time. Droste had spent every free moment with us. He obviously enjoyed being included in a family and surrounded by nice children. But we could not lose sight of our desperate situation. Droste was very seriously urging speed in our preparations for departure. He gave me a telephone number and an address in New York and asked me to contact him if I ever came to the United States. I have never understood why these were apparently not valid. Later my efforts to locate this man who literally saved us all from unspeakable horrors all failed. I have wondered if he became a late victim of the conflict.

I was faced with a dreadful discovery the next morning when I went to our "secret" chicken house to feed the precious flock and make up a box for their transport. Only one lonely hen greeted me with an anxious cackle! The door was locked but a trail of white feathers indicated the way through the flap that the birds used to reach their small outdoor run. Obviously someone had forced his way through this hole and committed the unspeakable crime! After searching everywhere without finding a trace of my charges, I followed the trail of feathers purposely laid out, and unmistakably leading straight to the soldiers' encampment on the lawn. Dissolved into tears, I ran to the house and told Margot the horrible news. She stormed out and with an angry red face accosted one of the soldiers. Several others listening to Margot's angry accusations soon joined him: "You—you—you Americans raped our hens."

I had followed and did not comprehend why amused grins should light up all those faces while the sergeant laughingly replied, "No, Ma'am, we sure didn't do that!" In the evening during Colonel Droste's visit, it dawned on us that there was a slippery word game involved in the use of "rape" versus "rob." Droste could hardly suppress a grin himself as he asked, "What did you say, Margot?"

We made final preparations for our departure the next day. Alas, the soldiers were still encamped on top of our salamis. We were gravely concerned when we detected unusual activities in their camp. They were taking down their tents in great haste and by nightfall only huge piles of trash and used equipment remained. The platoon's rapid departure left us with no doubt about the need of urgency for our own move. During all this commotion, the children found the piles of abandoned refuse to be an irresistible treasure trove. They scampered around with full cans of food, army blankets, trousers, and many other items that for us had become unheard-of luxuries. Shrieks of delight were everywhere as they hid some scavenged treasure on the baggage wagon while the adults were busily retrieving the long lost salamis, hams, and other important supplies.

All was recovered and stowed away in our transport before we each said polite good-bye's to the astonished homeowners and many other remaining refugees. They probably gave sighs of relief to see their numbers thus depleted, even though all knew that there was a strict order not to leave the premises or to travel on any road. Inez arrived and we soon cemented our friendship as we took our places on the rear axle of the last wagon. We were put in charge of the brakes, which were primitive but efficient and had to be operated manually.

We finally headed west on April 28. Our group was comprised of the three mothers; Pia, Margot and Mami, with sixteen children aged two to seventeen. Of these, there were seven Stillfrieds, four Matuschkas, four Kroghs and Inez von Aulock, all carefully driven by our nice Polish tractor driver. Margot's faithful housekeepers, twins Erna and Elli, opted to stay behind hoping to make it back home to Silesia sooner. Thanks to well-guarded canisters of tractor fuel, there was a sufficient supply of this precious stuff to keep us puttering along deserted roads for the next few days. Astonished faces stared at us in every village we rolled through, and several American military units passed and stopped us to verify the authenticity of our permit. It was quite an event to have refugees still travelling the highways, against all strict orders for everyone to remain in place. Invariably, these confrontations ended with an assemblage of GIs around the two "brake ladies" in the back. Particularly, Inez's dimples and passable mastery of the English language were an obvious hit. Then one child after the other tumbled out of the front wagon and a merry distribution of chewing gum and chocolates ensued before sending us on our way. It had become a game that we all enjoyed.

It came as a surprise when, in the outskirts of Naumburg, an inquisitive soldier lifted a corner of the tarp covering our baggage, became very agitated and called his superiors. The sight of U.S. army blankets and trousers carelessly stuffed into the back was ominous to them. Angry shouting ensued. Not even Inez's smiles could placate this hornet's nest. We were going to be searched thoroughly! Worst of all, the time allocated on our permit was running out and no telling when we could continue. During all this upheaval, Christoph confessed to his mother that they had found some guns and ammunition in the pile of abandoned debris and had hidden them in the back. Obviously, this spelled the end of our trip! But Christiane and Johanna suddenly announced an urgent need to "step out" behind some bushes. Afterward it came to pass that no incriminating items would be found. An elderly officer arrived and took one look at the masses of children and worried mothers. He had a kind heart and listened to the tale of the scavenging of the much needed, thrown away articles left at Syra by the departing U.S. soldiers. We were showered with more chocolate, gum, and candy and permitted to continue on our trek after a superficial inspection of the wagons.

Our most difficult task was finding shelter and accommodation for the nights. Luckily, Margot had names and addresses of estates of some friends and relatives where we knocked at not-very-welcoming gates. Every place was overflowing with refugees. With the assurance that we did not plan to stay and would leave again the next morning, the atmosphere cleared and people moved over a bit to let us squeeze into the crowds for a night. It had become obvious that we were just too many people to find refuge all together.

We passed Kassel into an area indicated as safe and far enough West to be out of reach of the Russian grasp. We obviously had to find a place where we could remain—but refugees and air raid victims were everywhere in town and the countryside. The large estate houses were all overcrowded. At one home of relatives where we had hoped to find refuge and were faced with an impossible situation, the owners told Margot about the Boyneburg, not too distant from our present location. Rumors had it that the owner had vanished with his family, hiding from the wrath of Polish workers who claimed they had not been treated properly. Our old tractor sputtered up the mountain to the Boyneburg. As we rounded the last curve and the buildings came in sight, the engine groaned to a halt emphasizing our decision to go no further.

We faced an assemblage of unfriendly-looking people, who told us to move on since there was no room for us. Their astonishment at what they saw was obvious, as one child after another tumbled out from under the tarpaulin as if to ease the weight for the old tractor. They followed a very determined Margot who marched on to face the crowd telling them we were here to stay and just had no place else to go to. Our Polish tractor driver, Antony, took charge conveying our determination.

We waited patiently until somebody went to fetch Frau von Loesch, we found she was also a Silesian refugee. She told us she was managing the farm for the Poles in "Communist" fashion. The usual "Hello" and excitement when refugees met assured us a stay. Apparently all Silesians are related or know of each other.

"You have an awful lot of very small children there," said Sigrid von Loesch, "but never mind, I have six myself. Everybody over ten years of age will be signed up for work. You start tomorrow at six in the morning."

She also knew how to assuage the irritation of the POWs who did not like the idea that we would be encamped in the elegant mansion. They wanted this arrangement for themselves and thought we should accommodate ourselves in the barn and labor houses. They let us move into the big house only on a temporary basis. However, we then stayed there, since shortly afterward the Polish workers left.

We again overcame the embarrassment of moving into the private living quarters of owners who were absent. We were assigned the large salon and a few rooms as we set up housekeeping. However, Inez and I were quietly spirited away and temporarily put up at the house of an old farmer and his wife. It was deemed prudent to remove us from the ogling eyes of the many rather wild looking former POWs who constantly milled around us. We were both assigned a place of work under the watchful eyes of the old foreman couple. The other youngsters were spread out. Christiane and Christoph became the dairy crew in the barn. Victor and Ruprecht were assigned to the pig barn and Mario became a shepherd. As far as sensitive noses are concerned, we certainly had drawn the

143

smelliest lot. Ten hours a day, Inez and I sat in a murky, cold and humid cellar sorting sound from rotten potatoes. The ratio was about one useable potato to about five mushy ones so one could multiply the stench accordingly. To this day, the discovery of one evil smelling potato in a grocery bag will transport me years back to that cold cellar! But we both knew we were quite safe there and used our time to do a lot of talking.

That huge potato mountain would have easily kept us busy the whole summer were it not for the good fortune of the POWs sudden departure. A week after our arrival, they opted to follow a repatriation call issued by the American occupation forces.

The departure of the nearly forty men who had previously done most of the work on the farm, but lately refrained from working, left old Herr Rimbach and two other German farmhands to cope with the large estate and the feeding of many hungry mouths. The place was now literally run by teenagers and children. Leaving out all but absolutely essential work, we had to concentrate on the feeding and care of the livestock. The herd of fifty cows had to be milked by hand. Christiane's hands still give testimony to this hard work. Inez and I were promoted from potato sorters to manure scrapers and general barn helpers. I became an expert in balancing a wheelbarrow with manure through rivulets of liquid ooze and onto some planks precariously placed over a huge mountain of manure. The objective was to tilt the heavy wheelbarrow over at the end of the planks. If you should let go or become careless its weight could easily pull you into the smelly mess below.

Our hands became callused from wielding the pitchfork, but in return, we received precious food supplies to carry home. This was the only thing that mattered during this period when nothing could be purchased. There was some time left between feeding and caring for the cows and calves, so we were assigned to other jobs. Inez and I had to clean the living quarters of the just departed POWs. It was not long before we found out that it had been more pleasant to work in the potato cellar. After literally wading, sometimes knee high, in trash and refuse, we managed to clear the place in a few days. Any idea of moving us all into that house, as had been previously suggested, was swept out with the filth. It would have taken much more than broom and scrub brush to make the place habitable again. We remained firmly ensconced in the "salon" and the other few rooms we had already been assigned.

A few weeks later, the estate owners reappeared. They were, understandably, not happy about our mass invasion. But Sigrid assured them that only our presence there had prevented a rampage and total destruction by the departing Poles, angry and eager to take revenge. She had placated them with a generous distribution of staple foods she had found hoarded in the basement. These supplies had been illegally withheld from the workers during previous years. After closing certain doors and passageways, rules were made so that we might cause the least disturbance possible to our landlords. We did want to keep friction at a minimum. Even though, admittedly, we could not resist taking a souvenir, for instance, a light bulb with the inscription: "Stolen on Boyneburg."

Sigrid, an accomplished agronomist, was capably managing the estate and our help and hers were imperative at this stage. Again, I was in charge of cooking. The first big meal, for which our cherished lonely chicken had been sacrificed, was tasty but eaten with tears in memory of our little pet. Meanwhile, "our" boys, meaning

145

Ruprecht and Christoph, had ganged up with their cousins, Mario and Victor, and in teenage fashion, were becoming a real nuisance. I dreaded their mischievous pranks. Tolerable ones, like being bombarded with pebbles that seemed to fly through the window and into my cook-pot, apparently from nowhere, and the eternal supervision and constant nasty smirks and jokes about us girls were quite galling. There was also ample opportunity for the many cousins to get into mischief. On one of the first days there, as they were snooping around and inspecting the premises, they had all disappeared. Suddenly, we heard dreadful screaming and the horde came running down the mountainside following a frightfully blackened figure that turned out to be Christoph. He had gotten his hands on a stash of black powder and was attempting to produce fireworks when the whole pile exploded in his face. All of his hair was singed away and, worse, he was blinded for weeks before our prayers were answered and he began to see again. Fortunately, he healed with only a few small scars to show for it.

Rumors about the impending peace circulated constantly. Peace, life, flowers—the profusion of these in May of 1945 surpassed anything I had ever experienced. Certainly the peonies, lilies of the valley and lilac bushes poured forth with as much abundance as in any spring. The veil of sorrow that had hung over the torn country had muted their message before. In the most touching fashion, the boys absolutely buried me with armloads of flowers on my eighteenth birthday. I guess they were good kids after all! Our young hearts wanted to rise with the jubilation of life heard in the call of the meadowlarks. At first, as if embarrassed, but soon becoming bolder, we would roam the forest on a day off, stretch out for hours in the grass looking up at the clear sky. No longer did we search anxiously for the silver speck of an airplane bringing death. Our realization of being alive revolved around the subjects that dreams of young girls have always been made of. Elisabeth, the landlord's daughter, had become Inez's and my friend. The three of us became quite inseparable as we reached out for the joys we sensed to be a young girl's due. Perhaps we had learned to find happiness forgoing fulfillment of so many wishes.

Drawn by the timeless call of youth, the first GIs soon appeared on the mountain of Boyneburg. They were not on a search mission or a call to enforce regulations, they simply came to visit. Strict rules against fraternizing with the population were still in force. Under the existing code of honor, young girls with any sense of decency should not associate with the "enemy." As if these rules did not apply to us, some of these young men almost became part of our large family. Hardly a day went by without the Jeep rattling up the mountain road bringing Chester, Harry and Joe and, on occasion, some other friends of theirs. Then a boisterous ball game with the kids often lasted into the night. When the youngsters tired out, we sat and talked on the veranda. We could be sure that the little "beasts" were hiding behind the shrubbery and counting the cigarettes we were offered. Giggles and comments would accompany any motion. We three friends would take walks and arrange horseback rides with the young men when our work schedule permitted. But the high point came when we piled into the Jeep for a drive up to the mountaintop. There the ruin of an old castle stood in a large courtyard with ample open space, ideal for driving lessons! Amidst a lot of giggling and laughter, the three of us took our turns in learning how to handle the steering wheel of the Jeep. We also organized picnics for which our friends brought many goodies.

On one occasion, when Sigrid had sent Inez and me to a field to harvest fresh peas by hand for everybody's consumption, Chester and Harry drove by and decided to help us with the picking. It so happened that the old Baron was walking by the field. Later that evening, Sigrid was handed a slip of paper. The Baron's relationship with her—as well as us other refugees—was such that he would only communicate with her in writing:

"Fraulein von Krogh and Fraulein von Aulock are picking peas with two Americans in two buckets, on field No. 5." The same slip of paper went back to the originator, telling him "Fraulein von Krogh and Fraulein von Aulock with two Americans are picking peas in two buckets on my order." The message of acknowledgment has been lost in time. For many years, Inez and I would exchange the little missive once a year for some anniversary. It was a hilarious piece of remembrance. I am sure that only the isolation of the place saved us from detection and the consequent wrath of the authorities and the population. After all, I barely spoke English and I certainly did not wear my American citizenship on my sleeve. It was on their last visit, when their unit was being sent back to the States, that Harry put his arm around me for the first time when we said our tearful good-byes on the veranda. A sad silence enveloped us all. But we also sensed that the days of playfulness would have come to an end. After the three men had departed, I had a sensation of relief at not having to feel guilty as my thoughts went back to Dominik. We three girls sat up talking till early morning hours. There was so much to guess and wonder about for us.

Although we tried to just be normal young girls who longed to enjoy our lives, order in everybody's existence was slow in returning. During the summer of 1945 rumors abounded, since there was no regular communication of news. We knew of the total collapse of the system and there were talks of the signing of a peace treaty. Then rumors of more war would surface. Electricity was finally restored, but there was no mail service and certainly no telephone communication. Newspapers did not exist either. During all this time, an assortment of strange people would appear, peddling news for whatever they could get in the form of shelter and food. One man, named Pflanz, ingratiated himself with Margot by telling her he had come from a reunion with her husband whom he claimed to have found well and not far from us. Professing knowledge about other missing relatives and friends, he soon manipulated Margot to give him money and valuables as well as precious food. It took a family fight, Pia and Mami against Margot, to convince her of his criminal intent and to get rid of him. We found out soon after that he was one of the many hardened convicts who had been released along with the unfortunate victims of the concentration camps.

Next, a man appeared on the scene who claimed to be an expert on spiritualism. Producing a Bible, he set up a sort of altar and had Pia tie her wedding ring on a thread, swinging it over the Bible. Reading his symbols, he assured Pia that her husband was still alive. This was the cruelest of hoaxes since she had almost certain knowledge of her husband's horrible death at the hands of the Gestapo following the plot against Hitler on the 20th of July the year before. By coincidence, the "pendant" proved correct in a couple of cases we knew about, so we used the method to inquire about others. He proceeded to claim certainty about Dominik's death as well as my father's. Papi actually appeared soundly on the scene only a week later. We quickly rid ourselves of this prophet, but not before he had dug deeply into our meager supplies.

Margot or Sigrid would invite me to go with them on short trips as they were trying to find news of loved ones. Sigrid still had not heard of her husband, who had last been fighting on the Russian front. We would either use some bicycles or saddle horses to ramble on from one estate to another for several days. We talked to all the refugees we encountered, piecing together their recollections, trying to find connections.

For one of these excursions, Margot and I had dressed in our colorful "Green Briar" skirts. We had to bicycle through a town occupied by an American garrison. As to be expected in a war situation, encounters between civilians and soldiers are not always problem-free. We tried to breeze through town quickly and made it without being stopped. We were on a lonely country road when the sound of tires made us look back and discover a Jeep with two GIs in it. We pedaled on, increasingly worried, as the Jeep persisted in following us at very low speed for the next mile or so. Real fear gripped us since there was not a person or habitation in sight. As the vehicle started to pass and creep alongside, our terror mounted. We both had only heard frightening things about involvement with the "enemy forces." When a hand with a pack of Camel cigarettes (a highly prized article for civilians in those days), was extended to us, Margot could only mutter, "Oh no, we don't smell." With my scant knowledge of English, I was able to explain to Margot, "You meant to say we don't smoke," while loud laughter rang in our ears as the Jeep sped away. But these associations were always a mixed bag.

On one occasion, I walked down to the military encampment at Wichmannshausen. We had been trying to

150

buy or trade for some food supplies and some medication for little Georg who was ill. I had not been successful and, as I stood behind the mess barrack, I worked up the gall to approach a GI in a white apron who was carrying a box of eggs. I actually begged him for a few eggs for a sick little boy and had to experience the shameful sneer of this man, who said, "So, you want eggs! Take them," as he smashed them to the ground and left with an ugly laugh in a face filled with hatred. It was years before I knew how such hatred had natural roots in the horrible atrocities Germans were accused of, acts I had no knowledge about, and which took me years to believe.

Soon after, we experienced the other side of the coin when a tragic accident occurred. Sigrid von Loesch was moving to a different village with her family. All her possessions that she had brought with her from Silesia were already loaded on her wagon. The two heavy draft horses, momentarily unattended by an adult, were nervously prancing and ready to run off with the load. A group of evacuee children was having a great time noisily jumping up and down on the loaded vehicle. My mother had just left with my two screaming siblings who were protesting having to go to bed. Also, the Stillfried children had been called away. Only the two younger Matuschka were still bouncing around and having a great time with the other twelve children. They barely managed to jump off as the ruckus became too much for the horses. The frightened animals suddenly bolted and ran with the shifting load and screaming children slamming into a gate-pillar. An iron post gored one horse and five children were severely injured. One girl lay under a heavy brick pillar. It took much effort to extricate her. Inez and I bicycled down to Wichmannshausen and stopped an army Jeep. Immediately, the soldiers commandeered the necessary help and

151

a medical team. The injured children were rushed to the field hospital. One little girl lost a leg that had to be amputated. It was a gruesome event, but the care and assistance we got from the GIs was exemplary.

As spring turned into summer, our work schedule changed with the season. We hated thinning the endless rows of sugar beets. Our backs ached and we could barely keep pace with the experienced farm helpers hired for this job. Then there was work with the harvest in heat and dust, as we had to shove heavy armloads of dried pea vines or other grain into the threshing machines inside a huge barn. Doing this kind of work for an entire day left us absolutely exhausted. We got a taste of it all. But we were not short of enjoyable weekends and evenings. We had our visitors and there was rejoicing at every arrival of relatives or just receiving authentic news about them.

In early summer, a stately coach crested the mountain road. The sight of it transported us to a distant past. Seeing the well-groomed horses, Inez let out a yell of recognition. Her parents alighted from their coach and her cocker spaniel that she had never expected to see again joyfully greeted her. They had traveled for many weeks in this fashion, following the rumor trail, to be reunited with their youngest daughter. We crowded together and gave up the room Inez and I had shared and they settled in to stay for a while. One day in later summer, an automobile appeared, and my father, whom we had missed for so long, was finally with us again. He announced that he would take us with him in the direction of Hamburg, where he had found an occupation and boarding in one room. Papi had borrowed the car and rented a summer cottage from friends for us in Holm Seppensen, not too distant from Hamburg. Housing was otherwise impossible to obtain.

We knew that leaving the Boyneburg would mean joining the hungrier masses. Food was very scarce, as was everything else. The value of the German currency now, shortly before its total collapse, was questionable and did not allow for any planning. As long as we had been working on the Boyneburg estate, we had not suffered too much hunger. We all worked for food and housing. But the war was over at last and, we were obviously all destined to go our own ways. Over the past year, unique and solid ties had been forged among us all. We knew these to be lasting. Yet, the separation was difficult. Each family had to leap into an uncertain future alone. Inez left with her parents. Once again their horses were harnessed to the stagecoach to take them north to Westphalia where they found permanent refuge with other relatives.

Before winter, Margot and her seven children moved into a small house in the village of Wichmannshausen where they remained until Wolfi's return. He had tried to stay home in Silbitz, but was forced by the Russians to leave before Silesia was turned over to the Poles and emptied of remaining Germans. Silesia became a part of Poland, in lieu of land taken from them by the Russians. People had no rights and were ignored or just bypassed in the process of decision making. So much for the adage that two rights will right a wrong! Pia and her four children stayed on at Boyneburg the longest. Pia had to face up to the tragic truth that her husband would never return and her home in Silesia was lost, too. Eventually she settled in South Germany, before acquiring an apartment in Bonn, where her by then grown children, active in the Foreign Service had settled.

Displaced Persons and Red Tape

I stayed until late summer with Margot to help out and then joined my family as we pressed on with our aim of returning to the Americas. This proved to be no easy feat. We began a struggle with endless red tape and were without any financial means. The adorable little cottage my father had found for us stood in an expanse of heather surrounded by graceful birch trees. Travelling to Hamburg was still quite complicated so Papi only visited on weekends. Constant trips to the city to visit the consulates or UNRRA (United Nations Relief and Rehabilitation Administration) in order to file for applications acquainted me with the misery of travelling. Late trains, cancelled buses, all overcrowded, made this a tiring endeavor. The children had long walks to school in Buchholz in all sorts of weather and were inadequately clothed. Above all, the food situation was dismal. Often, one stood in line for up to six hours after strenuous walking, only to find the announced item exhausted when reaching the front of the line. Food stamps were useless in the absence of supplies. So it was with everything one needed. Our spell of country living had spoiled us. On the other hand, we were able to visit some cultural events, which became available at an early stage. The approaching winter loomed as we faced the grim fear of the cold that would find us woefully under-clothed.

The cottage was not at all adequate for the winter season. Heating was impossible. The tiny kitchen had a small wood-burning stove that, most of the time, belched huge clouds of smoke that gave our skin a rather shaded appearance, not to speak of our clothing, furniture and everything else. Firewood was impossible to come by and we had to embark on foraging expeditions in the surrounding forest. As others had gone before us, not much could be found. We had to resort to "accidentally" fallen trees that we cut up and took home in a little handcart. Soon we joined the other folks along the train tracks waiting for a coal train to pass slowly, sometimes "dropping" pieces of coal. Occasionally, one could observe shadowy figures busying themselves on top of these coal trains which delivered the coal for overseas shipment as wartime reparations.

We were becoming quite adept in the occupation of "organizing." When all our endeavors failed and no farmer sold us anything, Christiane and I managed to scrounge a little cart full of sugar beets from some nearby fields, during a dark, cold night. It never occurred to us that this common way of "organisieren" (organizing) actually was pilfering. As usual, the excuse of "everybody does it" sufficed. Hunger can obliterate all other arguments. We walked our shoes thin, trying to buy or trade for some chickens. We had two rabbits that had been given to us in Wichmannshausen, but to get chickens was impossible. Christiane came home one day with a young gray rooster in trade for Papi's shirt. Our "Goodo-goodo-goo" became such a beloved pet that we were never able to butcher him, going hungry instead. I was tired of the constant trips to the authorities without results. I was tired of doing so much housework. Above all, I was depressed and unhappy, still having no news about Dominik.

At last, on October 15, we received a letter from Margot with the exciting news that Dominik had appeared safe and sound. I soon managed to find an excuse for a trip south to help Margot in Wichmannshausen. Arriving October 26th, after a grueling two-day train ride, I took up my occupation as cook and helper as if I had never been away. We were now harvesting and canning fruit, cooking syrup, etc. Many visits up to the Boyneburg with Elisabeth and the Matuschkas were included, and, of course, with Dominik who was helping out where needed. We had ample opportunity for conversation and I caught up with what had been his experiences during the last year.

After our brief get-together in Syra, where he had met his sister and sister-in-law and their respective families in the last days of the war, Dominik had managed to travel on to Berlin undetected. Youthful carelessness and his absolute determination to contact members of his family afforded him a few days with his brother Gebhard in Berlin. Gebhard, the priest, was ministering and aiding wherever he could in this devastated city. From Berlin Dominik was posted to an antiaircraft battery in Magdeburg. He got out of the constantly bombarded Berlin just days before the Russians stormed it. When he finally made it to Magdeburg that city had been declared a fortress. The shelling became so heavy on approach to the beleaguered city, the trains could not continue and they had to walk in to report to their unit. Incidentally, some twenty-five years later, we discovered that our neighbor and close friend in Virginia had been commander of the American artillery unit shelling Magdeburg. This small fact gave us many an opportunity to raise our glasses in a friendly "prost!"

In the midst of chaos, the officer in charge asked for volunteers to pull out two antiaircraft guns from the heavily shelled freight station. The railroad crews had revolted or deserted. Neither Dominik nor any of the three other volunteers knew anything about locomotives. They found a completely drunken railway brakeman slumped on the coal-car. He could not even stand on his feet. He lost several teeth when he stumbled forward and fell. Spitting out some of these valuables, he made them understand that he did not know much about moving a locomotive. After a lot of conferring and figuring, they got the engine going. Someone managed to arrange the necessary track alignment and they maneuvered the two guns out of the station and to the indicated location. All of this under constant heavy shelling! Soon after this escapade, General von Wenck commandeered his army to march to Berlin to relieve the Russian encirclement of that city. He did not succeed, but capitulated to the Americans and saved many of his troops from the Russians.

Dominik's unit made it along the eastern shore of the Elbe River to Tangermuende. There they found that all bridges had been destroyed. Thousands of retreating soldiers and refugees were trapped and the Russian army was rapidly closing in on them. People were guided in single file across the Elbe over a narrow emergency bridge. All military units were given a timetable to report to the bridgehead to cross with their guns, expecting and hoping to join with the Americans on the other side and immediately continue to fight against the Russians. Confused optimists tried to follow orders in their accustomed fashion. Enormous stashes of discarded supplies lay about freely. Their officer wisely advised them to discard everything else and fill their knapsacks with food supplies to ward off starvation. Dominik's unit, under command of an ambitious, well-organized young officer, was singled out to stay behind defending the bridgehead for the thousands in retreat. Some of the last ones were under heavy Russian bombardment as they finally made it across the Elbe. They emerged into the arms of war-trophy collecting American soldiers, some of whom had an assortment of watches displayed from their wrist to the armpit. They were marched on to Stendahl where some 200,000 prisoners of war were encamped without facilities, on the bare ground of an airfield, for more than a week. There was little food available, and they supplemented that meagre diet with what they had gathered on the other side of the Elbe, which now kept them alive.

At last, they were assigned to barracks and, in May, they were taken over by British forces and their condition greatly improved, particularly after they were dispersed among the villages to sleep in barns around Braunschweig. They worked for the farmers on huge asparagus plantations and were able to eat that delicate vegetable to the point of disliking it forever after. When this region was ceded to the Russians, the British occupiers pulled their POWs out on trucks and any other transport available. The Americans turned many over to the Russians, together with the units of "White Russian" soldiers who had been fighting with the Germans against Stalin. Those were handed over to their certain death!

Dominik recalls that, at release from the British camp, they were waved across without search, until ahead of him a supply officer with a very full knapsack caused suspicion. The knapsack contained a large hoard of cigarettes. With the admonition *"Du schlechter Kamerad"* (You are a bad buddy), he was relieved of his amassed very valuable assets, which were now distributed, one pack at the time, to the ensuing troops. Dominik declined since he did not smoke, but he noticed how some guys managed to cross back and forth again for an extra handout.

After his release, Dominik found himself totally in the dark as to the whereabouts of his family. Communications in the general chaos were impossible. He discovered that he was not too far from the home of an uncle and managed to get himself to his farm. The old General had lost his three sons during the war. He had news about Dominik's parents, who had taken refuge in Vilshofen in Bavaria. Also, his sister Angela and her little ones had joined them.

Dominik made his way there before going on the road again to contact other family members. Obviously, his planned career as an airforce officer was over. Now he considered farming. But first he was thinking of starting a transport business with the old Silbitz tractor and wagons, which had served so well in bringing us to safety. He meant to thus help Margot and the children. Meanwhile, Dominik's father had discovered a possibility for young soldiers like Dominik to go back to school and finish the war-interrupted Abitur. Dominik balked at the thought of schoolbooks this late in the game. This brought a firm parental telegram, "Come back immediately! Father."

One of my last days visiting Boyneburg, Dominik and I took a nice walk up to the ruin on top of the mountain, during which we had a very serious talk. Again, religion was the main topic that stood between us, but, astonishingly, this left me rather unperturbed. Dominik was planning to come up and visit us in Holm Seppensen. At the same time our big event was a short visit from the Silbitz secretary Kowollik, who brought good news about Wolfi's being safe and trying to join his family soon.

My return trip to Holm Seppensen via Hamburg was as dismal as possible. By coincidence, I met one of the young boys who had been digging trenches last year near Landsberg and had survived the ordeal. We passed the time exchanging experiences. Sitting for eight hours on my suitcase in bitter cold along the railroad tracks in Hanover was only made bearable by some delicious sandwiches made with soft white bread and thrown to us out

159

of a train window by British soldiers. At last, a train came by and I was able to squeeze into it. It was actually heading northwest and I made it home.

I was just recovered from the grueling trip when we were happy to greet Dominik and Ruprecht, who arrived together from Hamburg, with Christiane. With their help we were able to replenish our wood and coal supplies much faster. Despite the budding romance between the children Christiane and Ruprecht, my feelings toward Dominik were not blossoming. Actually they rather cooled off as I came to understand that only the distance and some subtle urgings from Margot had kept my dreams growing. Dreams they were, since Dominik and I really never had much of a chance to get to know each other, I discovered, and was saddened by the fact that we had too little in common. I felt, as if I was years older while he was able to hold onto his youthful cheerfulness. When, soon after, I received news of Inez's engagement to a fine, mature gentleman, I felt quite depressed and left out.

My family and I persevered in our determination to find an escape from this life of misery. One day it was with UNRRA (United Nations Relief and Rehabilitation Administration), the next day the Swiss Consulate, the Colombian Consulate, or some American authorities—but nothing ever came of it. We had to resign ourselves to the only relatively warm space around the stove in the minuscule kitchen. In the morning, our noses seemed frozen to the bed coverlets. Thick ice in the water pitcher made washing impossible. The bitter cold, unfortunately, had no soothing effect on the fighting spirits of my siblings. The nasty train trips were almost more bearable than our family life in the crowded kitchen corner.

Christmas was approaching and we all perked up

trying to do something about holiday spirit. We concocted a kind of bakery with the syrup we had made out of the sugar beets. There was enough conifer greenery around for decorations. Presents were fabricated out of whatever we could find and manipulate with some imagination. We managed to pack and send some food supplies to our poor grandmother in Berlin. We had recently received news that she and her sister, Tante Frieda, had been evicted from Tante Frieda's home in Silesia. These poor sick old women and the entire remaining German population of Silesia, including the many evacuees (some thirteen to sixteen million people), were forced out by a decision crafted at Yalta and Potsdam. Two to three million people died during this eviction that turned Silesia over to Poland as reparation for Polish lands that had been confiscated by Stalin. Oh, how little value there is in a single human life! Tante Frieda was blind, but the two old women were forced to march on foot for two months and arrived, nearly starved and frozen, at the home of a cousin in Berlin. Tante Frieda died soon after. Only a few weeks later, Grandmother was attacked and knocked down when a punk stole her pocketbook on a Berlin street. She died from weakness and the consequences of the attack.

Shortly before, Grandmother had found out that her only surviving son, my Uncle Heini had become a victim of the Czech uprising. He had been employed by Telefunken in Prague, was captured by the Czechs, hung on a butcher hook and brutally murdered. On my grandmother's side, the family originated from the Sudetenland, a heavily German populated province, now claimed by Czechoslovakia. My sparse memory of Uncle Heini is of a gentle, refined man whom we all liked very much. His lovely wife, Tante Josa, survived him by many years, they had no children. It became increasingly obvious to us all that the Stillfrieds and their relatives would never be going home again.

We assembled a few small packets for some starving soldiers who were always to be found desolately staring at the trains in the station. After being released from their imprisonment and camps, many roamed the devastated country looking for surviving family members. It was decided that we did not need all that food for ourselves and we were able to take care of two bedraggled young men on Christmas Eve.

I had constructed a small transparency in the image of the Madonna of Stalingrad. This very simple beautiful Madonna remained one of our Christmas decorations for years until it finally fell apart. By chance, I came upon the original drawing of that Madonna some fifty years later in the burned-out Berlin's Gedaechtniss Kirche (Memorial Church). It took my breath away. We had known the family of Pastor Reuber, the originator of this tragic Madonna likeness, in Wichmannshausen, where Margot befriended them. Stalingrad was such a horrible tragedy, not only for the population of the doomed city, but also for the encircled German army, sacrificed to the whim of one crazed man. For a Christmas service, Pastor Reuber had created the drawing on the back of a military map and pinned it to the wall of the bitterly cold dugout he shared with several other doomed and desperate men. He believed and held on to hope that he knew how to impart to his fellow men. One of the few survivors brought out the drawing from Stalingrad. *"Licht, Leben, Liebe!"* (Light, life, love!) Pastor Reuber never made it home. He died in a Russian camp.

As the year drew to a close, we still had no idea of

what the future would bring. The battle with the authorities was constant and I went at it with a vengeance. Survival in the bitter cold, on an often-empty stomach, was uppermost on our minds. Rations were cut again, to three slices of bread a day. The bread was often quite unpalatable since strange ingredients like sawdust were mixed in to give it some weight. Of course, other essentials such as milk, butter, eggs and meat were not available at all. It did not help much to know that we were, by far, better off than many other people. We did have a solid, even though thin, roof over our heads. We were together and safe. There were no bombs raining down on us and there were no Russians at our heels. It could really only get better!

I decided on January 17th, 1946, to again go on a "paper-chase" with vigor, by visiting the UNRRA camp where we hoped somebody with authority might be found. The children had been placed on DP (displaced person) status, as was my mother, but we had not received the papers to verify this. I could not help wondering, who actually had displaced us?

After a difficult trip to Hamburg, I spent the night with Papi's friends. I was to try for a ride with a truck to Bielefeld. The vehicle did not show up and other bus communications were cancelled, so I got on a coal train to Braunschweig instead. After a full day of freezing and waiting in bombed-out stations, I arrived in Braunschweig in the middle of the night, tired and hungry. The only accommodation to be found was in a wartime bunker, but in order to get a cot for the night, I had to first undergo a delousing procedure. This had become a favorite endeavor in the American Zone. DDT was a cure-all, probably even against hunger. It was lavishly distributed over everybody, even without request for such "kind service." The powder did give the dirty cot a whiter

163

appearance, however. At five in the morning, I was out again, sorting out my options of getting to Duesseldorf somehow. A lucky chance put me on a direct train that left at eight A.M. for the relatively short trip. After the usual stops, detours, and waiting periods, we made it into Duesseldorf. There were neither streetcars running nor any other transportation, for that matter. The one bridge over the Rhine that still stood had to be negotiated on foot. After several hours of walking through ruins, dirty slush, and ice, weighed down by my suitcase, I finally made it by nine P.M. I cannot try to guess at my appearance and condition as I knocked at the door of my relatives' house. I hoped to find haven for a few days before going on to Kevelaer and the UNRRA camp.

The first, absolutely forgotten, pleasure that was offered this weary traveler was a delicious warm bath in a real tub. After these years of skimpy washing facilities it seemed absolute heaven! I had been ushered into the bathroom so fast that I could only guess at the effect my appearance must have had on anybody's aesthetic senses. A sumptuous meal of little sandwiches, daintily served on table linen in luxuriously clean and comfortable surroundings, enhanced my euphoric state of well being. Even more, as the discreet sounds of chamber music caressed my atrophied auditory awareness. People here still actually lived! Was it possible that we too had taken such luxuries for granted a few years ago? Above all, they were kind enough to let me join the household for a process of "re-humanizing."

I hit it off well with my cousins and joined the household making myself as useful as I could. There was a lot of scrubbing, cleaning, and painting to be done in this very pristine household that had remained unscathed by the horrible bombings. We often went to concerts, the theater, or just visited around. They kindly put up with me for several weeks. Crowning my enjoyment, I also had time to read and they had a wonderful library. I was fascinated by the family epic, *Die Barrings*. A pronouncement made by the old father Barring stuck with me, "*Man soll sich nie zu sehr freuen, vor allem wenn es sich um etwas handelt was man sich besonders wuenscht.*" (One should never rejoice too much, particularly if it is over something one dearly desires.)

The two trips I made to the UNRRA Camp in Kevelaer brought no results. No one was ever in charge of anything. The place was dismal, having been established in some buildings of the mental hospital, Bedburg Hau. At first impression, the camp appeared to be a part of the institution. General chaos was the rule. People of different nationalities milled around as aimlessly as did the inmates. This was to be the next stop on our odyssey?

A story was circulating that the Brazilian Ambassador was visiting in order to handle some paper work for his countrymen. He was standing at the railroad crossing and an inmate of the institution, who also waited for the train to pass, asked him, "And what are you doing here, Sir?"

The man accepted the Ambassador's explanation of his status and aim with a compassionate grin, patting him on the shoulder, "That is okay; this is how the delusions began with me, too!"

Not having accomplished anything, I finally had to return home. I had imposed on the Duesseldorf hospitality long enough. Two days of the most inexplicable hardships brought me back to Buchholz and an exhausted walk on ice and snow, lugging my suitcase on to Holm Seppensen. I arrived late at night. There I found a much-loved friend visiting. We youngsters had always doted on her and anything she said. Now that I was reaching adulthood, I found myself much more of a critic of her many sugary religious and moralistic barbs. I saw how my ever-so-modest and unassuming mother diplomatically avoided confrontations, as she had always done, so that the mutual deep friendship was never breached.

The next morning an urgent telegram from UNRRA called me back to Hamburg. It sent me trudging all day from one authority to the next in cold and icy rain. Nothing was accomplished! It was one more false alarm so I headed back to do some urgently needed house cleaning for Mami. I found out that I had been very spoiled by that good life in Duesseldorf.

A day later, I was off to Hamburg again, this time to the American Consulate. Passing the Opera House as I made my way through the ruins of the city, I longingly studied the program of what was of course an unattainable luxury for someone not connected with the Occupation Forces. A pleasant-looking British soldier joined me and we had a nice conversation about classical music and opera in particular. It culminated in his inviting me to the performance of *The Marriage of Figaro* for that evening; he seemed to have easy access to tickets. How naïve it was of me to still not understand that nothing in life is free. After a beautiful performance, as we walked through the ruins back to the station, he became quite obnoxious. I was scared to death over his aggressive behavior, which was not assuaged even by his embarrassed apologies. I never saw him again. My mistrust of male motives increased as I encountered such situations repeatedly during my many train trips to the authorities. These brought me in contact with many members of the Occupation Forces. Respect, love, desire, (the latter supposedly after marriage), in that order, remained my creed. I had to learn that there were two types of men. I probably never quite accepted that the underdog automatically becomes easy prey and the vanquished have few rights. But, how lucky I was to be in an Occupation Area where firm resolve was usually accepted. Our early experiences with our nice GI friends had been so different.

In early March of the spring of 1946, just as we thought the worst of winter would soon be over and we could start enjoying the lovely summer cottage, we had to pack our bags again. Obviously, we were getting nowhere with the authorities. The only solution was to move to the UNRRA camp in Bedburg Hau. There, the consuls and other agents of many countries would make occasional appearances and one could possibly bring oneself to their attention. After all, what was the Displaced Person status good for otherwise? We also would be fed by the soup kitchen there.

However, first we had to come up with permits for train tickets for the entire family, no easy feat. It cost me several trips to Hamburg. Again, we had to pack our meager belongings that somehow had grown disproportionately due to our clinging to any halfway usable junk. We had to scrub and tidy up the cottage and, after a few hours of sleep in our clothes, we got up at three in the morning to march to the Buchholz station loaded down with our valuable junk.

An unbelievable battle with a multitude of people who seemed to revert to animal behavior when trying to board an overloaded train in Bremen caused us to give up and wait for another chance. I do not remember who had the brazen idea to board an empty wagon marked for the use of "RTO" (something to do with the Occupation

Forces). We planned to use our "DP" passes and to play innocent if questioned. It worked! Several train changes, trips in cattle wagons and an overnight in a bunker had to be endured before we made it to Duesseldorf with all our skimpy belongings. Papi went straight on to Bedburg Hau to make arrangements while we wallowed in luxurious baths at our relative's house. We enjoyed the hospitality of a friendly family and even took the kids to a great county fair, something we all had never seen. It was a lot of fun.

After this day of rest and cleanup, we headed on to the camp in Bedburg Hau where we were assigned cots and blankets in a huge factory-sized hall. Papi, who was "only" a German citizen, had not been granted the Displaced Person status. He had to return to Hamburg to his meager employment where he was trying to start an import business from scratch. It was a sad separation, the situation for Papi seemed so dismal. In our abode we erected three small compartments with blankets strung on ropes to achieve a semblance of privacy. A larger section became available for us after a few days. We fashioned an almost "elegant" compartment for ourselves, using the gray blankets again. The food was monotonous and, initially, filling—but far from sufficient. We were given a mess of beans three times a day or an occasional dried pea soup and a slice of white bread. We were able to supplement our diet a little by harvesting and boiling Brennesseln (nettles) that we gathered along the wayside. Otherwise, at least at the beginning, we youngsters found the situation to be a lot of fun. There were many interesting people, so much going on, and rumors about all those that had supposedly gotten their papers and departed kept the adrenaline flowing.

In the evenings movies or a variety show were presented in the British officers' mess. Of course, this was entertainment for the "Tommies" only. We young people stood and watched at the entrance, but occasionally, we got lucky and were allowed to join in, even at dances, which was great fun. It also meant that we were able to purchase some delicious Danish pastry to take home. Underdogs learn to catch crumbs!

No sooner were we settled in, and not yet even tired of the three times daily beans, when we were told that the camp was being dissolved and we had to leave. We started packing and I headed to Duesseldorf to finish up badly needed dental work. The next day as I waited at the station to catch the official transport from the camp, only Christiane showed up. The cancellation order had been rescinded or, rather, postponed. During the next couple of weeks this cat-and-mouse game intensified. We never knew from one moment to the next if we were to stay or to leave, or where we would be going. Then the news reached us that our lovely summer cottage in Holm Seppensen that had been uninhabited during our absence had been confiscated. We had no place to return to now if we had to leave the camp.

Christiane had discovered a riding stable where the British officers kept some horses. We would sneak over there to try for permission to do some riding. We found an understanding Colonel, but we had to stay out of sight of other officers. Christiane sat her horse beautifully while I took a not-very-elegant spill that fortified my suspicion that I had no right to claim proficiency in this sport. Meanwhile, I had become the focus of attention for some of the young men in the camp, in particular, of the blond Argentinean, Herbert. I could not figure out if I should be flattered or worried about this state of affairs. Until now I had escaped the usual association with the opposite sex except children or relatives. But this certainly put some spice into my life, at least until one guy once grabbed me and planted a kiss on my untrained mouth, an experience I found to be rather disgusting. I was informed that this was meant to be a "Freundschafts Kuss" (friendship kiss) offered after one decided to forego the formality of the German "Sie" (thou) and went for the familial "Du" (you). Strange customs these seemed! But in Germany and some other European countries, they still exist today. Actually the same is true in Spanish where one differentiates between "Usted" and "Tu" in similar fashion—but without such kissing.

All of us now spent days without any meaningful occupation often just stretched out sunning ourselves on the roof. I did, finally, find something useful to do by helping in the laundry, folding, and stretching sheets, etc. We also helped with the supervision of the many children in the camp. My sister, Christiane, once rescued a little tyke who had fallen into the air raid water reservoir. Several adults stood by aimlessly as he sank to the bottom. Christiane just jumped in after the child and pulled him to safety out of the slimy green muck. Fortunately, the boy was quickly revived. Christiane got an official commendation from the British camp officials and a generous ration of sweets, as well as a pair of shoes. Her celebrity status put some glamour into her life for a while but did not alter her sweet, childish natural demeanor.

One afternoon as we were sunning ourselves on the roof, a new, good-looking young man joined us. Hans-Udo and I were soon engrossed in unusually serious conversations and found we had a lot of mutual interests. He definitely was of a different caliber than those whom I had been encountering lately. His father was a scientist and

Hans-Udo had a degree in chemistry. He was a German-Argentinean DP.

During the short weeks of his stay, we spent many hours walking in the neighboring woods and countryside. On one such hike, we came to the ruined shell of the beautiful old "Wasserschloss" (water chateau), Moiland, in an overgrown park. Despite feeling awkward as intruders, we found the entrance, went in and were shocked by the devastation. The floor was littered knee-high with shards of the most precious porcelain, pieces of antique furniture and paintings. The destruction was wanton and complete. We could not understand why the Occupation soldiers who did this (as we were later told), had not rather taken the things home with them.

We came back a few times to walk in the beautiful overgrown park and think of times when all of this was still kept like a little jewel. Every day we walked and talked for many hours and sometimes even held hands. I knew Hans-Udo loved me, but he never overstepped the boundaries. My affection for him would have grown had he not left so soon to return to Argentina. The memories of the closeness we experienced remained like a beacon and gave me much security and faith in the possibility of valuable relationships with men.

When it appeared that we would be staying in Bedburg Hau after all, I decided to start a nursery for the many little children. The news about this endeavor spread quickly. Already, on the second day, my class numbered thirty. We walked, played in the sand, told stories and sang the many nursery rhymes I still knew. Communication was no problem. Of course, although only a few children knew some Spanish or Portuguese, we were all fluent in German. It became a great success even though we lacked toys, pencils and all other equipment.

171

Christiane was my good helper. I had to interrupt this routine for one more trip to Holm-Seppensen to collect and pack up what we still had there since the new tenants wanted us out. The few food staples we had saved for future use had disappeared. All else was soon packed and taken along to add to the other junk that comprised our earthly possessions.

A visit to the American Consulate advanced my efforts to establish my American citizenship and receive a passport. I also undertook a complicated trip to visit the Stillfrieds. Wolfi had finally been evicted from his home, and Silesia, and was reunited with his family in West Germany. It was so good to see him safe and sound, even though he was quite emaciated, having gone through severe hardship.

A short visit from Dominik gave the two of us one more chance to have some serious talks. However, these only widened the gap between our opinions. Before parting, Dominik said to me, "You will have noticed that I am very fond of you, but loving and marrying you would only be permitted me after you become a Catholic."

I had to counter, "I cannot believe that God meant for religion to stand between peoples' affections."

It was painful, but nothing could be done about it without my giving up my principles and being dishonest to myself. Life was so unreal, that disappointments, uncertainties, even pain did not quite touch my innermost being.

I then proceeded on a short visit with my friend, Inez, who, by then, was very pregnant and not feeling too well. We enjoyed our time together and I was royally treated in the wonderful Schloss Canstein. Inez's husband, Gebhard, took pride in showing me some of the very ancient books and furniture the family owned. I was sent off with a knapsack full of generous supplies for my family.

It was another nightmarish trip, often in cattle cars, to resume our camp routine. Many people had been sent out of the camp by then and constant insecurity hovered over us. Hunger was our daily companion, the rations had been cut again. Fortunately, it was summer, so we did not have to suffer from cold. At last, my family was assigned to private accommodations outside of the DP facilities. They were on their own again in very primitive condition, a situation they were to remain in until we finally managed to get them out two years later.

Meanwhile, I received the application papers for my citizenship. I turned nineteen in May and was now considered an independent adult. I could now definitely choose to be an American! At first, this all seemed exciting. I had to move to another town, Muenchen Gladbach, in the American zone. I was assigned a room and a little kitchen, which, however, was locked. I was to be on my own now with a very skimpy ration. The kitchen remained locked and unusable. Water was not available so I could not wash or cook anything and the loneliness soon became unbearable. My euphoria over independence rapidly evaporated. Within a short time I was back in Bedburg Hau and took the job of secretary and helper to Mrs. Barth, an American who had been married to a German. She capably ran the hospital for the foreign refugees in the UNRRA camp. I was glad to be back with some of my friends and was assigned a bed in a room with three other girls who were employed there.

The time with Mrs. Barth was valuable and I gained some new experiences. Besides working at the office, I substituted in the nursery kitchen to prepare baby food and helped in caring for Mrs. Barth after she had to un-

173

dergo a gallbladder operation. Work in the office gave me the opportunity to teach myself some typing. It began to dawn on me how inadequate my education was. I did not even understand the most basic secretarial concepts. Of course, since I did not complete the "Arbeitsdienst" requirement I had never even received my certificate for the "Hilfsabitur." That degree would have proven that I had had some formal schooling. However, I was not troubling myself overly much about such details. I learned how to sort and file papers and accompanied Mrs. Barth on her visits to the different buildings of the institution where some sick DPs were housed as inmates. It was a very sad experience and quite frightening to walk through the large overcrowded wards of the understaffed and badly kept asylum.

I got along well with Mrs. Barth as she gave me more and more responsibilities. Eventually, I was invited to some parties in the officers' mess, even to some dances. This was rather awkward since I was poorly dressed and very insecure about lacking all the social graces. But even this condition improved as I continued in a responsible, useful position. I had found a small group of friends and spent many good hours together with them in celebrations of birthdays and other little events. I lost contact with all of them soon after, as destiny spread us out to different countries on different continents.

The fact that my family was so bad off caused me great anxiety. I helped where I could, but had no real means at my disposal. My boss, Mrs. Barth, and I came up with the idea of putting my younger siblings alternately into the hospital for a chance to feed them for a while. They were both quite undernourished. Also, Christiane was in a rapid growth stage and badly needed improved nutrition. So for the remainder of my stay, I always had one of them with me. Harald seemed to be outgrowing his affliction and had become a somewhat "spoiled brat," but he still was in need of especially good nourishment which was very difficult to provide.

Meanwhile, two transports of about sixty persons each had moved most of the South American DPs out of the camp, no one knew where. Some Americans were still in Bedburg Hau and my office work entailed filling out lots of forms for them. Our paper war was in full swing, but we got very little response from our distant friends in Colombia or the U.S.A. Yet, so much depended on some kind outreach, some encouragement, and some modest assistance. We seemed to be relegated into limbo. We did not belong here or there.

Father clung to his habitual optimism. He saw himself, not only reinstated fully into his prewar position in Colombia, but he also expected the passage for him and the family to be paid by his old firm. When I was in the U.S.A. later, it took quite a while for me to understand the background and futility of his expectations. He was a German, perhaps quite nationalistic, as those who lived in distant countries tended to be. I do not know if he ever had become a member of the Nazi Party, but I strongly doubt it. We would have known that. It took Papi many years to grasp the fact that he had become "persona non grata." The hurt of never again hearing from his former close friends and associates he carried with him to the end of his life.

During this period in 1946, when we were so desperately trying to make connection with overseas, my case appeared simple. My godfather, Erik Klaussmann, had offered to pay for my ticket to New York if and when I got my situation cleared and found passage on a ship. Of course, questions cropped up. What was to become of me

175

when I arrived in New York? America and all it stood for were totally alien to me. Both my parents, believing in their good old friends in New York and sure of their desire to assist me in all ways, pictured my future in glowing colors. I would be going to college to learn English. I would have nice clothes, meet other young girls, and have a wonderful time as they all did. There would be plenty of food, warm rooms and cheerful parties. I simply could not imagine that there were young people in the world who had grown up and lived in such an orderly childhood and fashion. What would they look like, what were their thoughts and aspirations? What was a "higher education"? Well, at this point, I chose to stop reveling in dreams. First, I had to get there. We never questioned the fact, that I actually never had received a personal invitation or kind encouragement telling me that I would be received with open arms and find a home there.

And what of the rest of my family and friends, was I to leave them to starvation? How could I get food to them and without any money? Our family had never been given to shows of open affection, but real and firm ties united us through all our constant separations. No week went by without one or more letters from Mami and Papi when he was away. Our responses were prompt and timely. Distance could not take this from us. Leave-taking and separations had become so much a part of our lives, but leaving my family behind now would be particularly painful. I was really frightened, having learned that no ties are stronger than those formed during hardships. Leaving the misery, the hunger and the cold also meant leaving the togetherness molded by tragedy. There, too, were our friends with whom we had been so intimately united through these last years as refugees.

Strangely, I was experiencing a transformation in

our relationships. It was as if my accepting the American citizenship and following my endeavor to leave for the U.S.A. signaled a turn to imminent decadence. Wolfi and Margot's sons wrote critically about the horror of lipstick and makeup. Dominik penned a letter full of reprimands about the danger of becoming such an independent female and other, to me, totally incomprehensible, insinuations. His ideas were provincial. The winds of the vast world had not yet touched him, the European opinion about America was stalled in pre-war stodginess and fear of liberating trends which had not affected them yet. While I had just about had it with Dominik, I patiently answered all these missives, but the "perma" chill remained and did not lighten my departure pain.

The summer passed rapidly and, in September 1946, I received notification to appear in Bremen on October 10th for an interview at the American Consulate. One last traumatic trip by cattle car transferred me to Bremen. There at the American Consulate, I had to solemnly swear off any other nationality (as easy as changing your clothes!) and was now really considered to be an American citizen. It seemed unbelievable that the wheel was finally set in motion. My brief stay at the local, depressingly filthy, UNRRA hotel did little to enhance my confidence in the future. But nothing had been accomplished for the rest of my family. It would be two more years of ever increasing hardships, constant upheavals and insecurity for them, involving many wrong reports and much hopelessness, before we finally managed to get them out of Germany.

After a freezing, boring visit with relatives near Luebeck, I was accepted in the expatriates' UNRRA camp in Bremen. At last, I enjoyed the luxury of heated rooms and relatively clean surroundings. This was the last "holding pen" before we would be loaded onto a ship—but who knew when? Again, I was drawn to a bombed-out opera house and was overjoyed to get a standing place for a production of Verdi's *Il Trovatore*.

The place was packed. It was cold and the building only skimpily patched against the weather. From then on I would not miss a performance. I soon found out that, with my newly acquired nationality, I had ready access to tickets when I presented my passport, which incidentally was made out for a definite name change to Elko! At first I felt guilty taking advantage of this privilege. I was very sensitive to the envious glances of other people standing in line whom I simply bypassed. But the chance of even getting standing room was almost zero so I overcame my scruples and enjoyed several opera performances.

Winter was approaching. October turned into a muggy November and the wheel of our destiny was as bogged down as ever. My passage had been paid, my passport was in my possession, but news about transport on a useful ship was as confusing as ever. The situation at the UNRRA camp was most unpleasant and I was restless, miserable and terribly bored. Then a large group of about three hundred people moved in with us. I was horrified at their appearance. They constituted a medley of former inhabitants of the Balkans and central Europe. Most were men. Their grim expressions and loud aggressive behavior really frightened me. I sometimes overheard their sneering inquiries as to what business such a blond creature had there. I often had the sensation that someone might attack me if I turned my back. Particularly so, after I heard that many were former concentration camp inmates. I did not yet know anything about the circumstances of those camps. Why were these people being taken to the U.S.A.? I never read the papers and even doubt if such were available. No one ever discussed the happenings of the Nuremberg trials. The people I associated with were as ignorant about events that were obvious to the rest of the world. Our only interest was to extricate ourselves from the morass we were caught in, to be warm, no longer hungry and, above all, secure—somewhere.

I desperately needed to escape the unpleasantness. Once more I began travelling on the overcrowded trains. Now it meant fighting with over-zealous conductors who tried to deny me the use of often-empty RTO compartments that I was now legally entitled to use. Of course, no one took me for an American and who could blame them? I visited Inez and scrounged through all available shops to find some Christmas presents to leave behind for my family. The shops were as empty as ever.

When I was back in Bremen, my parents came for a farewell visit just as we received the news that our transport ship, the 12,000 ton *Marine Flasher,* which was to leave on November 22nd had broken down. The departure was postponed. We were now reassigned to the 9,000-ton *Marine Marlin,* due to sail on November 28th. My parents had to leave. Of course, the date of our departure was again postponed as we moved into December.

The war had been over for eighteen months, yet the misery everywhere seemed worse. The air raids and killing had been exchanged for cold and starvation while families everywhere searched for loved ones. Soldiers were slowly being released from prison camps to return to their bombed-out homes. Often they found that their families had been wiped out and they received no help or consolation for their wounds. Gray desolation was ever-present as I walked along the rubble-strewn streets

179

of this once proud Hanseatic city, Bremen. The freezing drizzle of late November evenings caused the dampness to permeate the streets and follow us into unheated buildings, intensifying the unfailing chill that gripped our malnourished bodies like vises.

Drifting along the Bremen streets, I followed a handful of people, gray figures with disinterested faces walking by, oblivious to the three pathetic, bedraggled men begging at the entrance to the cathedral. The men's well-worn, tattered uniforms barely hid the violence that war had wreaked on their young bodies. One had lost a leg, the other both hands and the third appeared blind; his face was badly scarred and disfigured. Their ashen faces and crippled bodies bore witness to the futility of their wasted young lives. They attested to the hopelessness of the shattered present and grim future.

I walked into the ruined cathedral, trailing the silent people. The rain followed us penetrating the bombed-out roof and the corner of the vast building where we huddled around an Advent wreath. In the fading light all faces looked as gray as those of the men begging outside. We were all beggars, hungry, aimlessly seeking as we observed the minister preparing for the humble ceremony. We were a handful of strangers brought together by the search for something we all had lost in the past years. Looking around, I found that the three veterans had managed to drag themselves into the cathedral, perhaps also hoping for some unexpected gift to be bestowed on them. In one corner an old woman was suppressing her sobs while somewhere a baby whimpered in its mother's arms. Otherwise, we were enveloped in heavy silence until the minister had cumbersomely arranged his prayer book and found dry matches to light a candle.

He haltingly began his simple sermon, as if unaccustomed to flowery words. Long interruptions of silence were interspersed with the few words he found himself able to say. But every word he said was heavy with meaning. When one of the candles on the wreath was lit, its small flame flickered hesitatingly at first as if having to absorb the moisture of the air surrounding it. Then the halo formed around the small light, steadying it and calming the wavering of its rays. A sensation of warmth spread through the dark vastness of the ruined cathedral reaching around the people kneeling or standing around the simple green wreath. The brightness of this one candle penetrated the bleak darkness. It shone up to the dark sky above us and shimmered through the drizzling rain coming down where once the roof had been.

The minister also seemed drawn into the magic circle of the small flame. While his words first had touched us like shy caresses, they became increasingly affirmative and purposeful. A surge of hope spread around us as he told us about the meaning of this first candle on the first Sunday of Advent. It would guide us on to the lighting of the second, third, and fourth candle on every consecutive Sunday, culminating in the brilliance of a blazing Christmas tree. Even though trees and candles were riches belonging to another era, there was no doubt in our hearts that our candles would be shining! I heard the sound of music, at first subdued, and then louder, but I did not realize where it came from until I found we were all joining in the singing of an old familiar Christmas song. The faces of the people who walked out of the cathedral that night were no longer gray. When I walked by the young soldiers, they nodded, one reaching out to shake my hand as the semblance of a smile spread over his face. We all carried an internal illumination with us. That one candle had warmed us all, the light of hope had been lit and we bore that precious gift with us.

Transport of people, coffee, and plantains in the Magdalena River, Colombia.

A steep mountain trail on the way
to Pinares.

"Trocha," a jungle path in the rainforest,
Colombia.

"Feria," a livestock market on Girardot streets.

Newly constructed residence on Pinares.

New pastures.

"Posada," the inn on the way to Pinares.

"Rastrojo," newly cut jungle for fields, 1930.

Traversing an uncharted river on the way to Pinares.

"Silbitz," the Stillfried home in Silesia, Germany.

Dominik and Elko in Silbitz, 1930.

The baptism of Christiane and Elko on Foehr in 1937.

Stillfried, Matuschka, Aulock, and Krogh. Refugees not yet aware
of the finality of losing home. Germany 1945.

SEASON'S GREETINGS
FROM
ELKO — CHRISTIANE

Stewardesses with AVIANCA, 1951.

The wedding of Dominik and Elko in Charlottesville,
Virginia, 1952.

Elko in the dairy barn on Snowden Farm, Scottsville, Virginia, 1953.

Farmers on Snowden Farm, 1954.

Scottland Farm, Scottsville, Virginia, 1964.

5

America Here I Come

There would be no more candle lighting for me during that Advent season, as we finally reached our departure date on December 9th. That morning at dawn, nine hundred of us were loaded onto trucks and driven to the station for a train trip to Bremer Hafen. In the afternoon, the *Marine Marlin* departed with us from a dreary Germany into a foggy future. I was assigned to a twelve-bunk cabin. The ship was absolutely packed with misery, but the joy of being at sea once again held me and left little time for departure blues. The food was excellent and ample and the crew extremely nice. I was spoiled during the entire trip and often allowed up to the command bridge.

Except for a handful of young people in a similar situation as mine, there were only a few Americans on board. As soon as we were out of the channel, the storm took hold of the ship and we were thrown about mercilessly. I was ecstatic since I have always loved rough seas, the wilder the better. However, it soon became impossible to enter the corridors or walk to our cabins. The ship carried a load of seasickness and misery. The nine hundred passengers (many Jewish from central Europe), were real "landlubbers" and did not tolerate the motion of the boat. Neither did they accept the available food. The kosher food demanded by many was not available, which caused serious problems for the kitchen. Once everybody was seasick, food was no longer an issue, but the cleaning crews were desperate. We heard constant admonitions over the loudspeaker about the real danger of an epidemic outbreak that could send our ship into quarantine. The poor seasick people could not even be coaxed up on deck for the daily rescue and lifesaving drills. The stench was unbearable. A few of us hardy water rats finally decided to camp out on deck under some tarpaulin in spite of the rain and cold.

Soon I was approached by a nice, Spanish-speaking steward who asked me to help out and take over the care of several children whose parents were too sick to do so. Again I found myself in the familiar situation of caring for children, but glad to be of some use. When the eleven-day trip was finally over, our ship anchored for the night along the festively illuminated Long Island shores. Sleep was impossible. Excitement alternated with bouts of fear about what was looming ahead. At last, the next morning, we were permitted to dock. Now I faced near terror—what would become of me?

It was a clear, cold day, December 20, 1946. Disembarking from the *Marine Marlin* took forever and so did the formalities. As I waited my turn, I was overwhelmed with emotions of an indescribably diverse kind. The real fear that gripped me was uppermost. None of my feisty show of self-assurance remained, so my relief at being called up by a lady who was awaiting me was understandable. Now I discovered how inadequate my mastery of the English language was. I did not seem able to form a simple sentence and communication became quite difficult. The nice lady was my godfather's secretary, Ruth, who explained that the Klaussmanns were away. The taxi trip through the city that was cheerfully decorated for Christmas was an impressive experience. I was driven to the apartment of Mr. Schaefer's mother on Park Avenue.

Never had I seen such luxury! I barely dared to sit down on the elegant furniture.

Having time on my hands and a few dollars in my pocket, I walked the streets for two hours looking at the displays in the fashionable store windows. I was in a daze that is difficult to describe, alternating with fits of uncontrollable nervous trembling and spells of joy. I could hardly compose myself. All the items we had not possessed or even seen for years were beautifully presented and available. At last, I could not resist entering a delicatessen to make my first purchase and walked out with some black bread!

I was overcome with the painful realization that all this abundance was no help for my starving family across the ocean. I knew that they garnered kernels of spilled grain on a farm to grind up in an old coffee mill, trying to produce some sort of bread. Misery and starvation had reached really frightening proportions for those who had nothing to barter with on the booming black market. An obvious division in the population had rapidly manifested itself. The bombed-out and the refugees had become a troublesome underclass versus those who still had their homes and plenty of possessions for bartering. I remember Mami's total desperation when the children, during one of their usual fights in the cramped living quarters, had knocked down and broken a porcelain wash basin which had been lent to her. Mami's frantic letter to me after this disaster really frightened me. Many in the population who could have done so failed to share. This was a sad revelation that I had observed before leaving the country to which I was related by blood.

I was painfully aware of the fact that I was now totally dependent on help from people who were real strangers to me. In a fit of depression, I returned to the apartment where I was told that Bernie Schaefer (who had been the senior partner of my father's firm) had left for a visit in the country. I was to be driven there for the holiday since my godfather was in Colombia.

After a luxurious supper and a night at the senior Mrs. Schaefer's apartment, an elegant car collected me the next morning. We drove to the station to board a luxurious train, actually with comfortable clean seats. The ride was to Cambridge, through a picturesque snow-clad countryside, where very friendly total strangers took me in for this large family gathering. I was generously included in all the holiday festivities, Christmas cheer and gift giving. I tried to help by wrapping presents and decorating and hurriedly made my own gifts for everybody, little prune-men with walnut heads and cotton beards—a very successful little gift since it was unknown to people here.

Even in all this cheer, I could not feel happy myself. The picture of my family and their misery was too strong and too present. I also felt like an outsider. I did not belong here. It became easier when I was put in charge of a small child, little Betty, whom I took out for sledding in the lovely, clean snow. In the evening we went to visit other families for more celebrations. On Christmas Day, I was almost in tears finding myself overwhelmed with all kind of gifts.

A collection by the people present made it possible for me to pack my first parcels to send to my family. This was my best Christmas gift! I visualized the possibilities of continuing to send parcels in the future. I must have started a one-man crusade. My family received several packages. These sometimes contained some rather strange items like white gloves, corsets, and silk party dresses, as well as high-heeled shoes, etc. But all these discards were real treasures to the recipients, at least for bartering purposes. And then there were the CARE packages, this gift from heaven that sustained millions of people in times of such hardship. Some were sent to my family and this mission was continued throughout the year and became a formidable lifesaver. I began regularly mailing parcels with things to fit all kinds of needs as soon as I had some money.

On December 26th, after all the festivities, Mrs. Schaefer accompanied me back to New York to deliver me to a nice couple, the Swenssons. I was to stay with them until the eventual return of my godfather. The Swenssons were the housekeepers of the Klaussmann estate on Long Island. They lived in a small, plain, but meticulously clean house in Flushing. Both had come from Sweden and their English was strongly accented. They were kind and tried to be helpful, but obviously had no idea what to do with me, nor when Klaussmann would return. I acquainted myself with the New York subway system and traveled about to get a feel for the city. I also visited a few people whose address I had been given while I was in Germany and I drifted on to Wall Street for a meeting with Ruth.

New Year's Eve, to me, loomed as another depressing event. Surrounded by old people, heavily pickled in booze, and who claimed rights for New Year's kissing (I was told), posed a disgusting prospect. Somebody had told me about the big "happening" of New Year's Eve on Times Square. The close subway station offered a convenient escape with a fast trip downtown. It became a memorable event. Through the festivities around me, I stood there among thousands of people, all strangers, and was overwhelmed by a sensation of absolute loneliness. Back at the house party later on, surrounded by a bunch of drunken old Swedes with groping hands, I developed a sudden headache and made a rapid retreat and escaped to bed.

I still dared to fantasize about college, young girls in pretty dresses, and carefree partying. It was Mrs. Swensson who insinuated a few days later the need for me to find a job. It hit me like a ton of bricks. How I had been banking on dreamy illusions!

After a sleepless night, I realized that I had to grow up in a hurry. Good-bye to college dreams and such nonsense! After all, my debts already amounted to about four hundred and fifty dollars for my passage and other small items—like the black bread I had bought.

Gathering my pride, I made some careful inquiries about how one would go about finding a job in a strange big city. I was told about employment agencies that would take care of such details. Going to work was the most agonizing decision I had ever had to make and there was no one with whom I could discuss my situation. Someone gave me the address of an agency and the next morning found me sitting on a waiting room bench, absolutely convinced that this would turn into a disaster. I had nothing to offer in the way of training or knowledge and my language skills were dismal. Who would ever want me? I decided to make myself older. Twenty did sound so much better!

Luckily, the lady who interviewed me was patient and drew me out to find where she might place me. It turned out that I seemed qualified to try for "nursemaid." I cringed at the word "maid." Neither in Colombia nor in Germany would this have ever been acceptable for me in those days. However, I could not help but realize the convenience of thus having free room and board, leaving all my earnings for more important disposition. Also, there seemed several job offers available immediately in this line.

All I had to do was choose and I was immediately hired by the best salaried offer. A young couple with a two-year-old boy wanted me on the spot. Mrs. Fleischer was a stunning looker, a former model and of a sweet nature which, I found out later, masked a rather limited, dull mind. Mr. Fleischer was part owner of an elegant jewelry store and was very friendly. Their little son, Ben, seemed adorable and spoiled rotten. A second baby was on the way in May. They lived in an elegant apartment at Central Park South. This was my salvation because, taking Ben on his daily outings meant I was immediately among trees and in the fresh air. Most of the apartment windows afforded only a look at towering walls displaying more windows facing a dark shaft of a courtyard. The electric lights were on all day long. It was quite depressing.

Learning to master the English language properly became my immediate aim. The reading of newspapers had been recommended to me and these were readily available. Sometimes it meant meticulously perusing an entire paragraph without understanding a word of its meaning. Being exposed to occasional newscasts on the radio accustomed me to the sound of the language. Unfortunately, most of the time this sound system was used for the reception of some, to my ears, painfully awful music, which Mrs. Fleischer favored. No sooner was she out of the apartment then I could switch to the excellent station, WQXR, that for years to come, offered me much needed musical sound consolation. My workload was considerable. Not only was I fully in charge of the little boy and all cleaning jobs, but I also had to cook if there was to be anything on the table for all of us.

Mrs. Fleischer did not hide the fact that she was not interested in any of these jobs. She slept late and went out a great deal. I had one afternoon a week off. As soon as I proudly held my first monthly paycheck of $125.00 in my hands, I went on a shopping spree and then spent the night packing parcels to send overseas. It was such great joy to be able to do this that I decided to divide my earnings from then on into three parts. I strictly held to this principle by using one third to pay off my debt, one third for overseas parcels and one third for other necessities.

Otherwise, although I put on my best face and was trilling away a medley of tunes and songs all day long, I was desperately unhappy deep inside. The weight of it once nearly threw me head first into a toilet bowl I knelt in front of as I scrubbed it with a rag and cleanser. It suddenly struck me as the most demeaning thing I had ever had to do, cleaning other people's toilet bowls! I cried bitterly under the weight of realization that there was no immediate way out of this situation. I could not tell anyone about it either, least of all my family who were going through so many hardships themselves. Probably their only consolation was the knowledge that I was safe and, presumably, happily living a normal life and planning for my education. My mother had always suffered from the realization that none of her brood had ever had the chance for such an education. She had studied art, was very well read and acquired learning during all of her life. I did allow myself an occasional spurt of optimism that perhaps this was really only temporary and soon things would get much easier with college, a nice home, friends!

I was advancing in my use of the English language and, with hope, again wrote a letter to my school in Hermanns-Werder, Potsdam, requesting the certificate of completed Abitur or verification of my school attendance as had been promised. I explained that I had not been able to fulfill the Arbeitsdienst (work-camp) requirement due to my American nationality. I could not believe it when I again got a letter telling me of my ineligibility. And this was two years after the war! Of course—I had not allowed for the fact that Potsdam was in the East, the half of Germany handed over to the Communists. America was not a favorite word in that region. I was obviously doomed to a life without any school degree. (What was I doing during all those years sitting on school benches?) Well, as it turned out, I never really needed to prove anything to anybody.

I went out to Long Island on my first visit to the Klaussmanns after their return from South America with suppressed hopes and expectation. He seemed as nice as I remembered him from my childhood days. He appeared a very optimistic person totally sustained by Christian Scientist principles. One never was sick. I quickly guessed being miserable would have been a sickness in his eyes. His first question, "I expect you have found yourself a good job," quickly put me in my place. I was glad to be able to confirm this. Yes, everything was fine and I was having a great time, but what of my family?

"Oh, I am sure they will be okay, too. Give them my greetings. Thank you."

This came from a man who originally had come from Germany, as did his wife, a man who should have been well aware of the situation over there. After all, we had also corresponded enough for him to know a little about it. But, in time, I learned that his mind worked differently than I thought. His old mother, who was quite infirm, lived in their house. She suffered painfully from abscessed teeth and many other maladies, but no medical attention was ever given her. She died with all these pains, even though she herself was not a Christian Scientist.

Back to my "happy" job, convincing myself that everything was relative and entirely up to me, I made a decision. I just had to be positive about my situation, regardless. It is through the strength of youth that one can actually make some conditions happen. I started to rely on my optimism, which had always been quite strong. After all, there was the beauty of budding spring with the first flowers in the park. There were lots of people walking nice dogs, and the Zoo was not too far away. Along Central Park, horses pulled carriages with happy people enjoying the early spring sunshine. But above all, I had discovered that I could go to a performance at the Metropolitan Opera for just one dollar. All I had to do on my afternoon off was to be there early, stand in line (sometimes in ice, slush and snow) and then when the gate opened, to use my strong young legs to dash upstairs to the balcony. I was part of a strange crowd of real music enthusiasts standing behind a wire fence to watch the entire performance. Never have I heard more boisterous applause than that emanating from our lofty chicken coop! The acoustics were tremendous, the view not so good. Thursday evening at the Metropolitan Opera became a regular event for me.

With much surprise I looked at the two tickets for prestigious box seats, which Mr. Fleischer had just handed me. "I want you to take Mrs. Fleischer to the opera tonight, maybe you can introduce her to this experience you enjoy so much, I will look after little Ben here."

This was exciting! I dressed as well as I could. Mrs. Fleischer insisted I wear a nice coat of hers and the two of us were off to a big evening, or so I thought—.

Very soon Mrs. Fleischer displayed great restlessness and persisted in asking me this or that: "What is she crowing about?" or "Look at her strange outfit!" "Ho, she is yelling again, what does she want now?"

People all around us kept turning their heads, and angry admonitions and "Ssshhh" were hissed, but to no avail. I was mortified and did not object, when after the second intermission, she decided we would go home. The next Thursday evening, back to standing at the "chicken coop" was great!

Conversations ensued while munching on our sandwiches at intermission and I soon found some soul mates. As a matter of fact, I met a couple of young Germans. Friendships developed out of this chance meeting and, in a matter of a few weeks, we became a nice group that met regularly in someone's rooms or a restaurant in the German quarter on East 86th Street. Over time this group became a real lifeline. There were some others in a similar situation as I, having just come out of Germany. However, most had a family or were in college and also working. We planned poetry, reading, music, museum, and philosophy evenings. We always engaged in very animated discussions. These were never political. I believe we all wanted to forget and go on with life.

Later, an occasional dance party could last into the early hours, always without alcoholic beverages. It was simply clean fun for our group of about twenty people. I also met two girls of my age, Traudi and Inge, who lived with their widowed mother and young brother in a modest old house near Long Island Sound. Mutti Engels became a great help and support for me on many occasions. I valued the down-to-earth wisdom and generosity of this widow who managed to raise her three children by fitting and sewing corsets for clients in her little house. We later took hikes and camping trips together with members of our group. It appeared, as the first year passed, that I had "arrived."

However, the news from Germany had not improved at all. The constant uncertainty concerning the acquisition of visas for my family persisted. Before my departure, they had lost the tiny apartment that had been assigned to them after leaving the camp. Now they had to accept an even smaller place, two small decrepit rooms on the third floor, under a slanting attic ceiling. There was no heat or running water; the only toilet facility was an outhouse a distance from the building. Four cots in bunk style and no other furniture were cramped into one 9' by 12' room. The second room, just as small a hole, offered a sort of couch, some boxes and a tiny cooking stove. The stove actually proved to be a blessing since it produced welcome heat during the brutal winter along with ample amounts of dust and soot. My mother had a desperate time of it with my siblings and their lack of interest in their schooling as well as their bad behavior and association with a rowdy crowd of children. Betsy became ill and was diagnosed with tuberculosis. My mother was relieved when she was accepted immediately into the hospital. Several months of relatively good nourishment and a warm, clean environment put pounds on her. Meanwhile Mami, Christiane and Harald could share a little more space in their living accommodations. Harald was now suffering from deprivation. His health condition had always demanded supplemental nourishment but nothing was to be had.

At least, I was able to—more or less—sustain them and a few others with the weekly parcels. I saved bacon drippings and had several friends do the same for me. These, filled into empty coffee cans, were much appreciated. That is, if the cans did not pop open so that Mami received a greasy mixture of spices, soap-powder (which sometimes arrived also in a burst container) and mixed in the "pielrojas." This was the disguised name we used to refer to the highly valued cigarettes. Coffee and cigarettes were an important item. A limit was imposed as to how many of these valuables could be included in a parcel. They were inspected just as the mail was being censored. Simple things like shoe laces, toothbrushes, nail clippers or nailbrushes, etc. were just as much cherished as I found out through lavish thanks from Dominik, Margot (a supply of diapers for the birth of little Henry was a real saver) and other friends.

When items like cigarettes became restricted, I devised my own smuggling techniques. Cigarette packs easily fitted in sugar or flour bags. But my greatest joy was to include some goodies like chocolates. I could visualize the joy of the children unpacking the parcels. Letters conveyed to me how they all waited to be assembled before this was done and each little surprise was greeted with shouts of joy. Some balloons caused a real drama when one took off in the wind over a field and Harald spent a long time trying to retrieve it, only to see it pop when stuck by a twig. I could see it all in my mind.

A lively exchange of ragged clothing went on between Mami and Margot with their children in different stages of growth. Sometimes children were also exchanged to give their respective parents some rest.

The Stillfrieds, too, were living in the most dismal of accommodations. Wolfi had found some sort of employment. He was deeply depressed at the loss of his beloved Silbitz and also beginning to talk about immigrating to Colombia. This was not an easy feat for a family with now eight children. Meanwhile, Dominik had given up trying to find adequate employment. Minding his father's orders, he decided to go back to school to finish his Abitur, which later enabled him to earn a master's degree in agriculture.

With little expenditure, I began to work on myself. A permanent for my hair, some makeup and a new pastel blue blouse did marvels for my ego. I decided to have my picture taken, following requests from overseas. The mixed bag of responses I received was astounding. My parents were delighted, others not so. A mass attempt to rescue my endangered soul was launched from the Stillfried side. Having committed the unthinkable crime of modestly using some lipstick, I seemed banned to perdition in that moral sinkhole that was New York. Unfortunately, Dominik again piped into the same line with a new reminder of why he never kissed me, etc., since a religious conversion had to occur first to pave the way for a kiss, a hug, marriage and childbirth. Oh, how little he understood my ardent need for a little honest affection, a real clean hug and kiss and a look from his beautiful eyes that would have sent me off into this lonely, cold expedition with a warm memory. I was not out for a conquest and I seemed to be very efficient in turning off advances by the male population. My hands-off attitude did not hurt my popularity, but neither did it warm my ego.

In late spring, my employers had moved to a nice airy apartment in Westchester along the Hudson River. Little Meg was born as I celebrated my twentieth birthday. At first, an old nurse, Nana, was hired to help with mother and infant, leaving me to cope with the running of the household and care of young Ben. A few weeks later, little Meg also became my charge and a great source of joy for me. The baby thrived beautifully and seemed all mine. Mrs. Fleischer sweetly went her own way. Mr. Fleischer, all kindness, had taken over as sort of father figure for me, stressing that I should always come to him with my worries and problems, which I trustingly did. He arranged for a dentist to work on my very painful, neglected teeth. He also had a doctor check on my back pain when it became so severe that I could barely lift the children.

Nana was asked to come back for a few weeks when I was overcome by exhaustion, and a holiday on a dude ranch was booked for me. I enjoyed swimming, horseback riding and horse racing there. I won a prize on a wild race sponsored by the local police, my horse almost trampling an intrepid bystander. He let loose a juicy string of invectives, but it did not stop me from reaching the goal. There were hayrides and a cheerful evening sing-along at a bonfire that involved me in a group of mostly young professionals. We all had a good time even though I felt like an outsider from a distant planet. I had not adjusted to normal life, carefree fun and absence of deprivation. However, with the help of some unfamiliar, strong highballs and a microphone in hand, I belted out "La Paloma" in Spanish during an evening competition. It took a tremendous effort on my part to overcome my terrible insecurity and shyness. I tried hard, but never enjoyed it, never really succeeded. Eagerly, I returned to New York and the pile of mail awaiting me. The one thing I lived for was the connection with the past and my family.

Correspondence with Dominik had begun in an almost intimate fashion again and seemed to deny our platonic relationship. Here was something to cling to, an invisible shield against the inevitable male overtures which I shied away from. Correspondence with my parents was voluminous, often relating to their many needs and the responses to my packages which had become a weekly event. Sensing my loneliness, my parents wrote to me frequently, often long letters. So did the children, quite often. They all worried about my having to send so many packages, entreating me to do something for myself instead, like saving for college. But their letters immediately continued with long lists of desperately needed supplies. I was quite aware of these necessities, having just left all that misery.

Noticeable was Mami's desperation that bordered on real depression as she tried to fend by herself with the hardships and poverty without Papi's help. He only could come from Hamburg on sporadic visits when transportation was available. There he tried to earn a bit of income as a business representative in an effort to keep the family afloat. My parents could not understand and I could not explain the reasons and my disappointment pertaining to having to obtain employment instead of continuing my education. This would have caused them additional anguish and worry.

However, after several months I finally had to make Papi aware of the ugly cloud of accusations that had been raised against him at his former place of employment. There would be no big welcome for him or resumption of his work with S. K. & Co. It seemed incomprehensible to us. After all, he had closed several large lucrative coffee deals with the (now discredited) German regime. The facts of the financial benefits to S. K. & Co., the accolades and many grateful letters from his former associates as to how much the firm had benefited from his work were all forgotten. Conveniently, the close friendship the families had shared for twenty years was ignored. Papi had become the unwelcome scapegoat. Perhaps he would now understand why I did not wallow in mutual affection for his former business partners. No letter from my parents arrived without inquiring if I had spent the weekend with

Bernie or Erik or if they had introduced me to this or that person. Neither did my parents seem to understand that my employment as nursemaid allowed me only one afternoon a week off—and that was all of my free time.

Pariahs Exit

We were all engaged in a wild merry-go-round to obtain the necessary papers to enable the family to leave Germany and to be accepted back into Colombia. I was involved in endless correspondence and telegrams with Colombian authorities, shipping lines etc. Papi, in his overly optimistic way, insisted that we should book passage, long before the needed papers were completed. Mami, on the other hand, had given up hope and did not believe in the whole thing anymore. Correspondence between South America, New York and Germany often took weeks and months. Another year went by filled with wrangling. Money for the passages had to be borrowed from Erik Klaussmann, using our farm property in Colombia as collateral. The exit papers for my three siblings to leave Germany and entry visas in their Colombian passports finally were ready. Now we learned that Mami would not get her visa unless she could produce her Brazilian passport, which had been lost in Silesia. Endless wrangling with Colombian authorities to obtain a temporary entry visa for Mami took us to the beginning of 1948.

Meanwhile, Papi's case was nearly hopeless. He had been categorically classified as a German and needed to go through many procedures before regaining his status as a free man. That seemed to be a process that might take years. He had left Colombia in 1942. The authorities considered him as evicted. The fact that he had gone of his own free will and had Harald, a sick child in Germany, did not interest anyone. Neither did the fact that German business people such as he would have been evicted and repatriated anyway on U.S. demand.

In our correspondence we had long ago devised coded messages since the mail was censored. Any mention of Papi was hidden under the pseudonym "Niko," the name of our favorite dog. We were all convinced that he would have to wait many months before being officially cleared. This left us with a big question concerning the destiny of Mami and the children on their arrival in Colombia. However, at the last moment, I had to find seven hundred dollars more on very short notice. Dear Mother Engels helped me with a short-term loan, after Papi literally managed to sneak out of Germany to join his family. Mami had a difficult time when she arrived in Brussels, Belgium, with the three young children. She found out that their ship would be delayed by a week, Papi's departure was still a cloudy affair. They had no money left for food for days while in the cheap *pension* where they stayed. But suddenly "Niko" showed up. He had been apprehended while crossing the Belgian border with a guide and admonished not to dare try again! However, he proceeded to do just that without the guide a few miles further south on the border—and he succeeded.

Lucky, as he always was, Papi had another break. He steadfastly believed this was all due to the lucky tie from me that he wore on such occasions. He even got a last minute passage on the ship! The Colombian authorities had written some unintelligible explanations about his case with his passport and these were misread positively. My sense of relief at getting their letter from aboard the Swedish ship, the *Seattle,* was immense. It took them south in clean luxury. They were overjoyed about it all and loved the good food, the warmth, and simple elegance of the new ship. A last big scare had marked their sendoff. Suddenly, after all the engines were working and lines cast off, progress stopped and another eight hours of tense waiting ensued. They were sure it was on account of their papers and that they would be hauled off the ship. But, fortunately, nothing of the sort happened and at midnight they finally set sail.

All of a sudden all my longing shifted to a different continent. My roots had been torn out of Germany with my family. Then a sense of urgency, a need to go south to join them as we all wished for, had to give place to the naked reality. I still owed a now increased amount of money. Any dream of an imminent departure to Colombia was put on hold indefinitely. The kidney and thyroid problems that I had been battling were under control. But I now experienced a sort of nervous breakdown and needed to recover.

The situation with my employers had become problematic when I discovered that the fatherly affection Mr. Fleischer had shown me began to manifest signs of a change into a "hands on" affair. Resigning was not easy. I loved the children and I did not know how to explain my rather sudden departure to Mrs. Fleischer. The most difficult part was to find a new job that sudden. I just could not face another household situation. I moved out and into Mrs. Engel's house.

Following up on my travel inclinations, I tried to get a job as stewardess on a ship. That proved to be quite difficult since I was not a union member. Gladys (a girl I met in the waiting room of the Maritime Union), and I sat and waited and hoped for the call of an opening for a position on just any ship. It was dismal. We were both totally destitute and did not even have enough money for a sandwich. The Union hiring hall was a most unpleasant place with an overpopulation of rather dubious characters. After three weeks of this unproductive undertaking we heard about the possibility of getting an "in" at a Scandinavian shipping company not allied with the American union. Off we went! Soon we had some unintelligible, Norwegian paperwork in our hands that proclaimed us as hired for the stewardess job on the *MS Bowrio.* The ship, a nine thousand ton freighter could carry a maximum of fourteen passengers and was departing the next day. Our salary, once we figured out Norwegian krona versus dollars, would be measly. No chance for a fast repayment of my debts, but the ship was going south and seemed to have a planned stop at a Colombian port. I saw my big chance to jump ship and be home. Another source for making money would have to be found there later.

With little time to spare, I packed the most important necessities and went on board. Gladys and I shared an adequate cabin. Under the guidance of a rather stern Chief Steward, we were in charge of the entire department. This meant cabins, food serving and, as it turned out later, when not enough passengers came on board, even scrubbing decks and wielding the eternal shipboard paintbrushes. Fortunately, another girl was in charge of the crew mess. We only had the captain and his young wife as well as the chief mate and chief engineer to care for. All of them spoke mostly Norwegian only, but I had an affinity for this race that is part of my ancestry and felt quite comfortable in these surroundings.

We carried very few passengers. My main charge was the captain's young wife, just married, pregnant and constantly seasick. She could not keep any food down; I would be called, even in the middle of the night, for an order of "fiske-pudding" or other outlandish foods. But to no avail. She later became so sick she was flown home from somewhere in South America. This caused the captain to become even more aloof and morose until once, when I was waiting on him alone and feeling sorry for him I approached him in conversation. He took offense at this improper behavior from an underling and told me so. Whereas, I blew my top and informed him that I had been used to traveling as a guest and sitting at the captain's table with my parents before I had to take this kind of job. He was astonished at my brazenness, but we became sort of friends and I was able to talk to him occasionally. He did speak good English.

A real friendship developed between Gladys and me and the first and second Engineers Knut and Jon. It became a custom that we four would go out together when we made port. Our trip took us first to Brazil, starting with the quaint harbor of Ancra Dos Rey's. From Bahia, we made a visit by car to Santos and the ship then headed south to Montevideo and Buenos Aires. With ample time in the ports to do some sight seeing while the freight was being unloaded and new cargo put on, this part of the trip was quite enjoyable. Entering the Rio de la Plata, tremendous waves and cross currents rolled us about like nutshells. The sight of our rotund steward trying to salvage the glasses and china that went sliding from one side of the pantry to the other and back was unforgettable. It ended in millions of shards on the floor surrounding our steward. He almost lost his stiff demeanor being thus exposed to Gladys's and my mirth.

In unbelievable stupidity, I had packed the wrong clothes. Leaving New York during a heat wave and thinking of the tropics, I had forgotten to consider that Buenos Aires was entering winter. Thus I could not enjoy many outings but I did meet once with Hans Udo, my romantic

215

friend from Displaced Persons times in Bedburg Hau. It was a sentimental reunion; however, I was not ready for more involvement and rather glad the ship only had a short stay in this port. To my great chagrin, no cargo came on board for Colombia so all my grandiose plans of jumping ship went up in thin air. A few stops on our way north took us into "hurricane alley," indeed we sailed into the tail of a furious storm. We had to tie our few travelers onto their bunks. Ropes were strung to hold on to along all passages. Dresses or uniforms would have blown off our bodies. Wearing a shorts outfit, I angled myself up to the top deck and found fierce joy in standing there holding on for dear life and screaming full blast while not a shred of this sound could be heard. It was simply carried away by the angry storm and howling winds. I loved it and had plenty of time to enjoy myself since the passengers were seasick and required no food. From there we had to limp back to port in Baltimore with a shifted load of cargo that had come loose during the storm and held us at a precarious tilt. We then headed up to Canada and into the St. Lawrence River to Quebec. Now it was nasty, wintry weather before we made it back to New York.

While continued travel with the *Bowrio* would have been quite possible, I decided to quit when we were back in New York. The emotional situation on board ship had put me in a quandary. Bluntly said, I had fallen in love with first Engineer, Knut, but so had Gladys—and in a much more aggressive way, while Knut seemed to waffle. Talk of engagement and marriage (I knew he wanted to immigrate to America) could not detract from the fact that he had to make up his mind if he really loved me, as he claimed. My philosophy was to give him breathing space and clear out, back into a hateful New York situation. The meager wages I had earned in Norwegian krona did not do much at all to shrink my debts and pay for a ticket to Colombia. I clung to the unrealistic dream of marriage and deliverance from the job situation when the *Bowrio* would bring Knut back from his next trip to South America. Of course, Gladys had stayed on the ship!

Meanwhile, my parents were engaged in a difficult struggle to find a foothold in Colombia, a home, and schools for the children. They were still desperately poor. Even Papi's constant reminders about how one could not protect one's self from wealth in the long run did not consider that this long run was beginning to look more like a marathon around the globe. That visualized wealth persistently headed in the opposite direction. After depositing Mami and the children in steaming hot Neiva where the kind Striepkes took them in, Papi headed for Bogota in search of a good position. Meanwhile, the children had to relearn Spanish and were enrolled in a private school Mrs. Striepke ran from her home. There were about sixty girls already so it was a cramped, loud lifestyle.

Mami moved her brood up to our farm, Pinares, for a breath of cool air and to relieve Mrs. Striepke as soon as school was out. She enjoyed the primitive lifestyle in the mountains, at least until the rainy season began and fog, rain and mud drowned all romance for the "montaña" (mountain wilderness). They were really too isolated without neighbors and help not available at all. When the open kitchen hearth collapsed, they had to repair it themselves. The children had to find and bring home the firewood.

As soon as feasible, after Papi had landed a position managing a furniture factory that he swore would make him rich in no time, they moved to Bogota to join him. A small apartment, borrowed furniture, patched old clothing, and at last, the prized possession of a small dachshund marked the beginning. Planning began for the inclusion of Wolfi Stillfried's family of ten. They were ready to relinquish Germany's miseries when it became apparent that Silesia would be lost forever. A rocky road lay ahead for both families for a long time to come. Pinares would again include the Wolfi family as it had done so many years ago.

Meanwhile, in New York, a trip to an employment agency put me back into the only position I was qualified for, the hated job of nursemaid. This time I was placed with a wealthy diamond dealer whose apartment bordered Central Park West. A fat teenage boy and a fat twelve-year-old girl, who was still wetting her bed and sucking her thumb all day, and five-year-old, rather cute twin girls were my charges, as well as housekeeping in the rather large apartment.

What I did not know beforehand was what the modern notion of "progressive education," according to the educator Mr. Dewey, entailed, or I would have rapidly put my gears into reverse. The three girls occupied a large room and I had to have them ready for school or kindergarten at a certain time each morning. Even though close to tears myself, I rarely managed to get them out on time. One girl would have a sock on, the other her shirt, then, before you knew it, everything was off again and thrown into the corner or at me, amongst wild shrieks of mirth.

Meanwhile, the older kids were fighting over something or other and Mrs. Schrump would dash in and out adding to the commotion with her admonitions of how I was never to lose patience, but just politely urge the children on. She usually left me with that when total chaos had ensued and we could not proceed in any direction.

I did not have to cook; a tall African American lady came in daily and was in charge of this realm and also of me, it appeared. She took delight in showing "my place" to this German who had to cross her kitchen in order to reach the tiny room beyond where the two of us had our toilet in a niche. That room must have been a broom closet and now it was my bedroom. Cook used my little cubbyhole for rest and changing. Eventually she softened her arrogance toward me. Having raised her own children, she did not mince words as to what was wrong in this situation. Otherwise, I was in charge of general cleaning and care of the clothes. Occasionally, I was simply banished to my quarters when Mrs. Schrump, clad in her elegant morning negligee, would entertain a male visitor in her bedroom. She did not hesitate to tell me that he was a world-renowned pianist. Big fat Mr. Schrump was a quiet and pleasant man who treated me kindly and would invite me to their meals and ceremonies during the Jewish festivals. Otherwise, he steered clear of the pandemonium in his home.

Christmas brought more loving correspondence from my still destitute family. None of us had been able to buy presents. But I was moved to tears when I opened a parcel that had been sent via Cecil Schuler with much Christmas love from my family. They all had contributed. There was a book signed by all of them with a touching inscription. Mami and the girls had embroidered handkerchiefs, obviously homemade from old bed-sheets and some table-mats. And the most valuable gift I had ever received, a beautiful fan made of amber and white marabou (ibis) feathers, a hunting trophy which my grandfather had made for his young wife when he lived in Cameroon. It was the only memento left to my father from his parents. I cherished it, because I knew how much it meant to him. I had managed to squeeze a tiny tree into my cubbyhole and was subjected to smirks and derision by Mrs.

Schrump who could not understand my childishly getting involved in this "silly" tradition. I celebrated quietly by myself but went to church not so quietly when madam became insulting and let me know in no uncertain terms what she thought of Christianity. This attack left me quite flabbergasted and determined not to remain in the position much longer, no matter what came up.

Next Knut came "up" on his return trip, but nothing had changed, and nothing was decided. I still believed his tender words of love and I clung to the mirage of marriage, which seemed salvation from my present miseries. Papi's and Wolfi's words, some years ago, of the futility of wasting money on a girl's education, since "they would marry anyway," persistently rang in my ears. There also was no denying that in those years, the career and earning possibilities for women were dismal. All of this made my situation difficult. I was in desperate spirits when another verbal attack from Mrs. Schrump pertaining to my nationality and religion started my blood boiling. It was as ugly and unreasonable as I had experienced a few years back from Frln Hornung in Hermanns Werder and it brought the bubble to a burst. Snapping back that I would not take any more of her abuse, I quit on the spot. No apologies and entreaties from her could change my decision.

After a short stay with the Engels, Papi, in Colombia, arranged to scrape together the necessary amount for my fare and I was finally off to Bogota in the early part of 1949. I stopped on the way south for a week of rest at the Schulers' nice new place in Orlando Beach. A few weeks earlier, Mr. Schuler had telephoned me in New York and invited me to the "Casino Russe" where his brother-in-law, Jean Gian-Carlo-Menotti, had the "honor" of making my acquaintance (it had escaped my attention that it was my honor to meet the famous composer!). Meantime, Papi and Mr. Schuler had teamed up in an enterprise. Together with another partner, they started a furniture factory—the certain way to inevitable wealth, as we were assured!

6

Home—or What's Left of It—in Colombia

At my arrival in Bogota, our happy reunion took place in the cramped little apartment, but we soon set out to find roomier accommodations. The ten Stillfrieds were on their way and, although no one had any furniture, a condition we refugees were used to by then, a roof over everyone's head seemed advisable. This was found in a nice roomy house near the "Parque Nacional" (national park) and once more twelve (or eleven and one half considering my ripe old age) lively children were packed under one roof. Wolfi had to look for employment and Margot needed schooling for the children. The older ones stayed in Bogota when Margot and the younger ones eventually headed for Pinares.

Much enthusiasm and big plans that promised a profitable farming enterprise once more undertaken with minimal funds and lots of optimism, kept everybody except the two mothers, who seemed to share more realistic views, in a state of excitement. Erik Klaussmann, who had advanced the money for the passages for the Stillfrieds, went into a sort of partnership with Wolfi, buying land adjacent to Pinares. This farm was named Silesia in commemoration of the lost home.

Bad luck persisted and within a year, it all fell apart. The first guerrilla insurgency in Colombia started in brutal fashion and right in our mountainous region. A bloody battle ensued between the police and an (at that time), still obscure band of "guerrillas." Their infamous leader was one of our former peons who now called himself "Tiro Fijo" (sure shot). Wolfi had to dispose of several bodies left on the Sorbetana, a part of Pinares. Cattle were stolen and constant attacks by the guerrillas made it impossible to stay on. The guerrillas had offered the useful "gringo" safe conduct and employment as farm manager. Of course, if he had accepted, it would have put Wolfi immediately at risk with the local police or the army. The dream of becoming wealthy "hacendados" (farmers) had found a rapid conclusion for the two friends. Papi continued with his furniture factory for a year longer without noticeable progress. After that, a small coffee firm did not pan out either. Wolfi tried a few small things and ended up as sales representative for the Schering Chemical Company. Enveloped in poisonous dust and heat, he traveled Colombia's many bad roads to sell their agricultural products. His older boys found employment; nuns took in the four girls for schooling.

Papi's projected wealth persistently eluded him and funds were scarce. Finally, fourteen-year-old Christiane rebelled against school. She had been shuffled from one to another German, Spanish and then English based systems so many times that it seemed hopeless for her to continue an education. Instead, she took employment at a small chemical plant to bring in a little money.

Meanwhile, I suffered bitter disappointment over Knut's persistent silence. He just seemed to have dissolved into thin air; my parents wisely avoided comments and were greatly relieved about this quiet dissolution.

Now I was lucky; I found a job at the airport information booth. A car collected me at five in the morning to start the day standing in the cold drafty hall of Bogota's

Techo airport, handing out information to a few international and mostly local travelers who often asked the most asinine questions. The wages were meager, but I had no housing expenses and I was home. We soon moved again, to a less costly house and took in a couple of children as boarders.

As 1950 dawned, the family gratefully perceived that we had begun to adjust to a life of some normalcy. Mami started visiting her old friends to play bridge. I arranged a few parties for the younger folks. But in general a deep split had occurred. People who had gone through all the upheavals of the European war had totally lost connection with those who stayed behind. An entirely different mentality was quite apparent. Mami learned very soon not to pay attention to inquiries about how it was during the war. No sooner had she obliged and started telling the ladies about it, they always tuned in, "Oh, but you would not know how difficult we had it here. Even gasoline and sometimes sugar were scarce," etc. Increasingly, we found ourselves admitting that we would not want to have missed any of "our" hardships. We had really lived and could be grateful for not having lost any member of our immediate little family. The experience of the bond formed during mutual extreme suffering can be quite compelling. That bond extends to the localities, the country where the collective misery took place. Trees, mountains, cities, people and memories are everywhere; they will stay with us forever.

Strangely, life had now gone flat for me. I suffered the withdrawal symptoms of now being just myself; nobody really needed me anymore. Actually, I caught myself praying to God to give me someone to take care of, someone who really needed me that I could be responsible for. Was I entering spinsterhood at my ripe age of twenty-three years and unmarried, when my friends already were blessed with growing families?

With friend Juanito, Christiane, Papi, and I ventured on a somewhat risky expedition, one last time visiting Pinares before it was totally closed off to us by the guerillas. We were able to drive on a normal road to Girardot and then on to a few more villages. After that, there was no road and our guide became a conical shaped mountain on the horizon we knew to be near Palermo.

We drove through scrub, overgrown desert-like country for two or three days, frequently having to traverse rivers of enormous width. Generally, these were quite shallow and could be powder-dry most of the time, being flooded rapidly if it rained up on the mountains. Once we got caught in the middle of such sudden a torrent of water and our engine stalled. We had to push the vehicle out—which was no easy task. After a wait of a few hours, the heat had dried the engine enough for it to start up again. After that, it became Christiane's and my task to wade ahead if there was water. The driver of the car following us knew that if the water went over our knees it was too deep for the vehicle. People were seldom seen; occasionally some scrawny goats greeted us curiously.

Once early on our trip when we arrived at a wobbly bridge over a canyon with strong water currents flowing below, we discovered several bridge planks missing and crossing seemed impossible. At least, until a bunch of decrepit looking men appeared scratching their heads.

"Si senor, this is bad, the river took the planks along. But we might be able to help you out." And, lo and behold, they reappeared with the neatly juxtaposed planks that correctly fitted over the gaping open space. Juanito whispered to my father to give them each a peso. Papi was incensed and rather inclined to use his revolver to disperse the "bandidos" (bandits). Luckily, my father could be dissuaded and so, after payment of our "toll," we were able to continue.

Our night accommodations were a hit-and-miss affair. Once we even managed to find the hacienda of friends. The entire adventure was much to Christiane's and my liking. A short stay in Pinares was uneventful. We found out that the Pan American highway, a project that had been on the drawing board for decades and was being built to unite and traverse North and South America, had actually progressed some kilometers. This road, which never made it through the Panamanian swamps and guerilla-infested Colombia, was supposed to go straight through Pinares. It had been a big incentive in our plans to settle in the area. Now horses had become necessary only for the last few hours of the once very tedious trip.

1950—The Holy Year

My job with Avianca suddenly improved drastically. Rome proclaimed the year 1950 as the "Año Santo" (Holy Year), and the company had big plans. They were going to be the first airline to fly across the Atlantic from South America directly to Europe. After outfitting two sturdy DC4 airplanes, the crew was the next important item on their agenda. The Colombian chief pilot of AVA with four American captains, two navigators and two stewards completed the crew of nine. Because I spoke three languages, a credit to our mobile life style and to Mami who had persistently impressed upon us the value of mastering languages, I was promoted to "Chief Stewardess." Having had no training for it, the stewards' department for this important enterprise fell into my lap like a golden apple with perks and benefits! I was to be on all the first international flights. I immediately had to learn the basics of being a stewardess.

My first assignments were to fly often on the domestic routes on the small, safe DC3s. These sturdy little propeller planes seemed to skim and hop over the high Andes peaks almost scraping the trees. I sometimes looked down and could only hope that no air pocket would slam us into a condor's nest. The mountains were always heavily shrouded in clouds and fog during the rainy season. I marveled at the relaxed attitude of our Colombian pilots and often experienced the most amusing events. Many were caused by "campesinos" (a friendly word for "hillbilly") traveling by plane, often for the first time in their lives. When I handed the proverbial paper bag to one of my puking customers, he proceeded to put it over his head, thus hiding under it. Once a man handed the steward two large paper bags to stash in the coat compartment. When hundreds of large crabs got loose and scampered about the floor and under the seats, pandemonium broke out and caused the small plane to vibrate heavily as the passengers attempted to save their legs from nasty claw attacks.

Once another mountaineer brought a large paper bag on and every time the plane hit an air pocket (an incident that always activated the rosary prayer activity of our devoted passengers), a loud "yippee" could be heard from the back. The furious passengers would gladly have lynched the poor steward who sat in the back seat, secured by his seat belt according to the pilot's instructions. Only upon arrival at the airport and after peeling off the paper sack was a well-hidden parrot found to have been having a good time mocking the terrified passengers.

The flights with an entire football team on board were nightmarish. These crude boors seemed to think a neat and, in this case, blond stewardess was placed on the plane for their entertainment. At departure, I had to stand up front to give the customary announcement concerning the flight duration, service, and other pertinent information. After the assorted fourteen or more pairs of eyes had examined me from head to toe, expressing their lewd thoughts in the loudest and nastiest way, I would break out in my customary furious blush which added to their amusement. Pinching, voicing ugly commentaries and even causing me to stumble by putting a foot in my way while I balanced a tray was routine fun for these morons. Many male passengers used the familiar trick of calling for attention from a steward by whistling, snapping their fingers or hissing as one did while driving mules. I observed the response of one of my stewards with mirth. He went down on his knees as if searching then turned around to the rude customer and asked: "Senor, are you looking for your dog?"

Avianca embroiled me in busy activities. Suddenly I had a real position and much independence. But first I had to learn the art of living and surviving in a regular hierarchy. There was a constant wrangling for position and influence among all sorts of intrigue, from the lowly cleaning personnel to the top chief of the department. I found myself in a rather privileged position with a lot of responsibility and the stimulation to improvise.

The first step was to come up with affordable uniforms for all the female stewardesses employed with Avianca. Our airline had trouble affording the high priced Pan America uniforms. So I discovered a dressmaker, a refugee from the Balkans, in a destitute condition. She and her family were moved to tears when I offered them the chance to sew uniforms for our girls. I cannot say that these came out perfectly, but they had to suffice. Our caps were procured from Pan American. High-heeled shoes and tight girdles were obligatory in those days. Soon we tripped along the planes looking like the real thing.

Next, stewards and stewardesses assigned to the international flights were sent to Miami for a two-week course. There we were instructed in such things as ditching and emergency procedures. Mostly we spent plenty of leisure time at the beach or shopping for the many items we were asked to bring back for family, friends and others. Otherwise, nobody really knew what we were supposed to be doing in Miami. It was a short, skimpy program that we could have absolved in Colombia. Back in Bogota, we became acquainted with our nice DC4 and its equipment. What an improvement over the tight DC3 this was! I was assigned to a few flights on the established route, Miami–New York with their regular crews from Pan American Airlines, for training. I did not like my stay in New York with its bad memories, but was able to collect what I had left at the Engels' house and to see some friends.

To remain hidden in the family fold was not my destiny, I started going international again which included Germany. Dominik and I renewed our correspondence as if no time had elapsed in our communications. I was flying to Europe, so a meeting between us became feasible. We both went to work on coordinating such a possibility.

Preparations for the first transatlantic flight were now in full swing. All members of the crew had to procure a lot of visas and entry permits for countries we might touch or fly over on our journeys. My passport needed to be renewed. Here I ran into the familiar situation girls had to face often. The American consul in charge seemed to be unable to oblige me with the necessary signature and stamp—unless I would go out with him. My haughty refusal did not sway Mr. Caine. He was perhaps accustomed to easier prey. We had only a few days left and no other stewardess was trained and prepared so far for this very important flight. Avianca was having fits and started high level negotiations with the Consulate. Luckily, I had gotten all my immunizations, a process which had taken weeks. In those days, one had to take shots against insect bites or virus exposure in any country we might visit or fly over: malaria, cholera, typhus, yellow fever and pox of any sort, so I was well poked and protected sometimes suffering nasty side effects. Just three days before the big day, Caine called me in and almost threw my processed passport at me. I was glad I never had any more dealings with him.

Meanwhile, the press had advertised the event to a high level. Numerous celebrations were scheduled for the entire week. As we nervously trooped up to the plane through enormous crowds, flashing cameras and jubilation accompanied us. The church dignitaries filed up in a procession for the blessing of the plane and for a "photo-op." I was to greet His Eminence, the Cardinal, as our first passenger to Rome. At the entrance of the plane he held out his hand to me which, uninformed as I was, I merrily shook. Luckily, I was well over the Atlantic when the front page of the newspapers exploded with this incident and angry inquiries were launched into the failure of the stewardess to kiss the ring . . . and how come a Protestant had been assigned this very holy first flight to Rome? After a repeat celebration at our actual departure from the port city of Barranquilla, we took off on schedule for the big adventure.

The plane carrying numerous church dignitaries, Avianca high officials, and plenty of champagne, made a scheduled smooth run. After having refueling and provisioning stopovers in Bermuda, and Santa Maria (Azores) and a very welcome overnight stay in Lisbon (Portugal), once again, I was a guest at the Palacio Estoril Hotel. Now circumstances were very different from what they had been in 1942 and much of a lifetime had been crammed into these past eight years.

At arrival in the hotel I was somewhat cross-eyed from exhaustion and plowing through masses of paperwork for my passengers while also helping with the room assignments. An anxious bellboy came and pulled me towards the luxurious, red-carpeted, grand staircase where I found my rotund passenger from Antioquia. His poncho was swung over his shoulders and he had opened his suitcase right there on the red carpet. He had spread out an assortment of goodies, hats, straw sandals, ties and other merchandize, neatly stacked. I had to almost battle with him in order to convince him that he could not open up shop here. His argument was that the trip turned out to be so costly that he needed to make some money and had brought these things from his store to sell.

I learned that this passenger was one of a group who were frequently assembled by private persons, often village priests. If someone had convinced fourteen people of the need for instant salvation in Rome or earthly delights in Paris, the organizer received a free ticket from Avianca. My enterprising Antioqueno had gone through many rosary recitals during the flight, he had not accepted alcoholic beverages and had vigorously complained about the absence of beans and rice on the menu. This was, obviously, his first experience with the world away from Antioquia. His friend, the little priest, was not

231

much help either. Fear and novelty of the experience had let him partake avidly of the plentiful champagne. The slightest air bump would send him flying back to my steward's department. I had difficulty keeping him out of my arms where he seemed to search for safety. I could not resist questioning his faith in the Lord during such outbursts of fear. In contrast, the Cardinal was a very nice and dignified gentleman. He waved to me with a big smile when a champagne cork I had just extricated from one of our fifty-four individual mini-bottles, went flying through the cabin and landed right on his tonsure. He offered to arrange an audience with the Pope for me, which I declined. On his return trip, he presented me with a Vatican document and a nice rosary.

Finally having arranged my fifty-four passengers in the luxurious Palacio Estoril hotel rooms, I had a quick bath before the crew reassembled in the elegant dining room. I chose a table as far as possible from our attention-demanding passengers. Even though we had tried to impress the need for a punctual, early departure the next morning, only half of my charges showed up. We had to hunt them down in any shop open at that hour. Often, when we had found someone and guided that person to the airport bus, he or she suddenly disappeared, having forgotten to buy another item.

Although the food served in flight was excellent, the service facilities on our plane were of a rather primitive nature. Liquids, both hot and cold, were stored in huge thermoses and the boxes stacked in the coat compartment or overhead racks contained the food trays. During a rather bumpy flight over Spain, I was reminded of the china event on the *Bowrio*, entering the mouth of the Rio de la Plata. A heavy thermos from the overhead compartment came hurtling toward me, while a bulky food-container below did the same from the opposite side and slid into my legs. I held onto the overhead rack with one hand. A few times, I observed how the steward seemed suspended in mid air with his head up against the ceiling, trying to balance a tray without spilling the contents. It was a comical sight. Needless to say, since the overhead storage compartments were completely open they would generously disperse their contents throughout the cabin during rough weather. Many loose items went flying and had to be rearranged.

My job, after assisting with the service for all the passenger needs, consisted mainly of going through masses of paperwork since I was chief stewardess and also the purser. Forget about the simple customs declaration cards now in use. Every country seemed to have the ambition to trump the other in its demands for the most intricate visas, permits and declarations of all sorts and in different languages. The passengers rarely managed to fill out their own documents and constantly needed assistance. This was particularly difficult during the shorter flight stretch between Lisbon and Rome. I barely found time to peek out at the beautiful Alps as we flew along them and I longed to go to Germany again. By the time we reached our destination in Rome, we had accumulated about twenty-five flight hours. One could easily say that we stewards had walked our way to Europe. The only seat we had for ourselves when the passengers allowed us time to rest was a collapsible narrow jump seat in the back of the plane.

When we finally arrived in our hotel in beautiful Rome, our excitement did not allow for recuperating. The chief pilot had invited the entire crew to an elegant dinner celebration at the famous Alfredo's. As the only female of the crew, I got the traditional golden fork and spoon with which to eat my "fettuccine." We all enjoyed the thrill of a tremendous high, at having just accomplished the feat of this first ever Atlantic crossing of a passenger aircraft from South America to Europe. Four days later, after catching up on sleep and doing a lot of sight seeing, I had absolutely fallen in love with Rome. Now we were on our way back. We had only a few passengers this time, but to my great astonishment, our Antioqueno was already returning home with a sanctified expression. He was quite engrossed in deep prayer. When I announced that we would land in Paris, where all passengers were to disembark to eat their lunch at the airport restaurant, he called me in great agitation and announced that he would not disembark, but stay on the plane. I could not convince him to set foot on Parisian soil. Somebody had told him he would lose the benefit of the Pope's blessing if he went to Paris. The captain was also unsuccessful, so our Antioqueno remained on board while we enjoyed an elegant lunch and many perfume purchases in the duty-free shop.

Again, we spent a night in Estoril before our hop over the Atlantic. The refueling stops on the return trip were on Isla do Sal in the Cape Verde Islands, and Trinidad. A more southerly route was chosen to follow the wind currents. Having ample time on my hands, I sat for a long time on an empty passenger seat and watched one of my most memorable sunsets. We flew into it for an interminably long spell. I was in a philosophical mood tinged with sadness due to the ever-recurring leave-taking. Turning away from the snow-capped Alps and leaving Europe behind had overcome me with emotions. A new onset of "Heimweh" (homesickness) sent me dabbling with poetry to fill my time and ease my feelings:

Verlorene Heimat:

Abendnebel senkt sich nieder
Auf das stille weite Land
Das mit blutend offner Wunde,
In der dunklen Sterbestunde
Die lang ersehnte Ruhe fand.

Die einst so lebendige grosse Stadt
Nun so lange schon zerstoert,
Ist nur noch ein dustrer Truemmer
Der im letzten Abendschimmer
Der Vergangenheit angehoert.

Veroedet sind die Wiesen lange,
Abgeholzt die alten Waelder.
Im Gestruepp der Steinbruch ruht
Nachdem des Tages Sonnenglut
Brannte ueber leere Felder.

Weht da nicht ein Hoffnungshauch
Durch die alten Gartenlauben?
Und ein scheuer Sonnenstrahl
Der sich durch die Blaetter stahl
Mahnt er nicht zu neuem Glauben?

My translation is as follows:

Lost Homeland:

Evening haze is falling
Over the silent, distant land
With the bleeding wounds still open
In this darkest hour of death,
It has found its final rest.

The once bustling, lively city
Now long ago destroyed,
Remains a dark expanse of ruins
Which in the sunset's glow
Is belonging to the past.

The meadows are deserted
Ancient forests have been felled
In the weeds the quarry rests
After the days' blazing sun
Burned over the empty fields.

Was there not a sigh of hope?
Stirring through the garden arbor
As a shy ray of the sun
Glimmers through the leaves
Urging promise of new faith.

Occasional sadness must be a part of all euphoria.
Life was wonderful! How fortunate it is to be exposed to
good music and beautiful art and to be privileged to find
joy in it all. I was still under the spell of the perfection of
Michelangelo's "Pieta," his "Moses" at the little church of
San Pietro in Vincoli, and the rich colors in the old mas-
ters' paintings. Then on to the overwhelming beauty of
such a sunset, after skirting the panorama of the Alps.
Above all, never to be short of Nature's rich offerings as

one always finds in any flower, in the smallest plant underfoot, to the giant trees. It seems surprising that we so often fail to look around and see it all.

With intervals of two weeks for a much-needed rest, I did all the bi-monthly trips to Rome until we had found and trained another crew. According to the schedule, we were to spend a night each way in Lisbon and two to three nights in Rome to rest, since the same crew flew the plane back. We often experienced unexpected delays and changes. Avianca, at that time, possessed only two planes for these flights. The necessary changes to arrivals and departures of our flights, caused by repairs and other incidents, made it a real challenge for me to arrange for the needed supplies for each leg of the trip. If Bermuda was supposed to prepare on-flight dinners, when we arrived late we had to call in for a change to box breakfasts instead. Then, as soon as we had radio connection, Santa Maria had to be advised of a change and so on for the remainder of the flight. Because of this uncertainty, the service crews at the airports did not always love us. Many an "Oh, horror, here comes Avianca," was thrown at us derisively. At times, we were stranded somewhere for days awaiting replacement parts. Occasionally hotel accommodations had to be arranged for the entire planeload.

I used my time well when in Italy—often for two or three days—and I methodically began to explore the country. Trips to Naples and Capri, or to Milano or Venice, among others, became possible. Travel by train through Italy was wonderful then and there was so much to explore while sightseeing, so many monuments, ancient ruins and wonderful museums. Of course, every street corner in Italy seemed to sprout a monument, a fountain or a museum with incredibly beautiful art objects. These explorations were also economical. Any little "trattoria," often adorned with a bead curtain at its entrance, would supply a carafe of local wine and fresh bread or perhaps a dish of spaghetti for the budget-conscious. What else did one need to achieve happiness? My communication improved as I began to learn a little Italian.

With the Portuguese language I had no luck; it was similar to Spanish, yet totally different. With much amusement I heard our tall, straight-faced Colombian steward Calvo relate the experience he had one time at the elegant Palacio Estoril Hotel. He had just decided to relax his weary limbs in a tub of hot water, when he slipped and grabbed a conveniently placed rope. Minutes later a pert little chambermaid appeared and just would not understand this naked man as he frantically tried to explain that this was all a mistake, he did not need help, he wanted her to leave "rapido" (quick)! To no avail, she kept on coming closer and the bath-curtain certainly did not offer enough concealment. Finally he must have uttered some Spanish word, that somehow conveyed to her that he had not rung the bell and she was really not wanted there.

In Rome again I was invited by an Avianca representative to an opera performance of *Carmen* in the ruins of the "Terme di Caracalla." It featured live horses on stage and a real thundershower to wet my enthusiasm and cool down some intentions my escort began to demonstrate with groping hands. I also got out of carrying his "encargos," the constant pain in the neck of becoming an unofficial mail person to transport other people's remittances, which often were contraband. These packages could be precious furs, gems, or even a handgun and many other unidentified items.

Flying over the Atlantic was usually a calm passage.

Even though we could not fly too high, pressurization not yet being perfected, we had enough leeway to navigate around clouds and storms. Once, however, we got into a tremendous storm; lightning was cracking loudly all around us. Alcohol consumption rose, as did the volume of prayers by the frightened passengers. I had been told that lightning never strikes a plane in flight since we were not grounded. I passed this wisdom on to my passengers. We were all quite shaken when we landed in Portugal. Joining the gesticulating maintenance crew and assembled pilots at the tail of our plane I was told by an ashen-faced copilot, that we had a grapefruit size hole in the rudder, millimeters away from the wiring that guided the landing flap. This news was not exactly comforting!

Flights over the continent were always much more tumultuous. Added to it, the passengers, in high spirits at the prospect of their impending arrival in Rome, were up and down from their seats constantly making service very difficult. As a last resort I sometimes complained to the pilot who immediately took care of the matter. He made the plane drop a few feet and bump to the left and the right, the "fasten seat belt" signs were now promptly honored and we could proceed with our service. Even though we carried a navigator, our trips occasionally seemed a hit-and-miss affair. One night on our return trip, we landed in what I knew ought to be the airport of Trinidad. I was somewhat startled to see very few landing or other lights below. As the pilot later described the landing strip, "*Como una procession de viejas fumando colilla.*" (Like a procession of old women smoking cigarette butts!) We made it down and, immediately, the copilot came back and whispered to me to keep the passengers asleep and not to turn on the cabin lights. We were at the wrong airport and had landed in Dutch Guiana, having been blown off our route by strong winds. This small jungle airport was not equipped for such large aircraft. Not even a ladder tall enough to disembark anybody was available. We were on our last drop of fuel and had to fill our tanks to proceed to Barranquilla. It is not surprising that we looked upon the adventure of the Atlantic crossings like real pioneers.

I soon discovered that I could have free flight privileges for my vacation and immediately contacted Dominik to see if we could arrange a get-together. He was very busy with his studies after following his father's wish and going back to school to finish his interrupted Abitur, as well as his studies for a degree. Of course, his financial situation was dismal, but we both were very excited about the idea of taking a trip together on a motorcycle Dominik had acquired. It took much planning till we could finally coordinate one of Avianca's trips with Dominik's and my vacation and work schedule. At last that day arrived and when I got off the train in Lugano, there stood a beaming Dominik to meet me. Four years had gone by since our last meeting. He did not appear much changed. Understandably in my profession, I had polished up to some sort of elegance and worldly sophistication. Would he reject me right off?

But, as we arranged ourselves on the motorcycle to travel the beautiful Swiss countryside and stay at simple little inns and munching on bread and cold cuts, the true, basically simple, me felt right at home. Even after being drenched by a torrential rain and having nothing dry left in our gear, we laughed it off. My Pinares training was obvious under any adverse situation. We were having a marvelous time. It was slightly embarrassing to find little comprehension when we asked for two rooms at the inns. Of course, they would have liked to pile in more peo-

240

ple. It always caused some haggling. Explaining that we were not married did not impress the innkeepers. We tried saying we were brother and sister in the next place, but it caused the same reaction. Well, we may have appeared as a couple of strange people, but after much insistence, we managed to get our separate rooms. We certainly must have raised several eyebrows among relatives and friends, however. Boy and girl together on a trip like this was rather out of the ordinary!

We concluded our trip in the grandiose Schloss (Castle) where Dominik's parents had found refuge. They greeted us with enthusiasm and much warmth. I was deeply impressed by the devoted, loving care that Mama Stillfried gave to her stroke-paralyzed husband, under rather primitive conditions, and without any help. She never complained and always had a cheerful loving smile. She nursed her severely disabled husband for six long years. I recognized, with much respect, how a deeply religious person found the strength to go through so many hardships without complaint or rancor. This observation gave a big boost to my desire to understand the Catholic religion. I had seriously been searching for this for a long time.

Dominik's parents had been offered refuge in a small ground floor apartment so that his father's chair could be wheeled out into the garden. I was a guest of the Duke and Duchess and was absolutely awestruck when we walked upstairs through the miles of corridors to pay our respects to the hosts. The salon was crowded with younger people, many family members and friends of Dominik's, who seemed to eye me like a bird in strange feathers. So this was "the American" who was perhaps laying claim to one of the few available male specimens left after the war! The Duke, however, was extremely charming and offered to show me around the next day.

I was guided to my huge bedroom and, as we walked down a tremendous staircase amongst hundreds of hunting trophies, I asked Dominik where the toilet might be. He bashfully waved his hand in a general direction densely studded with antlers. I still did not understand and finally he had to actually pull an antler to open the door to the small cabinet. That night, climbing the stairs again, it was quite cold in the old fortress corridors. But as I opened the door to my room, the warmth of a lovely fire made the room cozy. In an alcove I found a porcelain pitcher filled with wonderful, warm water for washing up. An invisible ghost had unpacked my suitcase. My blouses were pressed, shoes polished, slippers by the bed lined up to just step into them. My nylon gown was laid out on the bed so that I needed only to dive into it and under the covers, which I did. I popped straight out again since I had landed with my nylon clad behind smack onto a hot copper warming pan. At last, luxuriously ensconced in a feather bed, I turned off the light for a night of sweet dreams.

A short while later, I had a strangely uncomfortable sensation that caused me to switch the light on again to face not a ghost, but thirty-two pairs of eyes staring out of grim visages in my direction. I counted the paintings of this all-male gallery depicting church dignitaries in different habits, from different time periods. Not one indicated a smile, and as old paintings were done, no matter where in a room one stood, they would look at you. Oh well, let them have some fun—and, with that thought, I went to sleep at last.

The next morning, the Duke, true to his word, gave us an extensive tour. He obviously appreciated my fascination with a large collection of the oldest books and Bibles I had ever seen. Many were delicately hand-scripted and decorated. After a tour through rooms full of beautiful antiques, he wanted to show us some of his estate and his big hobby, an amphibian automobile. He drove rather recklessly into a lake with us in this vehicle, but it performed well. With much sadness we received, a few years later, the notice of the Duke's accidental death, after he turned over with this vehicle. He was a real gentleman of the old school. I consider it a privilege to have known him.

Engagement

We also visited some of Dominik's many relatives, who had migrated to this southern part of Germany. Of course, I realized that I was being scrutinized, as a future family member. Dominik's brother, Franz, lived close by with his family. After being forced to leave and losing his estate, Buchwald, in Silesia, he had taken on the position of farm manager of the Duke's estate. Sister Pia, with her four children, also had found a small house to live in in the vicinity. A group of the surviving families of the murdered members of the Resistance had formed. They attended yearly meetings in Berlin for memorial services which have been held since then at Ploetzensee-Berlin, where so many were killed by the Hitler regime. Pia's daughter met there the son of H. Haeflen, another victim. The two young people who had both lost their fathers in such tragic ways, later married. Several such unions grew out of these close relationships of the families of the victims of the Resistance. We also visited Dominik's brother, Ruediger; with his wife and two daughters, he

243

was also working on a farm. Brother Gebhard, the Jesuit, was in Berlin. He started "The Open Door" to alleviate suffering wherever he encountered it, often among people who managed to get across the border to escape from the Communist occupation. Dominik's sister, Angela, had immigrated to the United States with her two children. Angela was so traumatized by the events in Czechoslovakia, she feared Communists might catch up and harm her in Europe. A young Professor, whom she knew from pre-war times in Italy, helped Angela to get to America.

It was on our last evening together, when we were enjoying a walk through the moonlit park, that Dominik "popped the question" and we decided to become engaged—although, for the time being and by mutual consent, not yet "officially." Dominik still had to complete his agriculture degree at the University in Freising. This meant two more years of waiting and separation. He planned to emigrate to Colombia or the U.S.A. after that. Germany held no future for refugees struggling with poverty. He now had one sister living in the U.S.A. and one brother in Colombia, South America. It appeared that we might still have years to wait to get married and did not want to place difficult restrictions on each other. Could all this be carried out with an ocean and a different lifestyle separating us?

Religion had been taken out of the immediate focus. We had advanced to plenty kissing! It was understood that I would eventually embrace Catholicism, but on my own time and initiative. Subconsciously, I had always felt that this was my path, but now it seemed so sudden. I had been going out with other men, but I was not committed. To me Dominik was a secure harbor after all the storms. We had much in common in our previous lifestyle, and importantly, our long friendship and the secure knowledge of an honest, sincere commitment. Yes, love too had been rekindled. I departed the next morning very happy indeed.

Heading for Paris to join the Avianca crew for my free return trip, I learned that the plane had a three-day layover. I spent the time sightseeing and Avianca gave us one extra day since their flight was delayed twenty-four hours longer. How nice it would have been to spend this extra time with Dominik, getting used to the idea that we were now engaged. It all had happened so suddenly! My excitement over Paris was somewhat dampened when for the first time, I had difficulty communicating with people. I must admit I felt rather slighted that not even the feminine charms of a supposedly attractive young lady sufficed to elicit help or information as I was used to having in other places I had been. But a night at the beautiful Opera, where I luckily got a last minute ticket for *Faust,* soothed my resentment against the impolite French. Father's good Swiss friend, Dal Trumpy, invited me to an escargot dinner, a first time experience that did not agree well with my stomach. Otherwise, I took several short sightseeing trips, even one in the evening to experience the famous nightlife safely with a group of tourists.

When I arrived back in Bogota, I had to find out where my family had moved and I was rather pleased with the very elegant, large place where they were "house sitting" for the owners for two months. Of course, without much information from me, my family guessed that Dominik and I had taken "the big step." As my sister Christiane put it, if two traveled alone on a motorcycle, this was bound to happen. The buildup of events for so many years, of course, had to be also taken into consideration. Oh well, it was a joy to talk about it anyway. Life went on in its usual routine. Soon, except for the more lively correspondence between us, I sometimes found it difficult to feel engaged. Dominik and I were planning a repeat of our trip for the coming summer. It was obvious that we had to get together a bit more often.

As we began the year 1951 an increase in my workload became apparent. Avianca was branching out on other routes. More personnel had to be trained and two Constellations were added to our fleet. Retraining became necessary for our work in these machines, which I never liked. Their sleek looks belied their uncomfortable lack of space and the vibration during flight was unpleasant. Meanwhile, my family had moved once more. My sister, Christiane, had also joined Avianca and, with Barbara Adamovich who boarded with us, also was becoming a stewardess. We made a merry trio for the short time that we all lived at home. Conditions were extremely crowded if we happened to all be flightless at the same time and Heide-Betsy had to be moved to another bed. Of course, the three senoritas in their dashing uniforms became a focus of attraction.

One morning the three of us were getting ready for a day of flying, for which we would be collected by an Avianca vehicle at 5 AM. While it was still dark outside, we heard a cacophony of musical instruments and singing outside our window. All other house members were awakened in various degrees of consternation. I had a difficult time keeping my brother, Harald, from pouring a bucket of water over the romantic serenaders' heads. When the van arrived to collect us, the three of us had to file out passing our Don Juan and his musicians while constraining giggles. We never were able to find out which one of us was supposed to be the recipient of all this attention. My suspicion fell on Christiane, however.

Our stewards' department had become quite international. The pilots were mostly Americans but the stewards were multi-lingual, several from the Baltic States, who all spoke German. I enjoyed the rapid change of languages. Most of our passengers were addressed in Spanish. Our on-board announcements were now made through loudspeakers in Spanish and English.

Flights to Europe were still the choice engagements. Only two trips a month were possible on account of the many hours flown on each. This gave us plenty of time between assignments. Of course we returned extremely exhausted and required sometimes a twenty-four-hour sleep period to overcome the strenuous work and the two six-hour time differences in short succession. One woke up back to life totally groggy.

Dominik was able to find some time off and the poor dear spent his last penny on a trip to Rome to meet me. We went sightseeing and wandered through Rome. Heavenly weather, Villa D'Este with its many fountains, a little trattoria (restaurant) for a meal of bread, wine and spaghetti, Rome at its best, but somehow we felt that this was not a successful reunion as we separated to go back each to his own routine. Obviously, these occasional brief get-togethers with so little time for reacquainting were usually disappointing. We lived and worked under such different circumstances. The drudgery of a student's life was no match for the world traveler. I could not picture Dominik in the U.S.A. or Colombia. His was an entirely different lifestyle, so closely part of his upbringing and family tradition. But had his brother not adapted well in Colombia? After all, I would be there too wherever we would settle down. Surely we would manage . . .

With some pilot pressure, as rumors had it, Avianca switched to overnight stays in Paris on the return flight. I enjoyed seeing more of this city and its surroundings.

However, we never saw much of our male crewmembers while there. They had a way of disappearing in Paris. Many a time I had to be ready with a good supply of Alka Seltzer and strong coffee when they reappeared for the return trip the next day: "Señorita, please don't tell my wife!" It made me rather uneasy as I wondered about their ability to master the difficult return flight. I was relieved to notice that the chief pilot always seemed unaffected. Also a narrow cot had been fitted in for the pilots so that one of the double crew could rest up in between. No such luck in the stewards' department, we were one team only for the entire roundtrip.

The crew discovered the fun of "smuggling." Whether it was champagne, perfume or other goodies, just to be able to hide things from the authorities became a challenge. Once, our chief pilot was planning for a celebration and had bought a couple of cases of fancy "bubbly." The unfriendly little customs official in Barranquilla was trying to give him a hard time, obviously lusting for the good stuff himself. So "Mi Capitan" just told him, "You do not let me take this through, well then, keep it." With that he slammed both cases to the ground and we watched the golden liquid mingle with the dust on the floor. But, just as often, goods were confiscated and kept by the customs officials.

A few times, we had to escort unaccompanied children from Europe. A three-year-old girl, who was delivered to us in Rome, clung to me so desperately it was pitiful. I had her with me during the overnight stay in the hotel. She insisted on calling me Mama. I felt sad having to turn her over to her adoptive parents in Bogota. We also had to deal with sick passengers. One old lady, an apparent Russian émigré had an attack of sorts and indicated to me how I was supposed to give her a shot with a huge syringe and a very dull, thick needle. I simply could not penetrate her leathery skin. I went through the plane from seat to seat and finally located a passenger from the medical profession to help me before the poor lady totally collapsed. She had to be taken out on a stretcher on arrival in Bogota. I wondered how long she could live at that altitude of 8,500 feet. We had occasional incidents with alcohol abuse and I was glad for the male attendants in such situations. Generally, I was well respected by the passengers and crew and grateful for it, since I was aware of other flight attendants' different experiences.

When my vacation time was approaching, I again requested a free flight to Europe. I was able to take it in August. Dominik had just finished his exams and was getting ready to immigrate to the United States, but we still wanted to enjoy a trip together and visit relatives. He borrowed a small motorcycle for this event, since he had sold the old faithful one we had used before. This "little horse" let us down constantly with all sorts of mechanical failures. We enjoyed the trip in spite of it, often having to fill in with train rides in between. On the very last evening, zooming cross-country over rough fields, my "cowboy" rode right into an electric fence. The impact sent us flying, but nothing serious happened, so we could laugh it off.

We had a nice visit with Dominik's parents. We also visited Dominik's sister and brothers and their families. I hoped I was acceptable to them all as a new family member, but some correspondence ensued and, of course, the religious question constantly loomed prominently. Dominik shielded me from much of this. Again, having had a little more time together, our relationship benefited greatly from this trip. I was very touched when Mama gave me a present of small pearl ear-studs. Unfortunately, these were crafted for pierced earlobes and I realized I would not be able to wear them. Back in Colombia, I had them mounted together with an emerald, our Colombian gem, on a little pin.

My vacation culminated in one more adventure. After leaving Dominik, I had decided to visit relatives in northern Germany. Maybe I was craving some excitement. On a sunny day I accompanied my Uncle Bernhard to do some errands in Luebeck. On the way back we had to stop at the forest warden's house. While Bernhard dealt with the calculations on his planned tree cutting, I discovered a litter of the most adorable longhaired dachshund puppies I had ever seen. Golden balls of wool rolled about the room, needle sharp teeth nibbled at my fingers as a soft pink tongue busily worked on my face. I was absolutely hooked! When it turned out that the puppies were ready to be sold, a deal was closed and "Inch vom Grandelberg" had become mine before Bernhard had tallied up his tree investment. I had settled for the name, Inch, since by fancy pedigree, I was stuck with the letter "I". The men emerged from their office and I was ready to go, dog in arm.

When I told Bernhard that I planned to take the dog along with me, his mouth stood open. His expression of disbelief should have been filmed! I was leaving the next day for home from Germany via Holland and Belgium to Paris, where I was to catch my flight back to South America. This must have appeared one more proof that his cousins, who had left Germany some thirty years ago to live in uncivilized parts of the world, must be rather strange in their heads. But he willingly drove me to the veterinarian to get all the shots and certificates for my puppy. As is often the case, I began to consider the implications after the deed. I knew what I was doing was wrong. It was illegal to take a dog through all those border crossings without going through a tangle of time-consuming red tape. It was not permitted to take a dog on the plane and it was absolutely impossible to bring a dog into Colombia. There were quarantine laws, but no place to keep an animal in quarantine. Even if there had been one, I would certainly not hand over my precious animal for certain mistreatment and possible death. Worst of all—and I had not told Bernhard this—my wallet was empty. My last D-marks had been scratched up to pay the veterinarian. Fortunately, I had already purchased my train ticket to Paris, but there was no money left to pay for a dog fare in the freight compartment.

The next morning, I was dropped off at the train station by a gaggle of relieved relatives. They had supplied me with an ample picnic lunch to take along and were touched by my insistence not to accompany me to the train platform because I might get sentimental, farewells depressed me, etc. (Isn't she a sweet girl in spite of all!)

I had happily escaped the revelation of a telltale spot on the carpet and some teeth marks on the chair legs left behind by Inch who had scrambled out of his box during the night. And now, with the relatives gone, my odyssey began. In the lavatory, I stuffed my puppy into a flight bag and passed under inquisitive eyes onto the train. The compartments on European trains are made for eight persons each. However, I got the impression that people in Germany still enjoyed the huddle and standing for hours while being shaken back and forth, eating and even sleeping in such a position. I had experienced this during the war and right after. But this was 1951 and the train was still overcrowded. After an hour, a woman got up to leave the train and I managed to grab her seat. I had studied the people's faces and tried to analyze them for

251

"dog-approval." Inch's nose had poked out repeatedly; he was becoming quite restless. Brazenly, I spread a newspaper that somebody had left under my seat and hoped that this cramped space would do for whatever—and it did. With the newspaper neatly rolled up again, I had to now restrain the little beast on my lap. Never under-estimate the charm of a dachshund puppy! Within minutes, everybody in the compartment was cooing and fussing over him and my worries seemed needless. Magically a grapevine was established which carried the message of the conductor's approach into our compartment, always with time to spare, so I could stuff Inch into his flight bag.

Toward evening as we reached the Dutch border, most of the people in my compartment had gotten off, and the process of a border crossing with an illegal "passenger" began to occupy me. Anybody who has had dealings with customs officials and the usual bureaucrats who check passports and look into your face to verify that you are who you say you are, can appreciate the apprehension I felt every time I saw a uniform.

After passing the first checkpoint with the help of the few people still in the compartment, I became quite expert at the other crossings that I had to face by myself. Fortunately, it was night. Even the hardest official found it sort of touching to confront such a sleepy young girl who had piled a lot of (sometimes shifting!) clothing and coats on the seat while she looked for her passport. Early dawn saw us through the last border crossing into France. Inch and I were all alone in the compartment. With a sigh of relief, I put Inch onto the much-used paper and wondered about the gallon capacity of his pintsized body.

Our next step needed to be plotted. Political implications had to be considered. French people did not like Germans and they often disliked Americans even more. How would they take to a German dog? I could not expect my good luck to last forever. I had had the compartment all to myself as we rolled toward Paris. Just then a "uniform" loomed at the door, barely giving me time to interrupt Inch's activities on the paper and stuff him away. To my great consternation, he sat down across from me and looked me over rather inquisitively. He obviously intended to stay and make the best of a rather boring trip with few passengers on board and, O la-la, a nice looking young Mademoiselle at hand!

"Parlez-vous français?" (Do you speak French?)

I put on my most stupid face and stared at him blankly while a squeaky sound emitted from the region just behind me. Coughing and sputtering did not quite match the squeak, but did distract.

"Sprechen Sie Deutsch, mein Fraulein?" (Do you speak German, my lady?)

The "uniform" was bilingual; good that I had not talked to him before. Something reminiscent of a growl came from the lower regions of my back. I hoped that he would realize that I had not had breakfast and some people's stomachs can become quite musical under the circumstances. At that time, some needle sharp teeth dug into my restraining hand and emitted a louder growl. I heard the man ask perfectly clearly, "Do you speak English?"

My luck was running out. I hoped he would not resort to some international silent language so often used to communicate between the sexes.

Brazenly I plunged into an experiment. *"Yo unicamente hablo Espanol y no lo comprendo."* (I only speak Spanish and I do not understand you.) After all, there had to be a limit to the languages spoken by a simple train conductor!

It was with great relief after seeing his blank expression that I entered into a torrential discourse. With that I could tune out the ever-increasing noises that emitted from behind my back. This barrage interspersed with grunts and coughs soon became too much for the budding Don Juan. Twirling his French mustache, he pushed his official cap tight over his ears and marched out, leaving the insanely babbling female behind. I cleaned up the mess on the floor as well as I could, and was not too concerned when two more passengers joined us. They ignored us completely.

At last in Paris, I happily carried Inch out of the railroad station and brazenly walked him on my arm into the Hotel D'Iena, where I was to join the Avianca crew in prepaid crew accommodations.

"Miss, you cannot take a dog into this hotel!" was the last thing I needed to hear at this stage, but the lady at the desk was absolutely adamant. She also informed me that the Avianca flight, due to depart that same evening had been cancelled because of mechanical troubles, it had been rescheduled for two days later. My pleading that I had no money to go anywhere else fell on deaf ears.

For the first time rather subdued, I walked out of the foyer and down the street in a worried state. I was tired and hungry, and surely Inch was, too. Avianca offered meals to its crew only in the Hotel D'Iena.

After walking around the block a few times trying to assess my situation, I noticed that a different receptionist was now on duty. With a well-trained grip, Inch was stuffed into the flight bag and a self-assured Avianca stewardess marched into the hotel to be assigned to her room. Confined upstairs for two full days on room service only was not my idea of enjoying Paris! But my fellow crew members came through, as usual, like one big family and I had plenty of visitors and helpers.

It worried me when I heard that this was to be a VIP promotion flight for the German *Stern* magazine. The crew was on the alert to make special efforts and provide special service for advertisement reasons. Although I was still off duty and technically on vacation, I found a notice asking me to take over this trip in absolutely VIP style. I decided not to tell our captain, who happened to be Avianca's chief pilot, about the little passenger he would be carrying as a stowaway. However, I soon struck up a friendship with the *Stern* reporters who were also waiting in the hotel. Their help was assured and they became co-conspirators to help move Inch through the ticklish customs search at Orly airport. We had devised a web of diversions to spirit Inch through the departure proceedings. Somehow, the significant Avianca flight bag switched many hands in fast succession. There were many more similar Avianca flight bags around, so while one of the reporters was embroiled in French arguments, I hastily boarded the plane with Inch safely tucked away in his bag. He was becoming quite a good traveler. Needless to say, he kept everybody aboard well entertained during the long flight to Barranquilla. The plane was nearly empty since it only carried the "official" *Stern* party and a few extras. It did not worry me too much that a story and pictures might grace the pages of the magazine and some official reprimand could follow. After all, it was not my nature to worry prematurely or to think before I acted. But, as it turned out, Inch did remain incognito, thanks to the nice *Stern* team.

However, a big hurdle remained to be taken at our arrival back in Colombia. In Barranquilla we had to go through customs before proceeding to Bogota. I smiled a lot with the guys of the maintenance crew and asked them to watch over Inch while I went through customs clearance. I was not at all sure what I would do later, when the officials would be inspecting the plane. The Colombian custom officials were always a humorless, unfriendly bunch, very eager to prove their "machismo" (manly pride) and totally untouched by a stewardess's beguiling smile.

I stood in a long line since another international flight had arrived at the same time, and glanced through my vaccination certificates, a whole booklet of them, adorned with official stamps, to be presented to the authorities. No one dared travel without these documents in those days, as the dread of being quarantined in a filthy tropical hospital was ever present.

I stared at my papers and gasped in disbelief when I saw that my vaccination certificates had lapsed three weeks before, during my travels in Germany. Obviously, I was in serious trouble as I moved closer to the dark, unfriendly face of the official who was grumpily scrutinizing everybody's documents.

"Next one."

Only two people were ahead of me. I had broken into a sweat, not only on account of the horrid heat and humidity. My fear must have been quite obvious. Here I stood, with lapsed documents and an illegal dog in the plane.

"Next, senorita. I said, next!"

As if in a trance I handed him—not my papers, but those of my dog. The man scrutinized them intensely; it seemed forever, then I suddenly noticed that he held the document upside down. His rubber stamp came down with a thud, right over the beautiful clean seal and signature of the veterinarian. I realized that the man, illiterate as many, had somehow deciphered the "Dr." but not known what the "Veterinar" stood for. The rest of the German certificate was unintelligible for him anyway. With this one stroke of good luck, my dog and I had both been "stamped in." I felt quite jubilant and, when the plane was inspected, I could wave a legally stamped paper in front of the questioning faces. My dog-smuggling adventure almost called for a repeat-performance!

The interview for the German magazine, *Der Stern,* was a big event for our airline. Avianca was exploring the feasibility of flying to Frankfurt. A feature article in an issue of *Der Stern* was dedicated to the report on Avianca and its beginnings. This history was rooted in the pioneer work of the defunct post World War I "Scadta" airline. The friendship that Inch and I had struck with the *Stern* reporters brought me the assignment to escort them and fly on the promotional flights. My sister, Christiane, was also included in the team. A picture of the two of us in front of the "El Colombiano" plane was chosen for the magazine. It was a real fun time and we enjoyed ourselves, especially on a flight abroad with an overnight in Paris as guests of *Der Stern.* Mr. Henry Nannen, the *Stern's* chief publisher, editor and owner, invited us out to eat "mules." (At least, that was what his chief reporter, Henry Grossmann, called the mussels.) However, our joint French language expertise did not suffice to locate the "moules." We all finally settled for an evening in a cabaret instead.

7

America for Good

Meanwhile, Avianca had decided to station a crew for the New York–Miami–Bogota flights in New York. I was to be one of them, since my job of training the stewards for the Europe flights had long been accomplished. Our Europe teams were well established now. With much horror we learned a few month later, that one of the planes had slammed into the mountain at its takeoff from the Azores. All persons on board were killed; the crew members had been our friends, the stewards, with whom I had flown so many times on that route, I had trained.

While I did not cherish the thought of transferring to New York, it was a very practical move now that Dominik would be coming to the States and we were planning to get married in the near future. The wages in U.S. dollars was a real incentive, and a very important factor to consider. As to my family, Bogota had lost much of its interest for me. Papi had taken on a promising position as manager of a milling concern located in far-away Pamplona, near the Venezuelan border. My parents moved and Inch went with them. I was supposed to get him back once I was married and established. Our family was split up for good now and we had to go our own ways. Harald and Betsy were to visit a school from home in Pamplona. Harald had overcome his sensitivity to the tropics and no one would have guessed at what he had gone through.

Christiane and I found a room to rent for a short while until we both were transferred to New York. Together with Vicky Serrano, a third stewardess, we found a nice furnished apartment in Queens and set up housekeeping. Having grown quite close to my sister, Christiane, we had a very happy time together. Vicky also fit in well. All three of us were rarely at home at the same time. Soon the need for an automobile became obvious. I did not join in with this acquisition since every cent of mine had to be saved now, but I did get my chance at taking driving lessons in the girls' Chevrolet.

The flights via Miami to Colombia and back were rather boring, the full planes meant an increased workload for us. They had taken on a more routine and business-like character, which made the flights rather monotonous. Mostly so, that is! We had our excitements, particularly when a breakdown occurred in Miami and we were stranded. Even though Avianca's safety record was a good one, many of our passengers chose to see this differently. No wonder then, when we were faced with a fuming crowd after the passengers had been loaded and after a routine taxiing down the runway, our plane returned to the airport for the third time in a row on account of engine trouble. We now had a regular strike on our hands and nothing mollified the angry passengers who demanded to have a Pan American plane made available to them. In the name of public relations, this wish was granted. We waved them off with a sigh of relief after another barrage of verbal abuse and thumbs down for everything connected with Avianca. The Pan American plane taxied down the runway, and turned around to again disembark our passengers. The reason, engine trouble! Was it vicious when we gave the passengers a thumbs down for PAA?

Finally, before night set in, another PAA Turbo prop was able to fly them off while we returned with all the baggage on our now-repaired Constellation. It was an eerie flight in the totally empty plane where we crew members could lounge and sleep to our hearts' content. To give us one more jolt of excitement, the Colombian pilot, perhaps not used to night flight, almost lost us to the jungle on arrival in Barranquilla. He banked the plane so steeply that all the hand luggage came tumbling down on us. As I stared in disbelief, I saw the night-black forest below approaching us at frightening speed before he caught the big bird in the nick of time for a safe landing. Needless to say, we were quite shaken up and the copilot was fuming mad.

Dominik arrived in New York in the winter of 1951 while I was away on a flight to South America. My good friend, the photography student Traudi Engels, met him at the ship and brought him to the bus station. Dominik took a bus to Charlottesville, Virginia to be with his sister, Angela. Angela had immigrated to the United States and had married a friend from her University days. Giovanni Previtali was a professor at the University of Virginia in Charlottesville. They had sponsored Dominik for his visa to the United States. Dominik proceeded to find a job on a horse farm in Maryland. Under rather primitive conditions and with little opportunity to improve his English language skills, he started his new life "counting" horse apples, as we teased him. Dominik did visit us in New York once, but was not too impressed by the big city. He actually nearly set our apartment on fire by using a wastebasket as an ashtray! Several months later, he accepted a job in Virginia on Blandy Experimental Farm. I was able to visit him there. Dr. White, who had started an arboretum for the University of Virginia, offered to help Dominik get into the field of biology, perhaps with a scholarship. But that would have meant working for a new degree and years more of studies.

However, exotic trees, flowers, and weeding were not Dominik's calling. The need to establish a possibility for us to get married remained his uppermost concern and regular agriculture was his career interest. Our friendship with Dr. White and other professors and graduate students whom we met at Blandy Farm was genuine and continued from then on.

Meanwhile, I was flying regularly to Bogota. My family had no home there anymore, and we were stationed in the old Hotel Granada, an establishment downtown, next to a very old church steeped in Spanish tradition. I liked to enter this church any time of the day, just for a short visit. The deep silence even during Mass, the atmosphere of religious fervor, especially as witnessed in the devout faces of the somberly clad, older women who shuffled in on their "alpargatas" (straw sandals) and wrapped in their black scarves deeply touched me. They often looked destitute; they knew hardship and suffering; their lives were mired in poverty. But, here in the church, they appeared so serene. I always walked out into the sunshine with a feeling of peace, and was trying to understand the source of these emotions. My serious search for religious stability was quite touched by such experiences. Unfortunately, the result of religious training I had undertaken in New York pushed in a different direction and rather served to stimulate my old antagonism. Especially when the priest in charge refused to answer certain questions and put me down with the admonition, "You just have to believe it," without an explanation.

Otherwise, what little time we had in Bogota or Barranquilla was used to visit with friends. The at-home feeling in Bogota was lost since my family had moved away.

I was able to get a few days off for New Year's Eve and traveled from New York to Charlottesville to be with Dominik, who was visiting Angela. The blues caught up with me here, too. Somehow I felt like I was being uprooted again, but, of course, I was concerned not to let Dominik notice this. How was he supposed to understand these conflicts and torments in my personality? The talk now was that we should get married in 1952, regardless of our financial circumstances. I also realized it had to be soon or not at all. I was moving toward the marriage date in September as if in a trance. It appeared to me to be a jump off into a totally insecure future, the fulfillment of a preordained fate.

Dominik finally took a job as a farm laborer on a place called Snowden Farm, twenty miles south of Charlottesville, near Scottsville. The small dairy farm was actually located across the James River in a horseshoe bend created by its waters. The wages of one hundred dollars a month were dismal, but we were not too concerned about this. We knew how to economize, had learned to do without, and we could both work.

A Swiss carpenter in Bogota had crafted four beautiful pieces of furniture for me, which Avianca flew to the States. One cabinet was to house my treasured record collection and stereo set. The lamp gave a room distinct character; a chest became, and still is, our Christmas chest and a small stool is now beloved by four grandchildren.

So we now had our elegant basics. I had started to accumulate a few real necessities in New York, including a small sewing machine. Christiane and I decided to drive to Scottsville for a visit, with a load of my things, in the summer before the wedding. We had not announced our arrival, a typical surprise! We found the farm across the James River and we found the small cottage, my future home.

As we walked in, we were greeted by a swarm of black flies, which then settled on a huge pot full of rice and shrimps (or something like it), sitting on an old wood burning kitchen stove and left open in the heat of summer. Dominik arrived, apologetic. He liked to cook for several meals at once, he told me. I was surprised to find him still alive under these circumstances. Of course, everything was extremely primitive and housekeeping of the most basic kind to be expected of a man totally untrained in such a field. Christiane, seeing my aghast expression, began to rhapsodize about all the possibilities this three-room hut offered. Think of curtains? What about some nice picture here and there, and a chair, perhaps—! Well, this was not my real concern for the time being. But no use to bring it up at this time.

We had settled on the wedding date of September 6, 1952. Before that, I still had a free vacation flight due from Avianca that I did not intend to lose. Christiane, and I joined our aunt and uncle for a gorgeous trip through France. A young doctor friend of theirs, went along in Uncle's large car. We visited several Loire chateaux, drove down to the Biscaya, along the Pyrenees to Cannes and Nice. I enjoyed every minute of it, except for the spines of a sea-urchin which I had stepped on when swimming in the Mediterranean at Cap Ferrat and that were painfully embedded in my heel. I realized this would be my last fling for a very long time. In Cannes I refused to take money into the casino, but let the doctor try with my five dollars (of course, without luck). The desolate, greedy faces of the gamblers, many of them elderly, were a study in depression. Later, we walked behind the casino to the old cemetery where many of the impoverished suicides had found eternal rest.

Back in Germany, Christiane and I enjoyed a visiting tour and also looked in on the Stillfried parents. Mama seemed disappointed with my little brooch and Christiane was instructed to induce me to pierce my earlobes, apparently a wedding gift required it. I did not know more about this surprise.

Of course, I could not resist the temptation to gamble again on another dachshund-smuggling enterprise, a partner for "Inch" who was with my parents. This time it was a black and tan puppy acquired for a repeat of my previous experiment. I had fewer problems with "Puenktchen" and all went smoothly. I had to deposit her with friends in Bogota, until I had my last flight to New York. My only worry now was taking "Puenktchen" into the U.S.A.

Coming in from Colombia, even though she had all required inoculations, was a difficult endeavor, risking the puppy's quarantine if caught. However, all went well and we arrived a week before the wedding in New York.

Wedding

Vicky and Christiane let me load up their car to the roof with my possessions topped by "Puenktchen." I said good-bye to New York, hopefully for good this time and headed south. A multitude of emotions accompanied me on this trip as every young woman probably faces when taking such a serious step as marriage. Sometimes, I would feel like I was taking a dive into an unknown abyss. Then again I would feel that I was liberating myself by taking this plunge into an entirely different life-style. One thing seemed certain; I was giving up much of my accustomed independence. But I also was gaining in love the partner who seemed to need me—someone to take care of, as he would take care of me. Was I not also giving up loneliness by following a path that seemed pre-ordained? My distracted attention got me terribly lost in Washington, DC where I was spewed out into Arlington Cemetery three times before I found the proper exit to Charlottesville, Virginia.

Christiane and Vicky were to follow two days later to be my bridal attendants. Sadly, my parents and other siblings could not attend. There was no money for travelling. My father was able to send us one hundred dollars to help defray wedding expenses. His sound advice that wealth was not necessary for a good marriage reminded us how he'd had nothing when he began. Mami's contribution was priceless advice that we have always cherished: Never go to bed carrying a grudge against each other, but settle disagreements the same day.

Mami had a wealth of wisdom, which she silently carried in her unassuming way, never imposing it on others. We could not splurge; not even a wedding gown was planned so street clothes had to do. As for guests, we did not know anybody in Virginia. Dominik's sister, Angela, at that time quite pregnant with her fourth child, kindly offered to arrange for a very small reception with twelve of their friends after the ceremony. All of them were elderly and became very good friends of ours too.

We were doing some errands on the morning of the wedding, when I allowed Angela's husband, Giannino, to talk me into buying a wedding gown. It happened to be displayed at a ridiculously low price in a window we passed in town. The dress fit perfectly and when

Christiane and Vicky arrived I then had to chase them off to buy those horrible, pastel shaded attendant's dresses that would go with such an extravagance as a wedding gown.

As we were preparing for our big event, Dominik's nephew and niece, Nico and Astrid, went about decorating Dominik's recently acquired vehicle. It was a 1935 Plymouth hatchback that I derisively called "cucaracha" (cockroach). They adorned it with chalk, Coke cans, etc. As Dominik waited for the big moment to be driven to church, Mrs. Minor, a dear neighbor, fortified him with a couple of highballs. These tasted sweet and wonderful to Dominik; their alcoholic content was an unknown to him.

Meanwhile, I was running terribly late. Dressing would have been quite uneventful, at least until my bridesmaids instructed me to attach a pair of gorgeous pearl pendants in my recently pierced earlobes. These were the precious wedding gift that Mama Stillfried had promised Dominik his future wife would receive some day. Years ago, he had found the lost gems in a field. That long ago day, Dominik had accompanied his mother to the train in Kurtwitz as she was travelling to Breslau to attend some function. They were late and running across a plowed field which was a shortcut, when Mama dropped her jewelry case. They quickly gathered the spilled contents and while the small train's conductor held up the departure signal and the engine's bells were tinkling, he waited for Mama to get on. Home again the next day, she was very upset, having lost two beautiful pearls that were part of gorgeous diamond-pearl pendant earrings she had been given by her husband at her wedding. Dominik was summoned to join her in the apparently absurd task of searching for the pearls on the huge recently plowed field. It was a small miracle that he found them.

Thirty years later, at the time of the war's final horrors, by coincidence Mama had detached and carried the pearls with her in an apron pocket as they fled from their home where most other possessions were lost. It now became clear to me, why I had been given the two small pearl-studs after our engagement and had been enticed to pierce my ears. Now my recently "stabbed in Germany" earlobes had closed and started to heal again and, as we all poked them in a great hurry, my ears ballooned red and blood began pouring from both. The torture delayed me considerably, but I held my finally decorated head as still as possible to avoid pain, as I bravely marched into the church.

Dominik, meanwhile was aghast. There had been no time to advise him of my sudden change of wardrobe plans and, liberally highballed, he thought the wrong bride was hidden under the veil. Still, there were happy tears all around us. Old Mr. Jessup, Dominik's boss, cried, as well as the Whites, the Minors, the Luptons, the Newcombs and some neighbor ladies. Dominik's best man and attendants, John Endrizzi, a biologist from Blandy Farm, and Ottavio Gelmi, a young doctor and cousin of Giannino's, completed the picture of a regular wedding party.

With great disappointment, Angela's children, Nico and Astrid, saw us take off on our honeymoon—dog in arm—in his much nicer car, which Giannino had offered us for use on the short four-day trip. Their entire artistic endeavor with our "cucaracha" had been wasted.

Mr. Jessup had given us a three-night stay at his Natural Bridge Hotel, for a honeymoon, where we now headed. I experienced one last time the familiar embarrassment as Dominik asked the receptionist for "two rooms for Mr. and Mrs. Stillfried" while rice fell off his head onto the registration book and the receptionist asked with a grin, "Are you sure you want two rooms?"

Once more, I had to smuggle my little dog in and out of the hotel. Only four weeks later Puenktchen died of hepatitis; the immunization she had gotten in Germany had been insufficient.

We actually stayed only two nights at the Natural Bridge Hotel. Be it my restless soul or a sudden realization how completely grounded I would be from now on, I longed for a last peek at the ocean. So we dashed off to Virginia Beach, a close to 300-mile trip, for a one-night stay. On the way, I managed to cause a fender-bender on Giannino's car, which cost me some of my scarce money and half a day of repair time. To top it all off, I then proceeded to get a speeding ticket. The nice young officer was quite taken by Puenktchen, congratulated us effusively on our wedding, when I tried using my present state of mind as an excuse, but was quite adamant about the need to ticket me.

"You know, I followed you for fifteen minutes and you were driving eighty in a fifty-five mile speed zone; that is bad, I am really sorry." A bad beginning could only mean, that things would get better now!

Farmers at Last

Back from our long weekend, I started furnishing and decorating our little cottage with a vengeance. Very soon, it looked really "gemuetlich"(cozy). Mr. Jessup came to see us regularly, always bearing a gift. He would bring some curtains, flowers, or a basket of crab apples he had picked at the cemetery he owned. An antique wall clock also became a gift. He often assured us it would not be long before we would be moving into the bigger farm-house. He took real interest and treated us as if we were his children. We were grateful for the opportunity given us to get a good start on our future. Dominik was employed as a farm laborer. He conscientiously worked long hours and only took off Sundays when we would drive twenty miles to Charlottesville to church, after milking the cows, of course.

Holy Comforter Church was only a short distance from Mr. Jessup's house. He always expected us after the service, to report on farm business and to eat pancakes he cooked himself. His helper, Pete, was not in on Sundays. We enjoyed hearing this successful, self-made man's fascinating life story. Having started out with scant education, he sold Pepsi-Cola and milk from a pushcart. Later, he made a big profit on a railroad carload of apples from the Shenandoah Valley. He was able to sell them for a very good price after convincing his customers of the reason why the apples were not evenly red and round. His plausible explanation was that the trees grew on the side of the mountain, and the apples adapted to the steep uneven location to take better advantage of all the sun. Several of these stories only made us appreciate him more. He married and raised six children, almost all working with him in his business. Now he was the owner of vast holdings. The Trailway bus line, the Pepsi-Cola plant, the Monticello Dairy, two farms, a cemetery, parts of the Natural Bridge Hotel, banks, houses and who knows what else. His lifestyle was modest to an extreme, and his friendship genuine. What an inspiration for us he was!

On one of our visits, Mr. Jessup showed us a very old letter which was in his possession. With awe I held it in my hand. It was hand written by Thomas Jefferson to his brother Randolph and concerned the transfer of some dogs and a few other matters. Randolph was owner and living on Snowden at the time!

There were no employment possibilities for me in the area and Dominik's wages could barely suffice. My occasional help on the farm was unpaid so I supplemented his income with my wartime experience of making do with anything available. Cattle feed could be purchased in printed feed sacks, wonderful for curtains, aprons and an occasional skirt. Gardening, a flock of chickens, hog butchering, and all the really useful old farmers' customs were quite handy, and fun to try. I had learned during the war to cook with few resources but I finally rebelled at eating groundhogs, which were plentifully available. Even cooked in homemade beer as a stew, they just tasted disgusting and I had to give up on this cost-free "delicacy."

After a few months, Dominik was advanced to the position of manager when his predecessor left. Our salary was eventually increased to a hundred and fifty and later to a hundred and seventy-five dollars a month. Best of all, we got to move into the big house! Again, it meant furnishing the place. Ingenuity and, by now, a habit of making do, made it all possible. Orange crates were transformed into tables. Bricks and boards made shelves and we gratefully accepted a discarded old mattress that made a wonderful sofa after covering it with a Colombian blanket. And so it went. Dominik's wicker hamper that had survived the refugee days was sent to us. It contained pieces of family silver that Mama had saved and kept for him. Since he was the youngest of the family, he was the only one who had never received his inheritance portion or wedding gifts before the exodus from home. How happy we were to have a few elegant pieces in memory of it all. It nicely matched the few pieces of old Spanish silver I had brought with me from Colombia.

The house had four rooms and one bath upstairs, a large hall, a living and a dining room and a kitchen downstairs. A screened porch in the back where we always ate during the summer was convenient. Although not attractive, it was a typical farm homestead. A separate root cellar and smokehouse supplemented its efficiency. Four very large trees in the front were my special joy. The traffic passing the house to rattle over the old James River Bridge was only sporadic. But we did hear the train on the other side of the river which started blasting its signal at the beginning of the large river-bend and would not run out of steam until it had navigated the entire bend a long while later. It took quite some time, getting used to this racket.

Snowden Farm was located in that bend of the James River across from Scottsville. It comprised some six hundred acres, including woodlands, and it was run as a dairy with a hundred-head Guernsey herd. The cows were milked electrically by two men who also operated the rest of the farm with occasional help. One jolly farm fellow was in charge of a mule team. These handsome, but ornery, beasts could not be handled by anyone else. Once in a while they would take off over the bridge to visit Scottsville and Luis had to be found in order to collect them again. The milk had to be delivered daily at Mr. Jessup's Monticello Dairy in Charlottesville. Most of the cattle feed was produced on the farm with the help of a few machines. After Dominik became working-manager, we began to import student trainees for extra help, usually two at a time, and, at first, only from Germany. In the early years these young men lived with us and later in one of the two cottages, but were otherwise members of our household. We occasionally would face a clash of personalities, but in general it was a good experience that we continued during all our farming years. Later on, as we worked through a regular exchange program with Future Farmers of America, the trainees became an international lot. Our first helpers were University companions of Dominik's, who eventually immigrated and also stayed in the United States.

We were finally able to arrange for a belated, extended wedding trip to Germany in 1954 when we found a reliable substitute. I still had my savings from Avianca days burning holes in my pockets and it was sufficient for a trip. Mr. Jessup could never understand how we could be so careless as to squander time and resources on just having a good time on a trip abroad. He never took a vacation himself. But Papa Jessup even forgave us this frivolity. Our friend Bo von Schmeling, a young man with a Ph.D. in Agro-chemistry whom we had sponsored to come over from Germany, had his first employment on Snowden Farm. He managed and worked on the farm for us during our absence.

Dominik's father had died that spring after his long illness and now our uppermost concern was to visit Mama and take her with us for some travelling to give her a break and some relaxation. She had suffered much and was obsessed with other worries. I could relieve her of one of them, my religious affiliation, having recently joined the Catholic Church.

We rented a car and traveled with Mama to Northern Italy as guests of Giannino Previtali's parents. They owned a beautiful house on a mountain top vineyard not far from Bergamo. We spent a week there, then headed through Switzerland to Austria, frequently visiting Stillfried relatives on beautiful country estates. We finished the visiting tour with relatives in Luxembourg, again quite an impressive place. I finally got to know Dominik's much-revered brother, Gebhard, the Jesuit. He was a very positive, life-loving person who had the gift to impart much of his great faith to others. However, driving in a car with him could only be survived with the help of his guardian angels. No matter what the traffic conditions were, a beautiful vista, sunset, or cloud formation would cause him to break out in joyful exclamations, letting go of the steering wheel to look and point at the wonders at hand. He did all of this while continuing at rather high speed.

We had one last weekend alone in Salzburg, after dropping off Mama at her apartment. Originally, it was to be an Opera visit. But first we could not find accommodations except for a cubbyhole next to the elevator shaft in the romantic old "Gasthaus zur goldenen Gans" which was probably very "in" during Mozart's days. Our next discovery was that the high price made opera tickets unattainable for us. We had to settle for a night out with plenty of champagne instead. We got ourselves into such a condition, that we never knew how we found our night accommodations afterward. Our hangovers were tremendous. The kitchen fumes drifting up through the elevator shaft did their part to make us quite sick. But we had a good time alone for once.

Again we had a rather dismal tourist class cabin for our return trip to the U.S.A. It was a dinky, windowless hole, way up front on the old ship. But huge bouquets of flowers sent from different relatives must have made us look like celebrities—or was it the "title" with our name? The stewards' department showered a flurry of attention on us and a better cabin was offered after we left the last port in Ireland. We now found ourselves in a comfortable first-class cabin and with a cozy dining room table for two at no additional charge. It dawned on us that this called for ample tips at the end of the voyage. Our wallets were in their customary state of yawning emptiness by now. We had to revert to the embarrassment of having to confess to the chief-steward that he would have to wait for a letter with a little check from us after our next payday.

Mama came to us a few times for extended visits. We contemplated bringing her over to live with us, but this proved problematic in many ways, one being the cost of uninsured medical care that might become necessary. Admittedly, the dynamics of our different personalities also had to be taken into account. We heard with sadness a few years later of her dying alone in her primitive apartment, which she refused to leave for something better, even for the briefest visit with her children's families. However, we were glad that Mama did get to visit with us and, by then, our children, at our new home, the beautiful Scottland Farm, before her death.

Within weeks of being established in our Snowden Farm home, acquaintances and relatives started coming and, in no time, we had acquired a great circle of friends. We felt no compunction in making everybody work for his keep and contribute to our larder. Our cheerful parties became memorable events. The guests brought booze and also the food with which I cooked a good dinner. Many times a guest who had laughed about our getting sleepy early in the evening would be the first to fall asleep after a day's hard work on the farm.

I found myself in full realization of an early dream of being a farmer's wife, even though without all the elegant "trimmings." Of course, one of the first things was to fill the old chicken coop with an assortment of hens. We were embroiled in a constant battle with predators, like opossums, skunks and other varmints, which found easy access to our old wooden chicken house. The garden soil was very fertile and our dear neighbor an excellent teacher with all the necessary knowledge pertaining to when to plant what seed, according to the moon and other traditional wisdom. Already, in the next summer, I had my own vegetables, potatoes and berries to supplement the good old-fashioned apples from an old tree.

When hog killing time came around, I learned the basics from the neighbors and had Mama Stillfried's good old recipes to try and fabricate German sausages. The small cottage, in which we had started out, was not in use now. There a wood fire kept the pots boiling as I stuffed the pork casings I had cleaned and washed the night before, with the different fillings. No matter that I had no experience and filled them too tight. Many of the sausages exploded while cooking and fat splattered all over the walls and floor. But the smell and taste were enticing. We had a real "Schlachtfest" (hog butchering feast) the way I remembered it from Silbitz days. Several hams and bacon sides were soon hanging in the smokehouse where neighbors had shown us how to keep the perfect fire going.

The only near calamity occurred when I saw a handsome black and white bushy-tailed beast digging through my strawberry patch to get to the buried pig offal. Of course, I could not have that. I had seen Dominik's gun in the closet and also some ammunition. But how was I to load it? I just could not open the gun. I tried banging it over my knee and fell back as a bullet whizzed right by my face and slammed into the kitchen window. I threw the darned thing into the corner and have since hated guns more than ever. The skunk merrily scampered away. My trusted "machete" (the handy large knife with its multiple purpose) would probably not have been a good tool to use at such close range.

Years later on our last attempt to smoke several hams the fire got out of hand and the Scottsville Volunteer Fire Department immediately responded. They had to spear the lush hams, by now rather black, out of the still smoldering remainder of the smokehouse. Well, at least the hams were still edible, once you scraped off the blackness. The fire chief held up one ham and announced "Well done." It appeared that the entire town had come to help. So many cheerful people were there, what else could one do but join in the banter?

Baking large masses of sourdough rye bread was less painful. That turned out beautifully. It took some convincing to get the local mill to find rye flour for me. In those days, the only available bread was that pasty, white wheat bread. We had to acquire a small freezer when a poor cow slipped and had to be shot on account of a broken leg. The old lady was on the tough side, but we were assured meat for almost a year. We found ourselves in need of an occasional fortification. Beer and other alcoholic beverages were beyond our means so I decided to brew our own beer. I got started with relatively few items and the first batch came out sweet and potent. So I tried again—a little less sweet. One bottle tipped over and exploded. Blood running from my mouth forced us to drive to the doctor who had to put a few stitches in my lip. Here went our savings! It had not been such a good idea after all.

Attempts at economizing proved sometimes treacherous. We learned that lesson during the next exceptionally cold winter. Who needs heat in the bedroom? Just let us turn off the radiators! The explosion caused by hard freezing of the water in the old radiators almost sent us hiding under the bed! No, this was not the beginning of World War III as we found out, only the bursting of two radiators!

By 1954 we began to realize, that we were not actually getting on with our plans for the future. Financial restrictions looming ahead were our main concern. We understood how difficult it would be to ever become independent, or even to raise a family, on Dominik's meager employee wages. Our ambitions did extend a bit higher than what seemed available.

Meanwhile, efforts were being made by our family to have us join them in Colombia. Those became an attractive alternative when my friend, Erika's, husband, a wealthy businessman, who owned large land holdings offered us the management of several thousand hectares in the steaming jungle near Barranquilla. At that time, the guerrillas had not yet taken over the region and Colombia had not yet become the supplier for American indulgence. Drugs in Colombia were almost unknown. But the overall political situation did not appear conducive to an enterprise composed of a vast cattle ranch in the steaming jungle. Also, I did not think it a wise decision to undertake a change necessitating a new language for Dominik. Mostly we felt uneasy about the feasibility of raising a family under those rather wild and primitive circumstances. I had seen enough of the problems we would have to face in the tropics.

What ultimately caused us to give up the idea, was Mr. Jessup's determination. He said, "I am treating you like my children and thought you were happy here and planned to stay. Sell your ticket, Nick, I won't let you go! Why don't you buy my farm and make yourselves independent right here?"

It sounded fantastic and started us on feverish calculations. After all, we did not have a penny for such a purchase. Neither did we know enough about the business part of agriculture, and had no insight into the economics of a dairy farm. Dominik came to the conclusion that we would first have to make a trial run and rent the place before buying it. This seemed reasonable to Mr. Jessup. He asked us how much we would be willing to pay for rent. Dominik's inquiry about how much the yearly farm income had been brought forth Mr. Jessup's disclosure. He had been losing fifteen thousand dollars a year before this, and only five thousand since Dominik had taken over. He broke into a happy laugh as Dominik suggested letting him have the farm rent-free for a few years. Dominik pointed out to him that he would actually be converting the five-thousand-dollar losses into a gain.

"Nick, this is the darndest business deal I have ever closed. Let's shake hands on it."

Meanwhile, Dominik began to think hard about the enormous risk he was taking, particularly considering the shaky labor situation. There was no worse nightmare than the frequent calls at two in the morning when one of the milkers did not show up for work and a replacement was needed. That meant us. He decided to ask his friend, Emil Schmidt, who had immigrated to the United States a short while before, to join us in our enterprise as a full partner. Mr. Jessup was not too happy with the idea of a partnership in this small venture, but the deal appeared attractive to Dominik. Emil moved in with us until he married a few years later and started raising a family in one of the remodeled cottages. The two friends divided up the work alternating the routine of one week dairy, and one week farm work. I was the bookkeeper and errand runner, as well as substitute worker. I did plenty of dairy duty in those early years. I found this to be nice on the cool summer nights, but harsh in freezing winter when I damaged my hands with ice cold water. Milking at twelve-hour intervals had to begin at two in the morning so the milk cans could be loaded on the pickup and driven to Charlottesville on time.

We were quite pleased when our books showed good figures and an actual small income became obvious. The farm and its herd was constantly being improved with the know-how of the two agronomists. We could really take pride in our achievements as the date of our farm purchase drew near. Mr. Jessup had offered to sell us the place with only "one dollar down" and arranged a long-term mortgage, which we supplemented with a low interest government loan. Together with the Schmidts, we became farm owners in 1956.

These were exciting and stimulating times and Dominik and I were very happy together. While "maternal blessings" eluded us at first, our home never lacked for young people. My sister, Christiane, was often with us when between jobs. She had switched over to be a stewardess on KLM International and with her elegant appearance, brought us a whiff of the big world. She would immediately transform herself into a tractor driver causing goggle-eyed farmers to do a lot of drooling.

One memorable night, someone shouted: "The pigs are out," in no time we were all running after the critters across the field. Christiane managed to get hold of one tail and sit on the running animal, while I tried to hold on to a hoof.

After the chase and recapture of the animals, when we all reassembled in the house, Emil Schmidt and another young helper stared in disbelief at our attire. There had been no time to change from our skimpy, baby-blue nylon nightgowns! We all had to chase after cattle in the middle of many nights, when they got out and onto the highway.

Besides having young exchange students staying with us, we alternately housed and sent young relatives to school. First was our niece, Johanna Stillfried, who later became a nurse and married an American business-man. My brother, Harald, was shipped up from Colombia after he came home with dismal school records there. He was to work and try for a college degree in America. But this was a mistake in judgement. Harald got the wrong message and blew a summer semester on huge steak din-ners and other luxuries. Thereafter, Father withheld fi-nances and Harald was not at all passionate about a future as a dairyman. He worked for us for a while, then joined the US Army and made his degree in night school. He became a successful businessman, eventually he mar-ried and was sent to Germany by his firm.

My little sister, Betsy, who also had not benefited from the Colombian schools, moved in with us. After the years in an old-fashioned convent school, the only good school available in Pamplona, she arrived—a gangly teenager, dressed in long sleeves, high-neck collars and very buttoned up ideas about our frivolous lifestyle. She completed her high school diploma and went to a business school in Washington, DC. She also worked at whatever work she could find. Betsy rapidly loosened up and be-came a passionate vacation-job expert and skier in Jack-son Hole, Wyoming and other national parks. We later celebrated her wedding to a childhood friend and she moved back to South America with him. During her time with us, Betsy also did her stint as dairy helper and—among other antics—tried to raise a litter of baby skunks (deodorized!) which caused quite a few hilarious events. I almost had to evict her, when she came to the house highly perfumed, after a mischievous friend planted a wild little beast into the cage with her pets.

Angela's boys were often with us as was a niece, Agnes, her son and an assortment of other young relatives who came from overseas to learn English or to establish residency.

I always enjoyed the full house, and the many visitors who came. Friendships were forged that remain until this day. It created a wonderful combination with our local friends. That is, once we were "accepted," people simply ignored us for quite a while. We came from Germany, were Catholic and worse, we were just farm laborers, the lowest of the low!

The post office had a major problem with our name. Mail would arrive addressed to Graf und Graefin Stillfried (what was that?), Count and Countess (are they impostors?), or to just von Stillfried, or to Graf von and several other variants. Finally it leaked out that these were traditional titles, and our real name was Stillfried. Mainly, however, people found out during routine encounters that we were quite presentable after all and could look really nice when dressed in good clothes and sporting proper social behavior. The fact that we were foreigners and not "Yankees" was a real plus for us as residents of a small Southern community. Soon we had established contact with people connected with the German Embassy in Washington and with NATO. There we met quite a number of prominent people. We particularly found wonderful friends among the former officers and diplomats sent from overseas. We attended black-tie affairs several times and drove back in the middle of the night rather champagne-happy and always made it back for milking, after a quick change of clothes. Who needed sleep in those days!

As to be expected, Inch, the smuggled dachshund, was lost to me. My family in Pamplona could not part with him and was hoping for extra income with a dog-breeding program. However, I did get an offspring and eventually was able to breed longhaired dachshunds on the farm.

These were busy years and they were some of the happiest in our life. We were gratefully aware of the good fortune of our having been given this opportunity. It was a chance to build our own existence, even though it had to be without financial help. The challenge was enormous, but times were conducive to farming. We had not been spoiled before, never had had any money of our own and that made it much easier for us now.

Our Guernsey herd was rapidly improving through good breeding programs and producing astonishingly well. We began to look around for land that we could rent as we purchased extra cattle. The enlarged herd called for more grazing land so we rented farming land wherever convenient. We bought used machinery after much haggling and carefully assessing the price and condition; our cars were acquired for many years at Army surplus sales. Dominik explained that the motor was in mint condition, as I watched the highway zipping by through a hole underfoot. This did not assuage my misgivings. Never mind if the vehicle around the motor might disintegrate!

A trip to Germany was once again planned, as we were well represented on the farm by a capable friend of Dominik's. I had again suffered a recent miscarriage so the trip was to be a much-needed vacation for me. But above all, my sister, Christiane, was getting married in Germany! I would not have missed this event! We were relieved on this occasion to find Dominik's family members slowly settling into better living conditions. When we visited them and several friends, we saw normalcy—of a sort—in what was left of Germany. The year before Dominik had acquired his American citizenship! Our allegiance to our new home country, which offered us so much incentive, was normal.

After years of waiting and some miscarriages, our son Franz was born in 1960 at last. Gebhard arrived in 1962 and Christiane made her appearance in 1963. Our family was now complete. Enormous worries befell us when at his birth we learned of Franz's handicap. He was diagnosed as a severe case of osteogenisis imperfecta (brittle bones disease). The shock and pain over our much-longed-for first child's condition also made it quite clear that his care and needs would have to be considered and that we would have to reevaluate our financial future.

Franz was nine months old when the three of us made a visit to Colombia. I wanted to show that country to Dominik and, of course, our baby to my parents. At this stage, travelling with him was relatively easy. He was well encased and protected in one of those baby carriers. The change did us all good and Dominik visited his brother Wolfi and his family, as well. I did notice that Mami was having speech and coordination difficulties, but true to her nature, she rigorously denied any suggestion and got angry when we told her she needed to see a doctor. Neither would she listen to Papi in this matter.

A year later, Mami had acquiesced to see a doctor in Charlottesville, who confirmed the dreadful diagnosis, apparently without her ever fully accepting the finality of it. She suffered for five years with Amniotrophic Lateral Sclerosis. Fortunately she had been able to visit us for Franz's baptism and she attended Harald's wedding in Germany. We were unable to participate at this event on account of little Franz and our always-pressing financial considerations.

After the wedding Mami's condition visibly deteriorated. She died during her last visit at Snowden Farm in 1963 after visiting Harald and his wife and baby in Puerto Rico. My sister Christiane had left her twins and the baby with her husband in Germany for a short visit with our very ill mother, Betsy and us. Mami also saw our two little boys on that last visit. I was pregnant with my third child and experienced Mami's suffering due to her condition, at that stage as extremely painful. My sister Christiane had to return home to Germany. Betsy and I, with Papi, alternated staying with Mami until the end. She was buried in Charlottesville.

In the meantime the Schmidts had their second child, and as if we had to play catch up, our two families produced children almost simultaneously. It became quite obvious that our relatively small farm enterprise could not support two families.

Dominik's good luck streak was to help us to our next big step, that of purchasing big, beautiful Scottland Farm in 1964. A mad succession of events made for a year with a large measure of excitement until the purchase was accomplished. Dominik had always admired this best dairy farm in the county and enjoyed driving by and showing it to visitors. As he talked about this to our feed company agent, Mr. Lynch must have heard bells ringing. He told Dominik, "Why don't you buy the farm, it is for sale." Mr. Lynch quickly painted the possibility in glowing colors, after all he planned to become the real estate agent to handle the transaction!

My first reaction when I heard about these plans, was that of disbelief. I was totally involved in the care of my three babies and other duties and had no time to participate in the many meetings and discussions which now ensued. Once the ball was set rolling, however, there was no turning back. Even though, for a while, Dominik got cold feet because of a brutally dry summer threatening cattle feeding for the coming winter.

But in a year of constant change, we had finally transformed our part ownership of the Snowden Farm into sole ownership of Scottland Farm. We had originally purchased the six hundred-acre Snowden for approximately eighty thousand dollars with a loan that was far from being paid off. The acquisition of Scottland with its one thousand, twenty-five acres would cost us five hundred and seventy-eight thousand dollars. I had held my breath and voiced my disapproval when Dominik felt obliged to ask Emil Schmidt if he wanted to join in a new partnership. Fortunately, Emil must have thought us utterly insane for taking such a big risk. He opted to take his one half share of the Snowden Farm sale and bought a more modest place of his own with much less of an investment. We were now on our own.

After finagling all the necessary financing and a little extra for a startup fund, we felt like kings. We did not lack confidence in our chance to make a go of this project. In the dairy business, one always had a monthly income with which one could juggle the finances. We knew how to economize. My bookkeeping had only to adjust to larger numbers and I kept a tight rein on things since this was in my charge. Dominik figured if he left me to handle the money, I would certainly hold on to the cash carefully even for personal use. In particular, we learned never to be a day behind in payments of our obligations although we had taken on plenty.

My father had shown us full trust in sinking all of his small holdings into our business, thus allowing us to use him as our bank. Actually, he was our last resort and our purchase had hinged on his help. We were very grateful and punctuality in repaying him was a priority. He loved the farm, too and visited regularly until his death at Scottland Farm in 1970.

I always regretted that Mami never saw this beautiful place. How she would have loved the park, the garden and everything about it! She would have so enjoyed participating in our new comforts.

The transformation of a life of "hands on" farmers at Snowden to that of managing this much larger project at Scottlands was quite elating. We had a regular dairy crew amongst the ten employees but Dominik's presence and action was required everywhere in the operation. Fortunately, Dieter Henschel, our first, very capable student helper had agreed to join us as assistant. Together they were in charge of the breeding and healthcare of our roughly six hundred head of Holstein cattle. The dairy crew would frequently call Dominik out in the middle of the night for some cow care or even milking if one of them did not show up. It never was an easy job, but we did it and progressed well as "Virginia Country Gentlemen."

Eventually, together with a good friend from Germany, we bought back Snowden Farm, to run it along with our Scottland Farm, six miles distant. Unfortunately three hurricane-induced floods quite devastated the buildings and lowlands of Snowden Farm and proved that the re-purchase of Snowden had been a miscalculation. It eventually had to be sold again.

We were quite aware that our success story was somewhat unique, the times were conducive for our type of business. Scottland Farm was a showplace and many groups of foreign agronomists from Europe and others from underdeveloped nations sent by the World Bank, would arrive by charter bus to hear Dominik offer a presentation after showing the farm. Friends brought prominent visitors from overseas to show them our unique American success story and admire how penniless former refugees became owners of such a nice farm in beautiful Virginia. A Southern lunch of ham with all the trimmings was much appreciated on such occasions. When a school bus disgorged an entire class of grade-schoolers to teach them that milk did not originate in milk cartons, their attention was generally riveted on our St. Bernard dog, "Orson." Piles of ten or more small bodies would roll around over him, and he loved it. An ice-cream cup would lure them back to focus on milk products. Our Washington friends eagerly attended dove hunts or goose and duck shoots at the big lake, and great after-hunt gatherings and dinners. We were glad we had ample space to accommodate them for the night if need be.

I loved Scottland Farm. The old log house, built around 1790, had its special charm, despite wood-borers, beetles, cold drafts and all. It was nestled in a beautiful park with many ancient trees. The farm was nicely located and from an agricultural point of view had an ideal layout. This gorgeous estate had become our real home at last, for us and for our children, too. We had to work hard for it, but we were fully aware that our success story could only have happened in America. After my odyssey I had at last found an anchoring place. America—Colombia—Germany—Colombia—.

America—here is home!